Rainbows and Clouds

-A memoir

Dr. Suneeta Mukherjee
IAS and ICS (Retd.)

www.diamondbook.in

All rights are reserved. No part of this publication may be reproduced, stored in a retrieval system or transmitted in any form or by any means, electronic, mechanical, photocopying, recording or otherwise, without the prior permission of the copyright holder.

© Author

Publisher : **Diamond Pocket Books (P) Ltd.**
X-30, Okhla Industrial Area, Phase-II
New Delhi-110020
Phone : +91 (11) 40712200
E-mail : sales@dpb.in
Website : www.dpb.in
Edition : 2022

Rainbows and Clouds
Author - *Dr. Suneeta Mukherjee*

"This book is dedicated to my loving husband and soulmate Sudipto Mukherjee"

Foreword

I have known Suneeta since 1965 and it has been a delightful journey of watching each other's development through our careers and also the journey in our personal lives.

We both did our Masters from the Punjab University Chandigarh. We both excelled in sports: Suneeta in water sports, especially swimming and me in tennis. We both joined the civil services together: Suneeta joined IAS and I was in the Police. I know how proud Suneeta was of me being the first lady IPS officer. She combines the ability to share the success and joys of friends with taking pride in their achievements. Suneeta is a very steady friend and she is always there when you need her. Her friends adore her and she is always ready to partake in their struggles and share in their joys and sorrows. There is a lot to learn from her well-earned and well-shared life.

I was party to some of the important decisions Sudipto and Suneeta made in their lives and saw how compatible and happy they were together; I feel sorry that their dream life was cut short but I know Suneeta has the resilience to carry on.

I followed Suneeta's progress in IAS and marveled at her achievements as she moved from one post to another and from one challenge to another. I was very proud of her when she joined the International Civil Service and headed UNFPA in different countries. Facing diverse challenges and working with multicultural teams, she demonstrated that she had the capacity, fortitude and resilience to overcome hazards in unknown and difficult environments and differing cultures. Having done a stint at the United Nations myself, I could imagine the strains and turmoil she would have had to overcome.

This book is Suneeta's journey from both professional and personal perspectives. It is written more like a diary and provides the reader with a comfortable read.

It is written in a simple and interesting style and I hope the readers will enjoy sharing the journey of my friend.

Suneeta is unstoppable when she makes up her mind to do something and as you read about some of the challenges she faced, I hope you'll also share in the glory of her success.

I wish Suneeta and her autobiography all success.

– Dr. Kiran Bedi
IPS (Retd.)
Former Governor Puducherry

Endorsement-1

"Suneeta is an excellent raconteur. In this refreshingly readable narration, she has chronicled her life's joys, trials, and tribulations in a most readable manner. Coping with challenges, at the personal and professional level, and converting every challenge into an opportunity, seems to have been the bedrock of her life's journey. This feature seems to have helped her segue from the IAS to being a successful international civil servant. From its pages waft the evolution of a quintessential civil servant. Written in a very animated style, the book makes an interesting read. An equally inspiring read for any youngster who is at the portal of her career. A hugely appealing book."

Best of luck with the book.

– Shri Vinod Rai
IAS (Retd.)
11th Comptroller and Auditor General of India
Chairman of UN Panel of External Auditor
Honorary Advisor to the Indian Railways

Endorsement-2

Suneeta's life story as narrated is full of trials, tribulations and challenges that she happily faced and is for all youngsters to learn that when doors are closed you can always find windows that you can open. Where there is a will there is a way and there is always a place at the top, was her motto.

Her life story proved whether you are a civil servant in the country or an international civil servant, the challenges are the same because people are the same- whether white, brown, or black. Her short stay at AIIMS in her long career proved she could motivate her co-workers, succeed as a team leader at all levels and be loyal to the organization she served. She apprised the officials in the Ministry of Health that she represents AIIMS in the Ministry, though in the IAS, is not the ministry's spy at AIIMS because her loyalties are with the Govt. of India wherever she works. We as a team agreed on many points and agreed to disagree on others but to find solutions when running the complex organization called AIIMS, which frustrated many at all levels ending in or classical strike shouting "माँ बेटी का राज नहीं चलेगा". She found a perfect life-work balance and we are still friends sharing our joys and sorrows.

– Dr. Sneh Bhargava

Former Director and Professor Emeritus of the
All India Institute of Medical Sciences (AIIMS), New Delhi

Acknowledgements

I am delighted to avail of this opportunity to thank everyone who has helped me in my journey which I am documenting in this book.

My parents brought me into this world and gave me a loving and protected upbringing. Even now when I think about them I am enveloped in comfort and security. I wish to acknowledge my brothers Haramrit and Sawraj and their families for whom I care deeply. The army family has been a bedrock of support too.

What a hopeless place this world would be without friends; they mean the world to me and have supported me throughout. Most notably old friends such as Manju Madhavan and Sudha Sharma and new friends like Manisha Bhagat and others from Palm Springs society, Gurugram who helped me a lot especially after I lost my husband. An example is Anuranjita, who, although in Switzerland now, has helped me in launching this book. In fact, the Palm Springs community also brings joy to my life.

My dear batch-mates like Promila Issar, Kiran Bedi, Manjulika Gautam, Veena Chottray, Sudha Pillai and Chandra Gariyali amongst others who have been a great support and inspiration to me.

My new friends who shared my grief journey like Mamta who just started proofreading my manuscript and made valuable suggestions. My earlier friends like Neelam Prakash, Saramma Mathai and Deepak Gupta who are always ready to help me in my fortitudes.

My IAS family in service as well as in IASOWA. The support I have received from my HP IAS colleagues and their families is unprecedented.

My husband Sudipto Mukherjee, who meant everything to me. He did more for me than even my parents. He designed the entire layout of the book and happily added the photographs to the script. Unfortunately, I lost him to Covid and sadly, he will not physically see the final version which you hold in your hand.

I wish to appreciate my mother-in-law Mrs. Bela Mukherjee who was a lot like me and my father-in-law Shri P N Mukherjee, who left us too soon. My wonderful sisters-in-laws Prachee and Bonya and their families who are more of friends than in-laws. In fact, my husband's entire extended family, his nieces and nephews, especially Munna, Rashmi and Chotdi.

My children Mitali and Rajat who are now my support system and teachers. Rajat is aptly taking over his father's role of looking after me and Mitali also looks after me and even tries to mother me. My ten-year old granddaughter Arya, a budding author, full of new ideas and my writing guide. My son-in-law, Rudro, who is my strong and silent technology advisor as also is my nephew Amandeep. I cannot forget my absolutely adorable, Wall-E, my pet, a King Charles spaniel cavalier who is always smiling and a loveable stress buster.

I wish to thank my patient and cheerful assistants Pankaj Kumar and Jyoti who are my mainstay. Shri N. K. Goyal, the erstwhile GM of HPSEDC, who has given me his unstinted support whenever I asked for help.

Last but not the least, I wish to express my gratitude to my publisher and his team who have helped me in launching this book.

– Dr. (Mrs.) Suneeta Mukherjee
IAS & ICS with UN (Retd.)

Prologue

I was in a dream world, oblivious of what was happening around me, a kind of meditative state. I was in a large hall with over 1000 students and parents huddled together on carefully placed chairs, one next to each other, with a bare minimum space provided to move in and out, everyone trying to keep silent, and yet hushed whispers went around. I was sitting next to my closest friend Sheema (name changed), and we were holding the prizes we had received on our Annual Day in Feb 1966 close to our hearts. I got the first prizes in Economics and History and the second prize in English. In addition, I had college colours in NCC, Shooting and Swimming. Sheema had also won first prizes in English, History, and Political Science and recognition for Dramatics. So, with our prizes tucked in our laps, next to our hearts, our imagination afloat, we were two friends in a kind of purring state, whispering to each other, bundled together in a dark corner of the hall where we carefully selected and took our seats after collecting our prizes. It was a kind of meditative state where you were blissfully unaware of the buzz from whispers or the chatter of the dignitaries till someone was tugging me. Repeatedly.

It was like opening my eyes, and I suddenly became aware of a hand not only pulling but also almost tugging me onwards and two or three loud voices calling my name. Then, as I was pulled up and the prizes taken from my hand, I was pushed in front of the carpeted corridor to go to the stage, and then I could hear clearly:

"Suneeta Dhingra is adjudged the Best All Around Student of Government College for Women Chandigarh 1965-66."

I was given another light push, perhaps by another teacher, and I stumbled and almost fell face down to be caught by my father before I fell to the ground. He had been sitting in a corner and could see me stumbling ahead.

I reached the stage of being given a prize by Shri Krishna Menon, the then Defence Minister of India. There was thunderous applause, and I mumbled a few thank you sentences among tears as I was escorted back to my seat.

And then followed the speech of the chief guest, almost an hour, and suddenly I found that I was kind of suffocating, dying to burst out, talk, laugh and cry scream; I wanted people to hug me and congratulate me on my much deserved but least expected prize. But even Sheema looked straight ahead, having suddenly developed an interest in what the chief guest was saying, as did everyone else. Almost an hour after the chief guest's speech, I still didn't know how I sat through it when I was utterly claustrophobic and found it difficult even to breathe. Almost gasping for breath, I went out with my parents and reached home. One realization came to my mind. People don't necessarily share your joy and success.

I was a simple girl who didn't expect much from life. In fact, I just took life as it came. I had loving parents, and since my father was in the army, we moved from one station to another frequently. I remember being sad every time we left my friends in school, but my family consisting of my parents and two younger brothers, was enough. We got a lot of love from our parents, which was not necessarily reflected in material goods as my father was the sole breadwinner and also supported relatives from both sides who had come to India after the partition. However, the environment and the affection, along with our basic needs being met, left me completely satisfied and I never felt deprived of anything.

From this innocent girl who knew very little of the worldly stuff and of whom the class made fun of even at age 12 as I did not know about the 'birds and the bees', how did I transform into the girl who got this coveted prize which needed not only merit but also social connections which I apparently did not have?

From this modest girl, how did I transform into a successful IAS officer and then move to the coveted International Civil Services, where I worked as a Head of a UN agency in different countries. How did this transformation happen, was it planned or did it happen accidentally, or was it my karma?

What was my family like, how much did I support my husband and children and our extended families, and how much support did I get? How did I manage my home and office? Did my being a woman make it easier or more difficult?

I have written down various events in my life in this memoir which I am sharing with you. I am being completely honest in recollecting from and reflecting on my past. However, I find sometimes the same event is remembered differently by different people. I hope those who have been part of my journey will find resonance in my writing.

This book began as my daughter asked me to write my life story. She said I had many stories to tell, and I should pen them down for my granddaughter, who would grow up and read them. I do hope it will provide interesting reading for many of you. I hope my daughter and granddaughter enjoy it too, as when I began it was for them.

Looking back, what comes out are long series of events and activities, all culminating in some goals which were achieved even when I had thought them unachievable. However, I never gave up, and soon I could reach for the stars in the sky.

The strong pillars in my life were my parents and then my husband. I probably didn't even realise how much strength I drew from them. Now with all three gone, I don't know how many more projects I can support. We hope to help some poor children to study post-class 12 who cannot afford their further education. This I am doing in memory of my husband, who suggested supporting me after class 12. This is called The Sudipto Mukherjee Education Scholarship (SMES). I am grateful to my friend Sudha Sharma, my family consisting of my daughter Mitali Samanta and son-in-law Rudro Samanta, my son Rajat Mukherjee (Abu, as we all call him fondly), my sister and brother-in-law Prachee Mukherjee and Shantanu Chatterjee, for their support and contribution to this program.

As you go through my memoirs, you will find that it reads like a diary, but you will come to some conclusions as I share my life with you. A few critical things in my life were falling in love late and finding my awesome dream partner. How my life and career unfolded side by side and how I managed to juggle home and life and maintain good relations with relatives and colleagues in the mad rush of work and deadlines, it seemed then that time was so limited and work so enormous.

One of the critical challenges women have is multitasking with diverse responsibilities. As it is, we have some feminine interests in clothes, dressing up, gossiping, having fun, dancing, singing, etc.; and then, when we undertake full-time jobs we want to do them very well. I never wanted any man to say again that women cannot do the job well. My husband once commented that I wanted to keep the flag flying. Both my parents and husband felt that I subsisted on willpower. I hope I will have enough willpower to go through this book and the rest of my life without them.

I seek blessings from my readers.

Contents

Chapter 1

Growing up: Childhood and Teenage Years

(1948-1968)

Innocence and learning

In my thirteenth School in Class 7, I got my name. Not that I did not have one earlier, but Sunit became Suneeta in Govt. Model School, Sector 16, Chandigarh. There was a boy named Sunil, and as the teacher would call out names for the roll call, Sunil would stand up for Sunit, and Sunit would respond for Sunil. And the teasing would follow. Thus, Sunit became Suneeta, all because of one Sunil. And here I was, the youngest in my class and amongst the shorter girls and came to be called 'Githi.'

My father was in the Army, and we moved wherever he got posted. So, I went to Presentation Convent in Srinagar, where one had to take a boat to get to the school (now there is a road leading right up to the gates); a cantonment school in Gaya; Loreto in Ranchi and Canossa Convent School in Ranikhet. Many years later, I have gone back and visited my Schools in Srinagar, Ranikhet and Chandigarh.

I really do not recall my childhood very clearly. However, I have friends and even my brothers who seem to recall incidents and can narrate each detail with such precision that, at times, I wonder if they really remember them or if it is partly their imagination that speaks!

However, I do remember our stay in the picturesque hill station of Ranikhet. My father was in the Kumaon Regiment, and the Kumaon Regimental Centre is in Ranikhet. I did my class 6 and part of class 7 there. I remember our house in Dulikhet, and our dog, Blackie, who was taken by a panther. Later, an officer from the regiment shot a panther and we adopted her cub.

I remember that in Gaya, I was admitted just before the final exams; I failed in the final exams, which meant that I was to be held back. The teacher, however, mistakenly took me to the next class; When my mother

With my parents

met the principal, she felt I'd be able to catch up in the new class, considering that I had only joined the school just before the exams. Apparently, the maths syllabus was quite different from my previous school, and thus I avoided having to fall behind by a year.

My parents came with their families to India after the partition and had come through severe conditions, running for their lives in disbelief with what was happening all around. Having faced scenes of bloodshed and horror and the kind of hatred never imagined, they were haunted by those memories. In his last days, my father would sometimes hallucinate and imagine he was in the midst of all this. My mother was a simple sweet lady but with a great deal of native sense. Her whole world was her husband and children. She had been deprived of an

With my parents and two brothers

education because her brothers were embarrassed to be seen going to college with a girl, even if she was a sister, so she happily studied at home and got her graduation degree. She married a bit late and was staying with her brother and his wife and daughter in Sialkot from where she married and was on her honeymoon when partition was announced, so Daddy went back to get the families leaving her behind. She never mentioned all the jewellery she left behind. She was always happy to be in the background but quietly shaped our lives. Her brother was killed, and she often thought about the unnecessary bloodshed and horrors but did not ever make anyone's day gloomy.

Having come from this situation, my parents were now determined to settle in one place for their children's studies. They realised that for our future, we needed uninterrupted schooling, and they had to drop anchor at one location where my mother could stay with my two brothers and me while my father would move around as ordered by the Army. They choose Chandigarh.

Chandigarh was a new city that was being built from scratch. Later on, the city was designated as the capital of Haryana and Chandigarh. It was designed by the famous French Architect, Le Corbusier, and the Govt. was encouraging people to buy land and build their houses in the city.

Initially, we stayed in a rented house. In 1960, my mother and her brother bought a 3 Kanal (about 1200 sq yds) plot in Sector 8A, Chandigarh, for Rs 8000. Later, they felt they had made a mistake and wanted to sell it even at a loss, but there were no takers. The plot was in a premier sector, but it was full of trees and shrubs, with no other house in sight. They said it looked more like a jungle and, in their lifetime, did not expect to see a housing colony coming up here. However, my uncle was very keen to sell his share, so my mother bought it off him and repaid him in installments.

With great difficulty, she built a house there. In those days, construction materials such as cement and steel required Govt. permits. So Mummy would get on to her bicycle and visit one Govt. office after another to get these permits and then go to the suppliers, make payments, get the materials loaded on trucks, and arrange for delivery. And back at our plot, she would then supervise the construction of the house.

She looked after all our needs, taking us around pillion on the bicycle in the evenings to buy notebooks or materials for our craft projects. We would be in the kitchen doing mathematics with her help while she made breakfast. She had a small helper boy, and we never wanted even though she struggled with the finances for the house construction. She had taken out a bank loan, although my father was not in favour of it; he said none of his family ever took loans.

I, with my brothers, Haramrit and Sawraj, were admitted to Govt. Senior Model School in Sector 16 in December 1958. Later I went to College and University in Chandigarh itself. A memory that stands out sharply is that in my first-class test in January 1959, I got 6 marks out of 100 in Maths. My mother, always fearless and confident, started teaching me, and I got 16/100 in the monthly test of Feb. In March, I came running home with my mark sheet, calling out for my mother and screaming that I had got 64 in maths. The teachers, not expecting me to make it, had wanted to detain me. I had also passed in the Punjabi Language, although I had learnt the alphabet for the first time. Sadly, I promptly forgot them later.

The Govt. school at Chandigarh was a very different experience for me. The environment of a school in a protected army cantonment and an open co-educational school as well, was vastly different. I knew nothing about the 'birds and bees' and at the age of 11 heard and learnt about it at one go when two girls were talking about it, and realising I didn't know anything, they explained things to me. Of course, they told everyone of my ignorance and made fun of me. I charged home to my mother to check on the authenticity of what they had told me.

I had a happy childhood. I am told that I shared my treats and toys easily with everyone. My results were not brilliant, but my mother believed this was because we did not have stability in education and kept changing schools. I was a happy-go-lucky child and gazed with wonder at the beauty I saw all around, even as a schoolgirl. Chandigarh was a well-planned city, with colourful blossoming flowers on trees alongside the roads, providing shade and a feast for the eyes. We cycled to school every day, and in the evening, we went to Sukhna Lake for rowing and later sailing too. I remember my maths teacher, Mrs. Chawla, fondly. She was later to get in touch with me when I was DC Solan. My school life was uneventful, and after completing my matriculation, or Class 10 in those days, I joined Govt. College for Women (now known as Govt. College for Girls) in Sector 11.

My brothers, who were initially with me in the Sector 16 Govt. school, joined St John's School when it opened in Chandigarh. Meanwhile, my father took a posting to Indochina with the UN peacekeeping forces to be able to save money to build our house in Chandigarh. When I look back now, I remember I loved dancing.

When I was in Loretto Convent in Ranchi, I participated in group dances on an annual day, and I remember dancing at Dussehra in Ranikhet at army functions. I often just danced in the rain, and that love persists even today.

When I joined college, I was very disappointed that the dance teacher, Shobha Kansal, told me that there was no vacancy in her classes. Though those who know me today will not believe this, I did not have the guts to ask her again during the four years I was in college and looked

Dancing at the Dusshera celebrations

longingly at the room whenever I passed by with sounds of ghungroos and tabla beckoning me to take a peep at what was going on. However, when I started teaching in the same College, I asked her if she would still say that she had no vacancy or time for me. She was embarrassed and amused, but it was then that I learnt Kathak which I still love.

China attacked India in 1962. The Indian Army was ill-prepared and inadequately equipped with arms, ammunition, and clothing. The Indian Army retreated across the border in the face of heavy Chinese troop deployments, except at a mountain pass named Rezang La, and my father was intimately involved in this action.

Daddy was admitted to the Military Hospital in Srinagar with a stomach ailment when his battalion, 13 Kumaon, was ordered to move to Chushul, a remote hamlet in Ladakh, a stone's throw from the border. He asked to be released from the hospital, but the Doctors said he was not fit to be discharged. So, he gave an undertaking that he was leaving the hospital at his own risk and moved with his battalion.

The convoy of the forces going to the border got stuck in waist-deep snow, and the army men, guided by Daddy, used ropes tied at one end to the trucks and the other around their waists and pulled the trucks out so that they could move on.

Just before the battle started, Daddy sent his watch and gold ring back home, his only two worldly possessions;

and I saw Mummy go to the prayer room and have a dialogue with Guruji (my guess).

In the ensuing battle, Charlie Company of 13 Kumaon, led by Major Shaitan Singh, had the distinction of fighting to the last man and last round. 114 of the 120 men died, but not before killing more than 1000 Chinese soldiers. Major Shaitan Singh was awarded the highest gallantry award of the Nation, the Param Veer Chakra, posthumously. 13 Kumaon was awarded the Rezang La Battle Honour and is known as the Rezang La Battalion.

My father was decorated with the AVSM. Now that I'm more aware of gender issues, I'm pleasantly surprised that my father took my mom and me to his investiture

My father was decorated by the President Shri Sarvepalli Radhakrishnan after the Rezang La battle

ceremony at the Rashtrapati Bhavan (he could have taken one of my younger brothers). In the picture above, I remember chatting with President Radhakrishnan very amicably and also giving suggestions on how to improve the economy of the country, oblivious to the photographers trying to make me look around at the camera.

Daddy was always very important in my life. There was a very strong bond. He would call me from wherever he was. We would talk of patriotism and love for our Country; we both loved poetry and would recite patriotic poems to each other. So many things happened in my life because of my father. I did my Masters in English as he suggested, though I would have preferred Economics, but then doing English fitted into my plans of teaching in my college after doing my Masters. My love for poetry began with Daddy reciting Wordsworth's Daffodils to me.

Nowadays, in my seventies, I teach swimming to my fellow residents in our complex at Palm Springs. However, my swimming experience did not start well at all.

When I was in Class 10, one day, Daddy took us to Ambala Cantt. to teach us swimming. He put his hand under my waist and asked me to float; when he removed his hand, I started to sink, and he said I was too fat (at 52 kg) and could not learn to swim. And that was the end of my first swimming lesson. I was very hurt and just had to prove him wrong.

The Punjab Govt. organized a camp for advanced swimmers at Kanya Maha Vidyalaya, Jalandhar. This was advertised in the newspaper, and I signed up for it. Daddy was then in Indochina. The Punjab sports officer, who was Milkha Singh's wife, was my comrade in the secret that I did not know how to swim but had signed up for Punjab Govt. Swimming Camp for advanced swimmers. (there was none for beginners) at Kanya Maha Vidalaya, Jalandhar.

I did not tell the coach, a young Indian girl from the UK, Surjeet Somal. We lined up at the pool's deep end, and she called out: "On your marks, get set, go!" Everyone dived in, but I hesitated. She blew her whistle at me, so I also jumped in, started thrashing around in the water, and began to sink. Surjeet, who was in a dress and wearing pencil heels, jumped in and rescued me. She was screaming and was very angry with me, and I was in tears, saying I was so sorry and pleading with her not to send me back. She steadied me and let me stay on in the camp.

At the end of the 15-day camp, I did so well that I was selected to swim for the Punjab team. This is how vital Daddy's words had been. Another comment he passed later made me paint and briefly attend painting classes. As a result, all the paintings in our homes are by me.

My early years in college saw me participate in the inter-university swim meet in Calcutta.

Boarding a train to Calcutta for an inter-university championship, the coach is on the left, and the other 2 participants are with me, all saying bye to my dog.

Below is a picture of a swimming competition with the Chief Minister of West Bengal.

Sujeet Somal (Coach), Surinder Somal, me and Ranbir going for Inter University Championship in Calcutta

I also pursued water sports at the Lake Club in Chandigarh. I was the first girl member at the Chandīgarh Boat Club and loved sailing, which I learnt there.

The Punjab swimming team with the then West Bengal Chief Minister Shri Prafulla Chandra Sen after the competition

I won many prizes in water sports, and during one function General Thimaya came to distribute the prizes. I merrily chatted with him, and my parents were also impressed and amused.

Mummy was finding it very difficult managing her adolescent children. Though I don't think I was ever a major problem, but I was very friendly to my swimming coach and her sister, and they often came in the evenings, and we went to the lake together. Mummy thought I could go beyond what was permissible for me, e.g., come home before dark, etc. and then these girls would come and use her cosmetics and almost finish her one and only Channel eau de cologne spray, which Daddy had brought from Indochina; so new rules were made for me. My swimming practice was stopped as I was also getting my periods, I was told, and the rules regarding studying would be more strictly enforced.

Mummy now asked Daddy to come and take charge of the family instead of pursuing his professional career. He consciously gave up his chances of a promotion to the rank of Brigadier and opted for an administrative assignment as Col Adm in Chandigarh. Mummy was diagnosed with TB of the thyroid, which was operated on. However, we were told very little about family problems, and we overheard them or knew only something after it had already happened.

The emphasis was on keeping us happy and carefree. During this time, the war with Pakistan took place, and all our relatives from Amritsar were with us, and we got to know them. We would get into trenches which we dug in our lawns every time the siren sounded, and we actually had fun.

I loved going to the lake, but there was a little vacuum in life as I progressed to puberty. I pursued some other sports, participated in dramatics as well as debates, became an under-officer in the NCC, and made a mark in shooting, winning an award for the best girl shooter in Punjab.

Leading the college parade

With the academic awards I won in my college, and with the awards in extra-curricular activities, my father, who was home on leave on the eve of our prize distribution day, generally commented that I should get the award of the Best Student in the College. I told him that I had no chance. I was not even on the shortlist, as there were few girls who, apart from their talents, were socially active and well known to the teachers and the Principal, Mrs. Dhillon, and the Vice Principal, Mrs. Atma Ram. Thus, I was not even in the race!

The prize distribution day made a tremendous mark on the rest of my life! After receiving my academic awards, I settled down in a corner with my then best friend,

Sheema, to listen to the principal's annual report (boring) and then the speech of the Chief Guest, Mr. V. K. Krishna Menon, the then Union Defence Minister. My parents were in the 3rd or 4th row, and my name was announced as the best student. Since I was not expecting to be called, I did not even hear my name when it was called a second time. The third time, I was pushed by a teacher who got up to send me to the stage. I scurried to the stage like a rabbit and almost stumbled and fell before Daddy caught and steadied me on my way to the stage.

I learnt later that a procedure had been established which had scores for academic achievements and participation in extra-curricular activities. Additionally, a condition had been imposed that there should have been no academic failures in any year in College. This objective selection criterion brought me to the top. The girls we thought would get the prize did not qualify as they had failures in college. Thus, I got the best all-around Prize in Govt. College for Women (now called for girls) in 1965-66! This became my hallmark success, and I started believing in myself!

Receiving the Best All Round student award from the then Defence Minister, Shri V K Krishna Menon.

The first outcome of this was that my best friend stopped talking to me and another close friend Manju understood this so well that I became eternally indebted to her for her care and love. I had thought people find it challenging to be with you in your sorrow but are happy to be with you in joy and happiness, but this proved wrong. And Sheema and I were never so close again!

I had wanted to take up Economics but did English instead. There were two reasons for this. One, my father had done his MA in English from Lahore University, and he felt I would just happily drown myself in literature if I studied it. Secondly, I suddenly desired to return to my college to teach. English was a compulsory subject, and there were many vacancies for teachers. I could get a job there if I did my Masters in English; in Economics, there were only two vacancies.

The Punjab University campus where I studied was a large and sprawling campus with a super library, boys' and girls' hostels, which were all lush green, and a romantic ambience. There were large sparking fountains with some buildings of beautiful architecture. We had a tea shop next to our department, and it was quite a busy corner with students meeting up to chat. Alas, some of our teachers were not of the level they should have been. Manju took up Psychology, and I made

Kiran Bedi and me

new friends in the English department, Promilla, and Veena Jain, who are still my friends even today. We went on a camp to Shimla, where I met Kiran Bedi, a batchmate and friend to date.

This has been a critical trait in me. I loved friends; my mother said my father's frequent postings left me sad about leaving friends. In the later years, my mother would comment in the vernacular: "If you remove a brick from a wall, you will find Suneeta has a friend there!!"

The two years in the university were mostly spent in the library when we were not attending classes, most of the time drowning ourselves in literature right from the times of Chaucer to T S Eliot!! There were hints of romances, some of which matured. We learnt later that one of the students in our class married a young Professor, who later joined the IAS.

Some romances blossomed, and my close friend Promilla got married to Ranjit, also from our department. There was a guy interested in me too, very good by worldly standards, but somehow, I never felt comfortable with him around. He even met my Daddy; I said the same to my Daddy, which he understood.

My memories of the University include singing by some classmates who had melodious voices. One of them was Promilla; I also clearly remember Ravinder singing, and incidentally, he is settled in Gurgaon now and still a friend. I always loved poetry but now drowned myself in literature, particularly plays which I enjoyed very much. I did a focused study for exams and did well, especially in the second year.

One exciting incident I remember: I did not want to contest the elections to the student body but had been nominated. So, if I went, I would be voted for as it was too late to withdraw. But I wanted to see the election fun. So, I got a crazy idea: to disguise myself and enjoy myself. So, I dressed up as a boy and no one recognised me. The only time people looked at me curiously was when they saw Manju with me.

Soon our exams were over and the results were declared. We had to go through the Employment Exchange for jobs, and we had registered our names there. It was exciting to know that there were two vacancies in the English Department at my College. I requested the Employment Exchange to sponsor me, but when I went to the College, I learnt unofficially that the two people to be selected for this post were already decided. One was a guy who did his MA with us and the other was a girl we did not know. I was a bit disappointed and went for the interview in a cotton saree with zero expectations.

At the beginning of the interview by a high-level panel, I was asked why I thought I should be considered for this post. Without overthinking about it, I promptly answered that because I was the best all-round student in this very College. The chairperson looked hard at the principal, who fumbled with a "Yes, she was." She was mildly reprimanded for not having mentioned this in the brief, she had prepared. She explained later that she was under pressure to take those two candidates. And yes, you guessed right, I got the job! I was thrilled. It was a whole new life I was about to venture into.

Tender upbringing pays in the long run, even if surrounded with harsh realities (in my case frequent transfer of father and our continuous movements). I can always bask in the love of my parents.

❐

Chapter 2

Govt. College for Girls Chandigarh

(1968-1971)

Pure joy and happiness

I joined as a lecturer at Government College for Women in July 1968. Mrs. Atma Ram was now the Principal. Earlier, she had been the Vice Principal (though she was in charge of most of the extracurricular activities). Seven of us joined together, and 5 amongst us had studied together. This was a happy time. We enjoyed teaching young girls in College who were just a few years younger than us. We tried to dress up such that we would look older than our age. I just wore all of my mother's sarees till I got my first salary and started buying sarees to supplement those from my mother's wardrobe. My father bought a Lambretta scooter, which he taught me to ride, and very often, I went to College driving the scooter. Manju and I had a whale of a time riding the scooter though once I met with a nasty accident while trying not to run over a cat running on the road. My younger brother was envious, and I wonder now if I could have done anything to assuage his feelings at that time.

The older of the two, Haramrit, went to NDA, convincing my mother that his dream was to be an army officer. I don't think he was happy there, but we were constantly in touch and shared our lives through letters. Later my father got posted as Col Adm in NDA, and it must have been good for him with Mummy also visiting him.

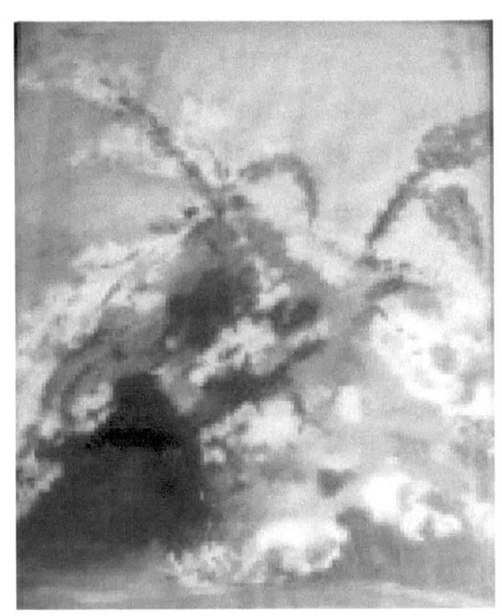

Daddy's financial condition was better as they had rented out the main portion of the Sector 8 house to Russians, after fully furnishing it, at a reasonable rent. Daddy brought a second-hand Fiat and took it with him to NDA. When we visited him, I found that he had bought paintings from an exhibition to put up on the wall; I looked at them and said that I could have painted them! Till then, my sole experience had been painting birthday cards, and Daddy said he would get me some paints. Daddy asked me to paint a bougainvillea bush in the garden, and I painted that. There was no Google in those days to check how to use oil paints, so when I returned, Manju and I took some lessons from an art teacher in Chandigarh.

Teaching in College was great fun but apart from teaching I was made in-charge for debates, dramatics, and sports competitions. This meant that I spent long hours in College. While teaching was over by around 1 pm, often I was in College till late afternoon or early evening for extracurricular activities. Manju's house was close to College, and I always had a late lunch or salad at her house. This period was packed with fun activities coupled with hard work. I went to the lake regularly, loved sailing, and enjoyed rowing a lot.

Manju was considering what she wanted to do. She did not want to get married yet. She was the youngest in a large family, and there was a natural expectation from our parents that we should get married. She finally decided to sit for the IAS examination. She was brilliant, came top in MA Psychology, and won a Gold Medal, so this should not have been a problem, only she never studied much. I offered to help her with European history, which I had studied and began to make notes for her. I would go to her place every day after College and spend quality time with

Enjoying Sculling in Sukhna Lake in Chandigarh (I'm in the centre)

her, and we were often discussing a lot of philosophical issues for hours on the phone. I loved going to the lake, and Manju joined me in this. We often went rowing and enjoyed our time together.

I was made President of The Old Students Association and we had an exciting Old Students Day with lots of games and fun and frolics. The Principal was very impressed and commented that whatever I undertook, I did well.

And then came a college trip to Sri Lanka. The girls were to be taken to Sri Lanka and some teachers were to escort them. I was selected along with the Principal and another teacher. Manju asked if she could come along and pay her fare; this was approved, so we were very excited as we prepared for the trip. I took my European history notes for Manju with me so whenever we got spare time, I could explain them and hand them over to her. In Sri Lanka we met the Prime Minister, Srimati Bandaranaike and wandered around the beaches and temples.

This visit was important in my life as it was on this trip that the seed of IAS was sown. One day I was handing over and explaining some notes to Manju sitting on the upper berth of our train. Mrs. Ram and another teacher were on the lower berth. She called me down and said, "Suneeta, why don't you sit for IAS?" I was surprised. Manju had suggested this a few times and I had said that

Our college team with the Prime Minister Smt Bandaranaike in Colombo, Sri Lanka, on her left is our Principal Mrs. Atma Ram

I did not know anything about IAS and was so happy teaching. She had understood. But Mrs. Ram refused to understand and said that she saw herself in me. When she had waited outside the room of The Education Secretary, an IAS officer, she wondered why she didn't take the plunge into IAS herself. She promised me that she would not fill my vacancy on a permanent basis and that if I did not like the IAS, I could always come back!!

Manju and I were thrilled. Our imagination and plans extended only up to going to Delhi to fill in forms, take the exams together and during the exams or soon after, make a quick trip to Agra to visit the Taj Mahal. We reached Delhi and rushed to the UPSC to fill out my form; there were hardly a couple of days before the last date! I got an urgent passport-size picture taken, borrowed money from Manju's brother, called my parents, and went to Chandigarh only after submitting the form. On this visit to Sri Lanka, the seeds of what was to become my professional life for more than forty years were sown.

Daddy did not seem excited at all about my new venture. He said that I was least interested in politics and never even read the newspaper except for the sports page. Nor was I interested in Governance or Governments. I later learnt that he had himself appeared for the ICS and got through the written test, but not made it in the interview, as the British presiding officer did not like an answer to a question regarding the Moghuls' rule in India! I wonder now: he never suggested to my brothers or me that we could prepare for and join one of these coveted services?

And then began the struggle and the hard work. Manju patiently taught me how to read the newspaper, beginning with editorials. On the very first day, she explained the historic relationship between Israel and Palestine; but for her, I could not have moved forward. I was really ignorant about world affairs and our discussions made everything exciting and enjoyable.

My brothers, one who was there at home, and the other who came on holidays from NDA, did not understand the need for my studying, and played loud music and had friends coming over. I struggled to study in the library, where we could not take our books, in gardens where small ants probably found my blood very palatable and in my home where there was loud music. Finally, my mother, who was a wonderful person, but worked quietly in the background, made arrangements for me to study in a room in our rented house separately. This enabled me to study. I never thought I would make it, and one day, I got up and made a painting (picture enclosed) of my struggle. And I heard in the background, 'Hum honge kamyaab', and felt a bit encouraged and hopeful.

A painting I made to reflect my struggle

My parents say I worked very hard, but I don't remember studying too much as I continued to teach till the end. We went to Delhi for just over a month. I stayed with my Aunt (Mausi) and her family in Karol Bagh and Manju stayed with her brother. I was a bit lonely but fine initially, but later got a fever and was very weak. My mama ji came over and took me to a doctor. I survived on paracetamol. Manju came visiting one day and soon she got the infection too. Anyway, we had one or two papers left. In my last paper, I remember passing out or maybe just falling asleep. My fever was diagnosed as dengue, something not known those days. In a few months, our results were out. Manju had made it to the Indian Revenue Service. The system was that the first few (say 10, depending on vacancies) joined the Indian Foreign Service and the next 100 joined the IAS. Then came the turn of Central Services, like the Indian Police Service, Revenue Service, Railways, Audit & Accounts, and so on. With Manju joining the Revenue Service and me not making it yet (since the full results had not yet been tabulated), I was sad. However, two lecturers in College, Kiran Sabharwal and Manjeet started giving me company, coming to my house almost every morning and going for walks to the lake. Mummy would give us a freshly baked hot cake which she did so effortlessly, and we would gobble it up.

I was embarrassed about what my students will think about my not making it to the IAS. I felt that they must be thinking that our ma'am could not even pass the exam. So, I started studying again to take the IAS exam. However, soon our results came out and I had made it to Indian

Postal Service, and I was off to Saharanpur for training. I had missed the foundation course in the Academy to which I went later. The stay at Saharanpur and training was relaxed and stress-free and I made great friends with Anju Chhibber and Milonee, my two other colleagues undergoing training. This was a really enjoyable period of my life. However, the second time I made it to the IAS, and was soon at the Lal Bahadur Shastri National Academy of Administration (LBSNAA) in Mussoorie.

My parents were delighted, though, as always, they found it very difficult to express themselves. Unlike modern times I don't think I ever heard them say, "I love you". When I told my Daddy, he stretched out his hand and said congratulations with the broadest smile and Mummy said very good, but I realize now how much it meant to them.

After retirement from the army, my parents were trying to set up a farm near Banur. My Mother bought that land when Daddy was about to retire. He longed to go back to nature and take up farming. But that was not to be. They lived in difficult conditions in a room they constructed, had simple meals, and led a spartan life. Mom would struggle on her bike and bus and walking combination to go there often but now that Daddy was back, they used a scooter, which was a relief. However, the soil turned out to be very rocky and augmenting it was a long-drawn and expensive process. Finally, Daddy managed to get a decent crop on one part of the land, which enabled him to sell it at a marginal profit. They then moved back to the main portion of the Chandigarh house.

With my parents and brothers as we grew up

When they were struggling with the land and all was looking bleak, I had made it to the services. Daddy asked me what I wanted as a gift. I was going to Mussoorie and had seen a yellow color coat for Rs.100, so I asked for that. He immediately opened his purse but did not have the 100 rupees to give so he got it from the bank. It was then that I realised how difficult it was for a single salaried man when his children were being educated and his new venture, the farm, was not doing well.

I had done my Masters in English Literature as desired by Daddy and taught happily for 3 years before I made it to the IAS. I only realize now that I had fulfilled Daddy's dream and, in a way, Mummy's also and made them very proud and happy. I realize this only when they are no more with us and I am happy that I could be a source of joy to them.

Teaching remains a pleasure and passion with me, even today.

I was so happy with life that I once remember telling Manju that I don't know why people talk of salvation. I love life so much that I want to be born again and again.

❐

Chapter 3

Indian Administrative Service (1972-1974)

Preparing for the challenges ahead

The training academy for civil services is the Lal Bahadur Shastri National Academy of Administration, named after our late Prime Minister and located in the picturesque town of Mussoorie. I joined the Academy in July 1972.

The IAS officers undergo two kinds of training: in the beginning a foundational course for 3 months, after which one goes to one's state (cadre) for district training, followed by professional training for 9 months. During the foundation course, other services also join, e.g., Foreign Service, Police Service, and Central Services. Those under training are called probationers.

The mornings started with yoga or horse riding, followed by regular lectures or presentation-based classes before and after lunch, and games in the late afternoon and evening, followed by a club meeting a few times a week before dinner. Off and on, there were functions like sports competitions, cultural events, singing, games,

plays and movies galore. I remember always being sleepy in class.

The boys and girls hostels were separate, with accommodation for about 30 girls in the girl's hostel.

Generally, two girls shared a room, and one or two rooms had a set of attached baths and toilets. My roommate, Manjulika Gautam, and I became good friends, and we are very close to date. And both of us are also close to Kiran Bedi, who lived in one of the outer rooms. Mussoorie gets cold in winters, but there were no geysers in the bathrooms; bearers carried buckets of hot water for our bath.

During my two terms there, I was the Secretary of the Mess Committee for one year and a Member of the Officer's Club for the other. The time was packed

with studies and activities. Our Academy Director was Mr. Rajeshwar Prasad (earlier the Director was Mr. Sathe), whose Shram Dan we remember to this day. On Sunday mornings, we would be clearing playgrounds etc. "doing service with humility."

Life was a breeze, rushing from bed in the morning and running around all day till you got into bed at night. I was surprisingly a bit detached; I don't know if it was a disappointment, probably resulting from unrealistic expectations. Looking back, I think I wanted more focus on the job we were expected to do. It was there understandingly in the later part of the training. I was good at horse riding, having done it before when my father was posted in NDA; I was also adept at Yoga and played some games. I did some rock climbing and rappelling too.

Shram Dan on Sunday morning

We often went on treks, and during one, I fell off when a tree branch broke and cracked my tailbone, which still troubles me. I was called Sarge (short for

A cultural evening

Sergeant Major) by some of the boys. We were in a similar age group, but maybe I was slightly older than some of them as I had taught for 3 years before joining the services; many people take the exam straight after completing their studies. We had a few VIP visits, and Indira Gandhi's visit to our hostel was memorable.

By the time our foundation course ended we were allocated our cadres. My cadre was HP about which I was happy. Though my first two choices were Haryana

Mrs. Indira Gandhi in the girl's hostel

and Punjab, I was delighted to be a little away from people I knew so well and thought I could function more independently. Also, HP is a beautiful state, and there was a lot of scope for development there, having been recently given Statehood. As a probationer, I was called Assistant Commissioner and posted to Mandi.

I had a nice and charming boss: Mr. R K Anand, who later became Chief Secretary of HP. I could have learned more from him, but he was a bit reserved. He showed a lot of confidence in me. I did not accompany him to inspect Police Stations or even sit in his Court and understand the processes followed though I initially did sit in his office; however I got his total support in my training and progress. He was wonderful, and I had a great stay in Mandi, learning from the SDM, GA, and DDPO with whom I got along very well. This included driving a jeep in the hills as one day they just asked me to drive; I had driven a car and scooter but a jeep in the hills and reversing? So, one evening at around twilight, Mohar Singh, the DDPO, just asked me to take the wheel, reverse on a narrow road and go back. With my heart in my mouth, I began to reverse and realized that the road was narrow, and there was a dark forestry slope next to us. A little wrong move would take the jeep tumbling in the forest, but when my feeble protests went unheard, I took charge and confidently reversed and started back. There was very little ground to reverse, and an inch or two more would take us down the hill, but Mohar Singh did not flinch, and I got confidence probably through his faith. He made his way through difficulties always and together with Mr. T R Sharma, the SDM (Sub–Divisional

Magistrate) they managed to handle sub divisional and district level matters quite efficiently though the broader vision came only from Mr. Anand.

We had powers of Magistrate 3rd class and then 2nd and then First class. The first case I decided on was a car theft case where the counsel for the accused, Mr. Kaul, was nervous and was advised to apply for a transfer of the case, as I appeared very tough. He's a Minister in HP now and still jokes about it and says he had the courage to wait for the judgement, which went in his favor as the accused got the benefit of the doubt due to lack of evidence. I remember being nervous even about framing a charge-sheet; the large room where I sat on a raised dais felt very daunting, but by the end of it, I knew civil and criminal work. I also learnt about the grass root

activities being carried out by the revenue as well as the development staff in detail. I was to learn later, when I did not have such appreciative bosses, on how wonderful it was to have Mr. R K Anand as my first boss.

We were back in the academy after 9 months, all a bit more mature and ready to learn whatever it would take us to match our field experience with the theoretical lessons and grasp the intricacies required in our upcoming jobs. During this period, I was a member of the Officers Club Committee, and we organized many sports competitions and other cultural activities. Almost all festivals were celebrated with a lot of joy and exuberance. Coming together again after a field experience with some joy and some pain but with many concerns gave us a chance to share, reflect, and ask questions. We were soon to embark on a journey where no matter how many storms we faced, we had to keep control of the anchor.

Heer (me on the right) with my acting parents (Promila and Ranjit)

I participated in the cross-country race, running for the first time in my life and got a trophy as the first prize. K C Verma, an IPS officer, coached me for it. I remember being very tired and a bit sick afterwards as I got exposed to the chilly weather. We organized many cultural activities and put-up Heer Ranjha as a musical. I played Heer and Nadeem was Ranjha. Promila and Ranjit played the role of my parents. It's interesting that though I loved dancing, I had never done a Bhangra but it seemed to be in my blood as I taught Bhangra to this group of boys and girls and had a little bhangra performance as part of Heer Ranjha.

So, studies, games, and cultural activities kept us busy. Once in a while, I went to the huge kitchen downstairs and helped in cooking or guided in making Chow Mein

or Nepali Alu, etc. This period went in a jiffy. I regret not going to the get-togethers at the teacher's houses sometimes and making strong bonds with them, though my friend and batch-mate Veena Chottray tells me that she remembers my going to Mr. Gurumurti's house and making Gobi Ka paratha one morning. We also enjoyed Alu parathas at Harri's canteen.

The president, Mr. V. V. Giri, also visited us during this period. One interesting and heart-warming fact is about some matches formed in the academy. Some were already engaged or in love when they joined. However, with about 100 boys and 30 girls, there were 3-4 boys for a girl on the average, so some romances flourished, some found new loves, and some dropped their old crushes.

Some of the early matches which matured were Anita and Badal Das, two of my favourites; Veena and Devdas, who had already paired up when they were in the

Revenue Services a year earlier; Gopal and Sudha who had a fairy tale romance; and Promilla and Ranjit who were already married when they came to Mussoorie but were a fav couple of many. Naresh Dayal and Pratima got together later and are a very popular couple. Also Tajwar and Rakesh, whose romance blossomed much later.

Veena and Devdas

I don't know about every probationer, but parents definitely look for the possibility of a match here, for

Badal and Anita Das

their daughters in particular. Like many others, my parents also visited the Academy on a similar mission but were disappointed that I did not have a special interest in anyone. Of course, I liked some more than others, and there were one or two I went around with more than others or was more comfortable with, but that was it. I remember I liked a guy's singing very much; another whose working style and aloofness were a bit mystifying, and in the end, another guy who coached me in the running (the first time I had run the cross country) and who was safe and engaged to his childhood love.

I had never had a boyfriend; some guys were interested in me, and I was happy to talk but never felt attracted enough. In December 1974, we went in groups of 15 to an Army Attachment. This attachment was for us to understand the conditions in which the Armed Forces serves and also how to call for the assistance of the army as aid to civilian authorities. It is here that I was first strongly attracted to an army officer. We were sent to Binnaguri, which is on the border of Assam and W. Bengal, for an attachment with 16 Rajput. The commanding officer was Col. T. K. Ghosh. Our liaison officer was Capt. Deshmukh.

Our group leader was Lakhanpal from Punjab Cadre and our team consisted of 2 girls, Sudha Khanna (now Pillai) and me. Some of the officers stood out, like Major DD Sharma and Major Harjeet Sandhu; the latter was from Chandigarh. But the person who stood out prominently was Capt. Sudipto Mukherjee, who, apart from speaking flawless English, had a chivalrous attitude to us, lady probationers. There was no electricity and no lamp with

At Army attachment with the officers on duty with us, between me and Sudha is Col. Ghosh and in the last row, second from left is Sudipto Mukherjee

us. Soon Capt. Mukherjee's lamp was in our room. Then hearing Sudha's complaint about no mirror to dress up, his large mirror was in our room, though his batman Chuna Ram, who came to deliver it, was not happy! He was and is always correct, and the only thing I saw him doing otherwise was offering to teach Sudha to drive on the CO's jeep. He bought tickets for us lady probationers for New Year's Eve and the gentleman probationers were envious, but he explained that he had minimal money, Rs 1200/month salary (Rs 800 was his mess bill and Rs 400 he sent to his parents); our gentlemen probationers did not come. New Year's Eve was fun, and I danced a lot with Sudipto. I had danced very little earlier and only remembered one army New Year's Eve where I had danced socially. To this date, Sudipto loves dancing, and despite all his dancing expertise developed later in life, his original style (Pammi, his sardar friend in NDA, taught him dancing and drinking and smoking) remains unmatched, unique, and very charming. I was attracted to him and told my diary that but was disappointed to see that he tried to flirt with me as much as he did with someone else (later he said jokingly ‘both were willing’ and “what did you expect from a 25 years old”?) So, I withdrew, aware of my attraction for him in the sports field. I was embarrassed with myself for noticing his long legs in the football field and other places. I realized that he was lonely, with no real friends, and missing his sister, who had moved to the US after her marriage. He seemed to be seeking people with whom he could relate.

On the last night of our army attachment, our train was late, and since it kept getting delayed, our farewell party kept getting extended! Sudipto drank innumerable bottles of beer (we disagree on the number even now) and sang as many songs as the CO asked him to sing. We were seen off at the station by our liaison officer. On the return journey by train, I was in a daze but poured my heart out in my diary. Back in Mussoorie, we wrote letters to each other, which, with the passage of time, became infrequent, and finally, we were only exchanging birthday and New Year greetings and not sharing much. In about a year, during his visit home, he had written to me that he had fallen in love with a Bengali girl who his parents would not allow him to marry as she did not belong to a Brahmin family. I advised him to wait, and either he or his parents would change their minds. Within a few months, he learnt something about her, making him change his mind. You see, he and I were destined to be consorts, not just passing ships! I reproduce a poem he wrote then, which aptly describes the intangibility of the relationship.

The Rubber Band

Fickle moments
To be etched together
Upon fickle memories
Desperate attempts.

To hold on the
To the present
Regardless of the past
Conscious of what may come.

It's all like
The rubber bands
That holds your hair
It can be stretched so much
And no more

Stretch it with care
Let us not let it break
For that will have about it
An irrevocable finality.

...Sudipto Mukherjee (December 1972)

We completed our training in Mussoorie and were to join our States for our very first posting. I was posted as SDM Kandaghat, my first independent charge. I was thrilled, I knew Chail in Kandaghat was beautiful, but alas, a batch mate posted to Nurpur did not want to go there as he had done his training there, and also, the politicians did not want him (they had not met me yet), and hence my posting was changed to Nurpur. I didn't mind at that time, as I was excited to undertake my first independent charge. One year in Nurpur aged me by at least 5 years, but I learnt lessons there which stood me in good stead throughout my service.

Tough times and tough learning last you a lifetime. IAS gave us so much, an opportunity to serve in your best capacity and a whole lot of batchmates who could be your friends and support system throughout your life.

❒

Chapter 4

SDM Nurpur (1974-1975)

One of my toughest tenures

I joined as SDM Nurpur in July 1974. My probation was over, and I was now confirmed in service. I didn't have any idea what the place would be like, but I was excited about my first posting. Nurpur borders Punjab at Pathankot; it's a part of Kangra District and the District HQs are at Dharamshala. Manju's eldest sister Kailash lived in Pathankot (she still does), and she had me picked up from the railway station for a cup of tea at their place before sending me off to Nurpur, which was about an hour by road. At their house, I learnt that some prominent people from Nurpur who lived in Pathankot wanted to meet the new SDM. So there I was face to face with some politicians; the most prominent among them was Mr. Sat Mahajan, then President of the HP Congress Committee and with Congress in power in HP, he was a very important person. However, he had lost the elections to an independent candidate, Kewal Singh, who was the local MLA. Mr. Sat Mahajan tried to orient me throughout the evening. I was mostly quiet (when uncertain, my brother Haramrit advised me to keep quiet and not say anything). There were veiled suggestions that if I favoured anyone other than the ruling party, I would be transferred. Actually, Manju and her sister had advised me that I should not worry about relatives and to work honestly and fairly.

I reached home at night and set up my kitchen with a gas cylinder my mother had given me and some minimum basic utensils. I had also brought a bed, a dining table and chairs, and a fridge, given to me by my parents as they had duplicates. With barely 600 rupees or even less salary, I could not imagine buying furniture, utensils, etc.

My financial situation was sad. Sumi was my peon-cum-chowkidar, and had his official residence outside my house. He received visitors, served them tea if required, and initially cooked for me. I was aghast when in about 15 days, my salary would be over on tea, sugar, milk, and rations. I had two small Pomeranians, and I was told that their food, roti and dal, and the tea for the guests and visitors used up all the money.

However, one day, I came home unexpectedly early and found that the person I had employed to sweep the house and her daughter, who cooked for me, were eating on my dining table; they were also wearing some of my clothes. This mother-daughter combo was related to Sumi. Nurpur was a tough station in terms of sensitivity and so I did not get angry or yell at them. I just informed them that I was making some other arrangements for my cooking and cleaning and that Surni would receive visitors outside. This step changed the situation at home,

which became peaceful and happy. However, it was towards the end of the first quarter of my stay that it was settled and a sweet young girl worked for me.

The challenges at work were stupendous. It was overwhelming, trying, demanding and at the same time, enervating. The immediate crisis was that the Govt. imposed a ceiling on land holdings, which had to be implemented. Surplus land had to be taken from landlords and distributed to the landless. The first paper presented to me by my steno, Shanti Swaroop (God rest his wonderful soul in peace), was a telegram from HQs in Shimla asking me to ensure the completion of all ceiling and land distribution cases in a month. I had read the Ceiling on Land Holdings Act; I had to give at least 15 days' notice to the landlords, hear witnesses, check records and then pass orders. There were more than 400 cases; how could I do them in a month? Anyway, that's the first task I organised: who would prepare notices and when; and then went on to estimate when the respondents would appear, looked at the time for examining witnesses, going through revenue records and then passing judgements. There was no way it would take less than a year. Often the Civil Courts also get involved and though they are trying to address issues, often the clients use them to gain time. I started work in great earnest. My steno would join me at 7 AM and we would work till 9.30 AM mostly dictating judgements. My office was a hundred yards from home. At 9.30 AM, I would go home, have a quick bath and change, have a quick breakfast and go to the office by 10 AM. But when the work started, it was as if a dam had burst and the flow threatened to engulf me. Politicians called me on behalf of landlords. They would ask me to exempt this or that landlord and said that if I did not oblige, they would get my successor to handle it. I would politely explain that they made the law, I was only implementing it, and I would be grateful if they allowed me to fulfil my duties. The land is the lifeline of people, and mostly it is ancestral; people are emotionally attached to it and no one wants to let it go. I found the lawyers to be a big opposition. They charged per hearing and thought and

I was standing in the way of their income as I wanted to minimise hearings and postponements. As I realised this, I met with the Chairman of the Bar Association, Mr. Gupta, and I explained my compulsions and asked them to charge per case as I was going to dispose of them early. This made some difference, but not much. Some respondents would not receive the notice; some sent medical certificates for themselves or their witnesses just to buy time. So, I started going to the field and called witnesses there. This was easier; often, there were no advocates and most respondents in the villages were simple and straightforward. I could finish most of the cases but did not distribute all the surplus land because of a stay given by the Court in some cases or the need for consolidation of holdings in some other cases.

But this was only one of my tasks. I followed all procedures as the Courts (judiciary was now separate) could easily pass orders against me. In only one case did they pass against me for causing loss to an individual. I had suggested this individual should not close the path through his land for a scheduled caste person. This individual removed one bush he had planted to close the path and said that this one minute of labour had cost him Rs. 10. However, this judgment came a few years after I had left Nurpur; the Govt. appealed in the higher (sessions) Court and had it set aside.

Manju visited me and her visit provided me a great deal of calmness and tranquility. She had decided to marry Madhawan and they both came together and I was thrilled.

As I write this, I ask myself: What was the main problem in Nupur? It lacked law and order, e.g., people believed in hoarding food grains, keeping unlicensed weapons sometimes and fighting unnecessarily. Govt. had introduced price control and there were price labels on essential items, including food grains. But wholesalers in Damtal, which bordered Punjab, hoarded food grains, and a few times when I went on a surprise visit based upon complaints received, all the godown shutters came down immediately and were locked. However, the crime rate was not too high; one day, someone was murdered, and I kept calling the police station and looking frantically for the SHO. He was not available; there were no mobile phones in any case for me to call him wherever he was. The constable on duty said that SHO did not tell them where he was going. He told me later that he had gone to Pathankot as he sought orders from Mr. Sat Mahajan in such cases. I was shocked. This, I felt, was insulting. I was responsible for law and order in my subdivision. Luckily for me, the SP was Mr. Mallik, who had worked with my Daddy in the army. When he visited, he asked me how the police were functioning, and I mentioned that the SHO did not listen to me or even meet me. After this, the attitude of the police changed completely.

One day a whole lot of people came to me and told me that Tikki (it's a potato roll with a nice tamarind sauce) Wallas were selling Tikkis for Rs 10 each (they would normally have been Rs 2). An easy way out, I told them, was not to eat them, but these 2 guys had the licence to sell Tikis at the bus stand, and people requested for cancellation of their licences. Strictly speaking, Tikki is not an essential commodity and I tried not to be harsh, so I gave them a show cause notice. In turn, they galvanised some people from the city, which included other disgruntled elements, and took out a procession to my house, threatening to set fire to my vehicle. Let me tell you about some other disgruntled elements.

A lot of these elements were parents of class 10 and 12 school children and their friends. In March, during final exams, I got a call from a teacher who said, in a

choked voice, that mass cheating was going on in the board exams, and people had knives and firearms and were threatening them. The school was about 500 yards from my office, and the tehsil and police station were between my office and the school. So I just got up, left whatever I was doing and went to the police station. One policeman was at the front desk (without a uniform), and no one else was there to come with me to address this problem. I could not find anyone reliable at the tehsil either, so I went to the school. My steno Swaroop was with me. There were people inside and outside the hall assisting students. Teachers seemed helpless and one of these teachers had called me. Some people ran away, some were apologetic, others adamant. The correct thing to do was to make a report and the children would, in due course, be disqualified. When we started making the report, the parents and everyone who was assisting started begging and pleading for mercy. All teachers recommended leniency. How can I be lenient, I asked?

Oh, they said punish these children if you want. How can I punish? I'm not authorised? So, one of the parents said we would put black marks on their cheeks for the rest of this paper. I just shrugged my shoulders and left. The mistake I made was that I did not have a written complaint nor did I remember the name of the teacher who called me. There was a lot of annoyance in the home of the few girls and boys who had black marks put on their cheeks with their pens; it was misrepresented, with a question even being raised in the legislative assembly.

Enough about Law and order, let me tell you about the developmental work. I dreamt of doing so much for the poorer people but was stuck in the daily hearing of the land ceiling cases and also other revenue cases. I did some work on setting up minor irrigation schemes, better seeds, and timely fertilisers and also some help to the cottage industry, but mostly I was firefighting addressing problems. I remember going with my team to a remote village no officer had ever gone to, resolving some food supply issues and starting the women there on weaving baskets, mats etc., and tied up their sales with a cottage emporium. Maintaining quality, however, remained an issue.

I must tell you what I learnt was my greatest handicap. Why did the SHO not talk to me? Why did he not discuss the murder case with me? Why did he remove his cap and look the other way when he saw me? And why was the block development officer (BDO), Mr. Nahar, so indifferent and non-communicative? Why did he not even look at me when I spoke to him?

Mr. Subhash Mallick, the SP, after talking to the SHO, told me that the problem was that he was reluctant to accept a lady officer as head of administration of which he was a part. The BDO said at my farewell, later, in a choked voice, that he had not co-operated with me for a long time as I was a lady officer and that he was very ashamed of it. This was my first real experience of facing discrimination. And from here, I would see it for the rest of my life. Even though I would soon establish a reputation based on my work, at every posting, there were the same doubts about lady officers, and it seemed I had to prove myself all over again.

When it came to politics and politicians, there was Mr. Sat Mahajan, the President of the Congress Party, the party in power in the State, the Independent MLA, Kewal Singh, and Vikram Katoch, who was known as Chota Parmar. Dr. Parmar was our respected CM of the State. Vikram Katoch had been an aspirant and was supposed to indulge in a lot of politics but did not trouble me. Mr. Sat Mahajan was trying to ensure he won the next election. So if Kewal Singh came to my room, he would call me at once from Pathankot, where he ran a pharmacy, to ask me why Kewal Singh was in my room. I was aghast. I said he's the elected MLA from Nurpur. But this also meant that there was someone in my office who would inform him that Kewal Singh was here. That, someone, was the Licencing Clerk; there were a lot of complaints against him. So I replaced him with another official from the Tehsil and also kept the DC informed. And then, lo and behold, one night, when I was sitting in my lawn and doing some files and also going through ceiling cases, the DC's

Mr. Kaw and me

car drives in with Sat Mahajan. We got 2 more chairs and sat there in the lawn itself with mosquito coils.

Let me tell you about my D.C., Mr. M K Kaw. God rest his soul; he recently passed away. He was brilliant and supposedly had done his matriculation at age 10. He was good at everything: he wrote books and poetry, played games very well (badminton, etc.), sang very well, and was so great at his work that I always looked up to him in awe.

I had heard that when he was posted in Delhi as SDM, he had many problems, and though he was brilliant, he was also star-crossed, and often things went wrong for him. During my early months in Nurpur, there was a privilege motion in the assembly against him, and he wanted Sat Mahajan's help to settle it. He tried to appease him, but Sat Mahajan's interests were only in Nurpur and not any other part of Kangra District of which Mr. Kaw was the DC. So there was a flurry of questions and accusations, including why I changed the Licencing Clerk, who would help Mr. Mahajan during elections. They asked me to reverse those orders; otherwise, Mr. Kaw would reverse them, resulting in loss of my self-respect, I was told. I refused and said that such political reasons hindered me in discharging my duties. I told Mr. Kaw that he would not reverse my orders as he knew I was not wrong and we belonged to the same service. Mr. Kaw told Sat Mahajan that he could only write my confidential report after a year and then he would have a chance to act, but Mr. Mahajan could have me transferred at once and recommended that he do that. I was shocked and could not believe that this was Mr. Kaw speaking. I got up and said I really don't want to do this job and went inside to ask for tea for them but really to give my anger a few minutes to settle. Mr. Mahajan was waiting at the door, and as I came out, he said he was sorry, and he would never interfere in my work. I was amazed and I asked what had happened? He said that his daughter had married and had gone abroad, and when I reacted and got up and went away, he was reminded of his daughter! Here is how gender acted in my favour too. Mr. Sat Mahajan and I remained on the best of terms after this and he never called or asked for an untoward favour. I was very sad to attend his funeral a few years back. His son Ajay later became his father's worthy successor as an MLA from Nurpur.

Let me tell you about a law-and-order situation. We had the Panchayat Samiti elections coming up and the two parties were bitterly divided. I was not worried or scared and had the full confidence to do the right thing. There was talk of the possibility of shooting and killing, but I was calm and told everyone to vote peacefully.

On the day of the election, who do I see? Mr. M. K. Kaw was there with Mr. Mallik talking to people outside my office and Courtroom. Several people came in with them. I vacated my seat on the dais for him and went to my retiring room. I could hear him talking to people, finding out about the plans for the election and checking who was expected to create problems. I was clearing my files in the retiring room. Soon Mr. Kaw joined me and I offered him tea. He asked me or made a statement conjecturing that I did not like his coming here. I replied, "Sir, it is your District. You can go wherever you want." He explained that they had information that there would be law and order problems and there were so many people who had weapons, licenced or unlicensed. I said I know that there is apprehension, but I've done my homework and I don't think there will be a problem that I can't handle. However, I said, "it is good you are here. I'll have an opportunity to observe you". We had tea together, and soon, much before the elections started, I saw the DC and SP leave, satisfied with whatever enquiries they had made and also expressing confidence in me.

I must tell you how I first met Mr. Kaw: someone I admired a lot. But we did not begin well. In July 1974, I reached Nurpur to join my post as SDM and started work. I called up the DC office in Dharamshala and requested for time to call on him and also get instructions. I went on the appointed day. We did not have vehicles then how did we work? we borrowed the BDO's vehicle when needed and used any conveyance available: e.g., I also had to travel by trucks, by fire engine, etc. I went by bus from Nurpur to Dharamshala and walked to DC office. It was windy and rainy and I had worn a synthetic saree (so that it dries quickly) and had my umbrella. So in a slightly wet and clinging saree, I was a bit self-conscious when I reached his office and climbed the dais where he was sitting with his reader and Ahelmad. I wished him good morning and he did not seem welcoming, asked me why I had come. 'Oh,' I said, 'I have been posted as SDM Nurpur and have come to call on you.' I thought that he had not placed me! But he went on to say that Nurpur was such a tough place and what will a girl do there. He mumbled softly that women were best at home looking after family and producing children. Grimly, I asked him if he had any instructions for me. And he told me to go and meet the G.A., Mr. K. K. Mahajan and ask for instructions. I went and sank on a chair in Mr. Mahajan's room, who seemed to understand what I may have gone through in my first meeting. I then decided that I would not ask for help from Mr. Kaw ever again and he would see how a girl/woman could work.

So, you will understand my discomfort when he came without announcing. He did not trust me, I thought, so when they left before the election started, I was happy as it showed that there was some kind of trust in my capability.

After this, my relationship with Mr. Kaw was better and I started getting rid of my annoyance. I will tell you about the head clerk whose family was in Dharamshala. He was drunk every morning when I reached the office. Often, I found him sitting at the gate when I reached the office in the morning and his reason was that his family was not with him, so he had nothing to eat but drinks. What an excuses! However, all my counselling failed, and I wrote to DC requesting his transfer to Dharamshala, where his family lived.

I had not spoken to Mr. Kaw about this and was surprised at his response on receiving my letter. I expected him to say something like, "See, these women officers cannot handle their staff," but I was surprised to see that Mr. Kaw had suspended my head clerk on my letter and fixed his headquarters in Dharamshala so that he could be with his family. After this supportive action came the assembly question about black ink on children's faces, which he handled well after checking with me!

DC inspects SDMs offices once a year and this becomes an occasion to discuss programmes, find out problems and seek solutions. DC came to inspect my office and complimented me. We sat in my retiring room having tea; he asked me if I had any problems and needed his help, and I said no. He said he was very surprised that I was not coming up with problems. Other SDMs made big lists even before he came. He had noted that I had no stationery in the office and needed a lot of paper to write evidence, he looked at me, and I hesitated. He said, 'Come out with it' gently. I took his word that he would neither make fun of me nor ask questions, nor talk about it again. And he promised. So, I told him that the probationer attached to him should not visit Nurpur. He said OK and left. I'm sure he understood, as Krishan Lal did not visit again. Krishan Lal was a probationer in Kangra who had been conferred judicial powers for Nurpur during his training and thus came to Nurpur often. Initially, I was very nice to him and he was having all his meals at my place. Soon I started noticing that his demeanor was not right. While I could handle his flirtatious tendencies, I could not stop his talking loosely to local officials about me. One day he came to my home at night and I did not open the door and told him that it was too late and he was not welcome. He picked up my dog (Pomeranian) from the lawn and said he was taking my dog away. I did not call for help or shout for the chowkidar, as I was avoiding a scandal. Nurpur would have been delighted to gossip about me. As you can see in the discharge of my duties, I annoyed a lot of people. I sent my driver in the morning to collect my dog from the rest house where he was staying. After I spoke to DC, Krishan Lal never came to Nurpur and Mr. Kaw did not make fun of me or talk about it. Krishan Lal was caught by CBI in some fraud /money laundering cases and terminated later; he had enquiries against him even for multiple marriages, but that's his story.

Ultimately, Mr. Kaw was an awesome boss. I cannot close this chapter without mentioning the Executive Engineer (XEN) PWD.

While I had good relations with officers of other departments, I became close to Mr. and Mrs. Punhani, XEN PWD. This friendship lasted throughout. I was

Mr. Punhani's family with us after my marriage

Rowing in a small boat in a pond outside my residence with Mr. Sat Mahajan on the left and Chief Secretary U N Sharma on the right

also friendly with XEN Electricity. This is important as usually the PWD officers do not get along with the IAS officers and create problems for each other, but in this case, they were my support system! I also had the Chief Secretary, Mr. UN Sharma, visit me and in a small boat, I rowed him and Sat Mahajan the small pleasures of being in Nurpur.

I was completing my tenure, my staff accepted me, and people began to appreciate me. I was, however, called Jhansi ki Rani after I sat on the bonnet of my jeep in front of a procession threatening to burn my jeep. When my brother Haramrit's marriage was fixed, I took 15 days' leave and tried to round off my work before leaving as my tenure was ending. I got my posting orders in Chandigarh and went back to Nurpur to collect my luggage and say goodbye.

1972

2017

SDM's residence in Nurpur

A fitting epitaph to my tenure in Nurpur was given by Mr. Sat Mahajan. He said that he visited a remote area where no officers went as it involved a lot of walking on foot. He was so surprised to see that I had been there and addressed all their problems by going out of my way, he said that I had not told others about it and advised me to do some PR. He said Ravan's P.R. was bad and even though he did not touch Sita, he is condemned and Ram is worshipped as he had a good PR even though he turned Sita out!! He said that there was only one person who could win the election against him and that was me as I was so popular with the work I had done!

I went to pay my regards to DC and was treated with warmth and hospitality by him and his wife. I then said farewell to the Chief Judicial Magistrate and when I laughed at his jokes, the constable on duty conveyed to the constables in Nurpur, "This Madam also knows how to laugh!!" but I was a sadder person after having seen and borne and also done so much.

Many years later, after retirement, I visited Nurpur and was happy to see that people still remember me. The house is the same and I posted the two pictures; the first one was taken in 1975 and the second in 2017!

Probably my toughest posting, but it also provided a lot of learning which has lasted me a lifetime.

It was almost like being chiseled into different shapes till you were all new in your original like shape but a sadder person.

❒

Chapter 5

Deputy and Joint Sec. Personnel (1974-77)

My Soulmate and Shimla

In July 1975, I was in Chandigarh to attend my brother, Haramrit's wedding. When I went to book the 16 Rajput band at Chandimandir on my father's request, I met Sudipto again at the house of Major Sandhu. I was not the same person after Nupur; I was more mature, a little sadder and a bit disillusioned. I was also not keeping too well. Sudipto came home the next day to meet my parents. He, too, was more mature and quieter but still very loveable and charming. He charmed everyone: my brothers, Manju and my parents. Since my father and brother were also from the army, there was a lot of army talk and everyone was comfortable with each other. Manju's parents and my family members had never seen Manju so relaxed with anyone, they thought that Sudipto and Manju were special friends. They did not yet know about Madhavan! Manju's eldest sister Kailash in Pathankot was preparing dinner sets for our weddings which she hoped would happen soon.

Sudipto was also sad, not about not marrying Moyna, but generally: because he kept wanting to leave the army. He had resigned once, but it had been rejected.

He had landed himself a job in the tea gardens. Having been posted in Binaguri, he had made friends in the tea gardens and got a job with Jardine Henderson, about which he had been very excited. The reasons he gave for leaving the army were "nothing constructive; we are only preparing for war" and disappointment with the perceived dishonesty within the army. I personally feel that as an intellectual, perhaps he should have joined some other wing and not the infantry. He also said that he could not sleep well and only slept in the early morning hours. We started going to the rear side of Sukhna Lake, he on his motorbike and I on my scooter. We first went there as I wanted to share the beauty of the lake in my city, and he had said he found nothing great in it. When we went together, he found it very peaceful and serene. We started sharing our disappointments and sorrows, our joy and excitements. This became our meeting place.

I was full of tales of Nurpur and unlike when I met him earlier, I talked and he was interested, concerned, and listened patiently. I liked this empathetic boy even more but was no longer feeling romantic and settled in for a comfortable friendship.

I had been suffering from giddiness and unsteadiness. I went with my parents to the PGI. Dr. Chuttani was the Director and had served with my father in the Second World War, so we had easy access. After plenty of tests and consideration, a young senior resident doctor, Dr. Jaswant Rai, concluded it was spondylitis, a newly emerging lifestyle disease. It usually does not happen to active people and I could have got the wrong posture during sports, e.g., horse riding. This is a common problem now with people hunched over their computers in inappropriate postures. However, it was not a known problem then. I did not like the words used: 'degenerative disease', 'can control but not set back the clock' and so on. Talking about my health to Sudipto was a new and comforting experience.

For Haramrit's wedding, just 5 of our family members (including Manju) went in the car. There was no large Barat, and we partied with relatives and friends on their return to Chandigarh.

As I had mentioned earlier, the band was from 16 Rajput. For the reception, Sudipto came in a black bush-shirt with small white polka dots and sat between my Mom and me on the lawn outside our Sector 8 house. He is a rum drinker and was drinking rum and coke while people were singing. He was also smoking cigarettes. I belong to a Sardar family where smoking is taboo, but guests do smoke (my brothers did too but not in front of our parents; for that matter, Sudipto also did not smoke in front of his parents). Soon his cigarettes were over and he asked his unit bandmaster for some who gave him bidis, so low and behold, Sudipto was smoking bidis sitting next to my Mom. He has later justified this by saying that at that time, she was a fellow officer's wife.

My parents were very keen to at least announcing my engagement on that day, and one senior officer IAS officer who was unmarried was to come over that morning for the purpose of a formal meeting for matrimony with me. From all accounts, everything appeared perfect. I was, however, unsure of things. This gentleman was a DC in Delhi and that day, section 144 was imposed and he could not come. Whilst this discussion was taking place, Sudipto gently commented that their unit band would not play at my wedding, which supposedly was to happen with this guy!

Marriage over, it was time to go to Nurpur, pick up my stuff, say goodbye, and come back as my posting orders had come as Deputy Secretary Personnel in the Secretariat in Shimla. In fact, I was being posted as the Deputy Managing Director of HP Tourism Corporation and had been quite excited but later learnt that Sat Mahajan had put his foot down. Even though we were on good terms, he knew I was not at all pliable. I knew nothing about my job in Personnel but would learn soon and acquire expertise for my life.

I must tell you more about Sudipto and me. A day before I left, Sudipto mentioned that he would like to go to Shimla and drop me there. I said that was not a good idea as my parents may drop me at Kalka as the train left from there and that the Punhanis would be at the Shimla railway station to pick me up. I was going to stay with them till I got a house. However, Sudipto did not seem convinced and was smiling as he bade me farewell before he left our place.

The next morning, my Daddy and my brother loaded my baggage in the car and drove me to Kalka. They put me on the train which goes from Kalka to Shimla. It is a lovely toy train, stopping at remote stations tucked away in the lush green forests of the mountainside. I settled down with a magazine, and within 10 minutes, Sudipto was saying Hi. He was in the neighboring compartment. I asked why he had come and he said, "for the pleasure of your company". He looked relaxed and charming.

He wore a check bush-shirt and black trousers and his smile was infectious. We soon relaxed and settled down to an easy conversation which was quite impersonal. He did not try to hold hands or say anything romantic. The only personal element was that he asked me to sing and when I said I can't, he insisted, and the moment I sang one line, he burst out laughing and has never asked me to sing again. When we reached Shimla, he stretched and shook my hand and was suddenly gone, allowing me to meet the Punhanis alone.

In fact, after that, I was never by myself, Manju was already a part of me, and we had a lot of telepathy. Sudipto said that he now planned to come to Shimla on weekends; when I looked a bit alarmed, at least alternate ones, he added. He was about 3 hours away and came by bus or motorbike on weekends. We were very happy together and drifted into an easy companionship. The problem, however, was that I was staying with the Punhanis initially, and one day, when both of us went for a movie, we took a longer route to go back. It was dusk and getting dark when we met the Punhanis, who teased me for a while for walking in "Andheri galliyan".

They were kind of guardians and asked me what was going on with us and remarked, "We know you guys will never marry." I asked them how they were so sure as I myself had not yet come to that conclusion. They said they were sure I would marry an IAS officer. There was an IAS officer who kind of joked and when people asked him if we were related, he would jokingly say, 'Not yet.' I would laugh and say that there was nothing between him and me! Actually, I was completely content with Sudipto but wondered if this was love. I was happy in our relationship and soon, I got a small flat in Brockhurst and shifted there, a 2-bedroom flat, my first home in Shimla. My parents gave me a dog, Pixie. I always loved dogs; Princey and Bully, the two dogs I had in Nurpur, had died of distemper and I had been heartbroken. My parents had then given me Pixie, another Pomeranian who we grew to love a lot.

There is an interesting story which Sudipto manipulates a bit while narrating. Manju started calling me Motu; compared to her, I was plump, so I also started calling her Motu in retaliation, but soon it was an affectionate term we used for one another. Somehow Pixie also began to be called as Motu. Sudipto says when he came into my life, I replaced calling others Motu and called him Motu. Actually, the story goes like this: he was very fit and I was plump (54 kg, 5.4″ height) as compared to him, so he called me Motu. I, in turn, called him Motu too and then others ceased to be motus!!

Let me talk about the office. Our Chief Secretary, who is also the head of Administration in the State, was Mr. U.N. Sharma, a hardworking man who was glued in the evening to his drinks. He had a lovely wife who used to say that he could put a straw in a bottle and drink it up in one go. She dreamt of the house or orchard they could have bought if he was not drinking! Thankfully, they managed to buy an orchard in Chail, which they sold off after he retired. He was my boss, very officious and good but never had the time to brief me properly. So, who briefed me? My Section

Officers. I was Deputy Secretary (Personnel) and there were two sections, Appointments 1 and 2; their Section Officers being Mr. Bhupinder Singh and Mr. Sood. Both were great in themselves but very different. Section 1 dealt with the appointments, postings, and service conditions of IAS and IPS officers, Head of Departments and Section 2 dealt with the Public Service Commission and policy matters. With reservations for Scheduled Castes and Scheduled Tribes and especially Backward Classes, this section became very critical during my tenure. I worked here for 3 years, two as Deputy Secretary and one as Joint Secretary. I learnt a lot here and this knowledge would help me for the rest of my professional life too. Mr. UN Sharma was relaxed. He told me to go to Chief Minister directly and clear my files with him. This was the beginning of my writing strong apolitical notes!

One of the main things a politician can do to scare or harm you is raise a transfer. This requires very little or no justification. Thus, many officers do not complete their minimum tenure of 2 or 3 years. Officers with children going to school or college do not want a change in between and often toe the line of the politician. The problem is that in this way, the politicians can scare you. Later in life, my daughter Mitali had a nanny named Dwarko. Dwarko would make up a fictitious character who she called Budha Baba to scare Mitali. Transfers were a "Budha Baba" for most Govt. officials. If we could handle this Budha Baba, we could work better without fear or favour. I was always clear that I would not worry about my transfer and this gave me a whole lot of strength. Thus when I got letters addressed to CM from MLAs, and they were marked down to Chief Secretary (CS) and then to me, I would find out the facts of the case and then put it up to Chief Secretary with a note defending those whose tenure was not over and proposing changes in cases where it was justified. CS, instead of signing this, would ask me to go and discuss the file with the CM. Dr. Parmar, the then CM, was wonderful, more like the British and in my Confidential Report, right from my training in Mandi, wrote "an Outstanding Officer." I was lucky, Dr. Parmar trusted me and was strong enough to sometimes not listen to those proposing the transfers. CS was happy that I was able to manage this tricky issue of postings. I was to learn later that even the senior officers are sometimes so insecure that they do not allow the junior officers to go to the Chief Minister.

Now about Sudipto and me. I shifted to my small flat in Brockhurst, and my brother Sawraj came to stay with me. He was also preparing for the IAS. He and Sudipto got on well, and it just seemed normal for us to sit together in the evenings on the weekends that Sudipto visited. One night when it started raining, Sawraj asked Sudipto to stay over and Sudipto stayed in Sawraj's room and Sawraj slept in my room. On his next visit, Sudipto had a fever and he was cold and shivering. So, I bought him anti-malaria drugs and B Complex with Crocin. Sudipto said he would never eat medicines without a doctor's prescription. Also, contracting malaria was a punishable offence in the Army because it meant one had not taken the laid down precautions. He was so adamant and I was so hurt that when we were walking on the hillside, I threw the medicines down the mountain, never to be retrieved. I did not know that he had such a stubborn streak in him. He used to call me "almost MBBS" and yet he would not take the medicine I was so sure of. Anyway, he went to a doctor later who gave him the same medicines he had thrown (even though the test was negative). Such rare incidents apart, we talked a lot and were very comfortable, but the relationship had plateaued while my parents continued to suggest boys for marriage. I had once told them when I was in Nurpur that it was awkward for me to ask for leave unless I have a very valid reason, so why don't they see boys before calling me. I even went on to say that I would marry anyone they chose. But that was not to be.

Sudipto said he had to go to Mhow to do a BSW course, and would be back after 4 months. I would miss him so much. But before he left, I was to go to Chandigarh and he proposed I get off at Kalka, and we go to a Haryana Tourism restaurant in Panchkula, Red Bishop, for coffee. After our coffee, we went to the lake on his motorbike and for the first time, he held me and kissed me as we sat near the water on the hard stones. The first expression, but not much was said in words. Before he left, he gave me an audio cassette he had recorded for me, saying that I could hear that when I missed him. We went around on his motorbike for a few rounds and then he dropped me at Manju's house and left. That was the 30th of August and the 31st was his birthday.

This cassette was the catalyst that would change everything. I would hear it every night in Shimla just before sleeping after the lights were off. It would always stop at the end, and I would rewind it the next day to play from the beginning. Meanwhile, Sudipto would call every 4th day. The telephone connection was through Army exchanges from Mhow to Indore, Indore to Bombay, Bombay to Delhi, and Delhi to Shimla. He would give the operator a bottle of Rum to get the call through, and this is the extent of what you may call corruption. Never again and nothing more.

The telephone operator in Mhow who would put the call through was named Albert. All officers who had calls to make knew Albert. Whenever Albert was on night duty, there would be a bunch of officers waiting by the solitary telephone in the Officer's Mess. Albert would ask one officer to pick up the phone and weasel his way through the operators in the intermediary exchanges to put the call through. He would not hesitate to use all kinds of excuses with these intermediaries: mother is seriously ill, sister is getting married, grandfather has expired, or simply love story hai. Sudipto was quite sure Albert would listen in. And sometime during the week, he would meet up with the officer and say things like my sister is getting married, can you help me with a bottle of Rum, or my mother is sick and the doctor says she should have brandy; and of course, the officers knew it was a polite way of carrying out the transaction.

Now what was in the cassette I have it even now. He told me how important I am in his life and in different words and ways, he ended by saying that I was like a diamond and any light that passes through the diamond became so glorious. He stopped there, no "I love You" or "Will you marry me?". But I would feel nice and warm and comforted hearing just what he had to say. Then one day, when I was about to switch it on, I saw it had stopped halfway. I was aghast! I thought Sawraj had heard it and with our sibling rivalry, he would surely tell my parents.

Mummy and Daddy had always told me to tell them in case I liked someone and they would be hurt if they heard about Sudipto from Sawraj and not from me. I was frantic; what shall I tell them? He may not be intending to marry me, I thought. But I could not afford to wait as Sawraj was going to Chandigarh. So, I dropped a line asking them how important caste and religion were if I decided to favor a boy I liked. They called me and asked me who it was. I would not tell. So, they asked where is he, I answered that he was far away, still misleading them as they thought Sudipto was posted in Chandimandir and did not know that he had gone to Mhow. They were disturbed and I said, "I'm asking you before he has asked me," and "I'm 28 and not 18 and not going to run away." Despite my trying and saying different things, they guessed as they always knew all my friends and said it could not be anyone else. I requested Manju, who was posted in Delhi, to go to Chandigarh to meet them and find out as they were not communicating with me. Manju went and said they were fine and were talking of Punjabi rites for the wedding.

So all would be fine and I should not worry.

Meanwhile Sudipto called and I was so edgy waiting for his call, I also did not know how to tell him. Anyway, I knew I had to, so I told him that Sawraj had heard the cassette and I had to tell my parents. He was amused and asked me what I told them. I said that I did not know what to say as I didn't know what he wanted from this relationship. He laughed and said, "stupid girl, I want to change the rubber band into a gold band." refer to the poem on Page 67. I was in seventh heaven and realised that, for some time, this was what I wanted. All my objections about not marrying an army officer, as I had missed my Daddy too much, were gone and I basked in the idea of spending my life with him. I actually started feeling beautiful. Once Manju had commented that I was not pretty and I had actually never found myself pretty till that day.

Now my parents said that they wanted to meet Sudipto again. I said it was impossible for him to come and that they had met him so many times. My Mother said that they had never looked at him from that angle. My Daddy remembered his dress and smoking bidis! So, there I was, telling Sudipto what my parents said. He readily said he would come on Saturday as they had a 3-day mid-term break. Apart from leave, the other problem was money; air tickets were very expensive then, more than a few months' salary, and hence were not affordable. So, he sold his motorbike and came to Delhi. Though my parents did not know or suspect it, I went to Delhi. We went to Connaught Place as Sudipto wanted to buy me a ring. We went to Zaveri. Diamonds were unaffordable and he wanted to buy a diamond ring. We purchased a pair of small gold earrings, promising ourselves that when we had sufficient money, we would buy a super engagement ring. We actually did that 8 years later! We came back that night by bus to Chandigarh. The bus reached Chandigarh at around 4 in the morning, too early to go home, so we went to Ranjit and Promilla's house, woke them up, and had a cup of tea and chatted with them, they were one of my closest friends. Sudipto went to his regiment in Chandimandir, and I went home; ostensibly, I had just arrived from Shimla. Sudipto came around 11 AM and sat with my parents talking about the army while Mummy sat for some time there and later was preparing lunch. I helped her with the lunch, and after it was over, they again moved to the drawing room. Meanwhile, my Mom spoke to me separately and said that he does not seem interested as he is not talking about marriage, and was I sure or was I presuming that he is interested. I requested her to ask him as I was sure, but she said that Daddy would be most annoyed if she asked. I asked her in an impatient voice how she could worry about Daddy's possible annoyance when we would miss this opportunity. I said they know he has come from Mhow to meet them, so how could they have a doubt? Anyway, as Sudipto got up to leave, I went in and Mummy asked him finally, "Beta, will your parents agree?" He looked surprised at the question but said, "Yes".

Daddy laid down three conditions. First, he said his parents must agree because a wedding also unites two families, not just the couple. Second, he said that marriage is essentially a Kanyadaan so that Sikh rites would be followed. And the third condition was that we should not meet each other until we married. This last condition was broken within the day!

I took a bus back to Shimla from Chandigarh. Sudipto knew the approximate time of my bus, and had one of his senior officers, Maj D D Sharma, drop him on his scooter to Kalka so that he could join me on the bus to Shimla from there. He told me his parents would never agree as they did not agree even with a Bengali girl as she was not a Brahmin. I said okay, let's try and write to them together. He wrote to them mentioning that I was in the IAS and telling them about my parents and ended by saying that I would make a good daughter to them.

We were delighted to get a telegram from my in-laws congratulating us. My father-in-law also wrote to my Daddy in his beautiful handwriting and that started a dialogue. Sudipto's parents agreed to Punjabi rites in Chandigarh as long as they could carry out Bengali rites once we went to their house. The date was fixed for 22 Feb 1976. Sudipto's course was finishing at the end of January. He would come back to his unit and then take leave to go home and come with his family. I told my friends and actually won a bet with Mrs. Punhani, who had insisted that I would not marry Sudipto. She had to give me a pair of gold earrings, I settled for 'baalis'.

In the office, I now had the additional charge of Joint Secretary (Home) and both charges required extra hours, especially during assembly sessions and I could not go back home and do any shopping for my wedding. My parents did most of it and that was fine. I went home just 2 days before my wedding and on 15 days' leave. My brothers and friends came. We saw Mughal-e-Azam, which was playing in the theatres and went for a facial. My mother remarked jokingly that I should have come with the Barat. That's all.

On the 21st night, Sudipto called me from Delhi Station; one had to go to a different platform to book a call and then wait for the call to get through. The baraat reached Chandigarh early in the morning by Kalka Mail. Manju joined the reception party with my brother and Daddy and the baraatis were put up in Panchayat Bhavan. The reception of the baraat was scheduled at 9 AM., At around 7 AM, the ladies in the baraat came to put haldi and chandan on my body and hair. Now I would have to wash my hair again, I thought. However, before I could do that, Manju said Sudipto was waiting outside and wanted to meet me and maybe go for a walk. Oh my God, I thought, I just couldn't go, but he was insistent, so I sneaked out and forgot everything as we walked to the lake and back. My Daddy was frantically looking for me. He thought I had wedding nerves and had disappeared. Anyway, there was no time to talk, Daddy being a stickler for time, I did not press for answers and went to wash my hair, bathe and dress up. Somehow, I managed to get ready in time.

I was out right in time for the Jaimala at 9.00 A.M.

Manju had brought me a diamond Tikka which she helped me to put on, but it caused heartburn amongst other family members.

My grandmother was still alive and it was great to receive blesssings from my mother and grandmother I was in seventh heaven. The baraatis liked the food and the doli left after lunch.

My Chief Secretary, Mr. U. N. Sharma, drove from Shimla in his car, as opposed to an official with a driver. Mr. Sat Mahajan came, as did many colleagues and friends.

Sudipto's unit band played, with same Band Master, Hav Subuddi, who had lent him a pack of bidis during Haramrit's wedding, except that there was no such transaction this time around!

Mummy and Daddy looked exhausted and we left by the night train to begin our new journey.

Sudipto's family also went through an Ashirwad ritual, where the elders bless the bride. It is actually like an engagement done before the wedding in the Bengali scheme of things. Since the Bengali wedding was to happen again in Gaya, the sequencing was okay from their point of view.

We came back home for dinner, where Daddy and Baba got to interact for a bit.

Baba and Daddy having chit chat just before we left

16 Rajput families as part of the barat

Sudipto's CO, Col Waraich, and the officers of his unit were also there.

Never say Goodbye

One doesn't realise how beautiful the world can be... Love can bring joy and light anywhere...all my dreams about an ideal man seemed fulfilled.

❐

Chapter 6

Joint APC

(1977-1979)

Post marriage: it was a bliss to be alive!

Thus, on the 23 of February 1976, I began my journey to my in-laws' house, where in due time, I was overwhelmed by the love and affection I got. However, it took time to grow to know each other and, more importantly, to appreciate and understand each other. My mother-in-law had not come for our wedding in Chandigarh, as this is the tradition among Bengalis. However, my father-in-law,

his elder brother, his elder son, then a Colonel in the Army, and daughter-in-law, along with other relatives, had come. Officers from Sudipto's regiment, 16 Rajput, also attended the wedding.

Initial interactions with the wedding party started on our way back and were not great. We were on the train going to Gaya - Manju and I were in one compartment, and Sudipto insisting on being with us was a bit frowned on. Also, some other comments are normally passed in a wedding. My little or minimum knowledge of Bengali was also put to the test. I was not too well on the train, nauseous, and had a headache. However, as we arrived at the station, I got into my bridal dress and got down to a welcoming band playing at the station. Ma received me at home and touched honey to my lips, ears, and eyes. Sudipto promptly put honey on her too! Symbolically, Ma was saying see good, speak good and hear good and Sudipto said, "you too." This was too sweet and interestingly new for me.

Bengalis have a tradition of "kaal ratri", where the couple does not see or meet each other for 2 nights or so and does not meet even during the day. Sudipto kept pleading with his mom, saying that I knew no one there, let him meet me and so time and again he would come up. As you probably know, I am a person of action and it is difficult for me to be so inactive. I was happy when I heard Tinku, Sudipto's younger sister, say that her clothes were not stitched well and she was to wear them for bahu bhat at their form of reception from the boys' side. I quickly altered her clothes using Ma's sewing machine. This created a bit of surprise, "she knows how to sew," exclaimed Nau-ma, Maa's elder sister. Sudipto promptly added, "She also knows how to brush her teeth." Sudipto and I both wore mukuts during the pheras. Sudipto requested Ma, 'You were so sad that Didi (Sudipto's elder sister, who had been married many years earlier) had to sit with contact lenses on, the smoke from the havan going into her eyes. You couldn't do anything then, but you can now "please finish the pheras early", he requested, as I also wore contact lenses and the smoke from the fire made my eyes water. When I was asked to touch his feet, I kissed them (of course, no one else saw it).

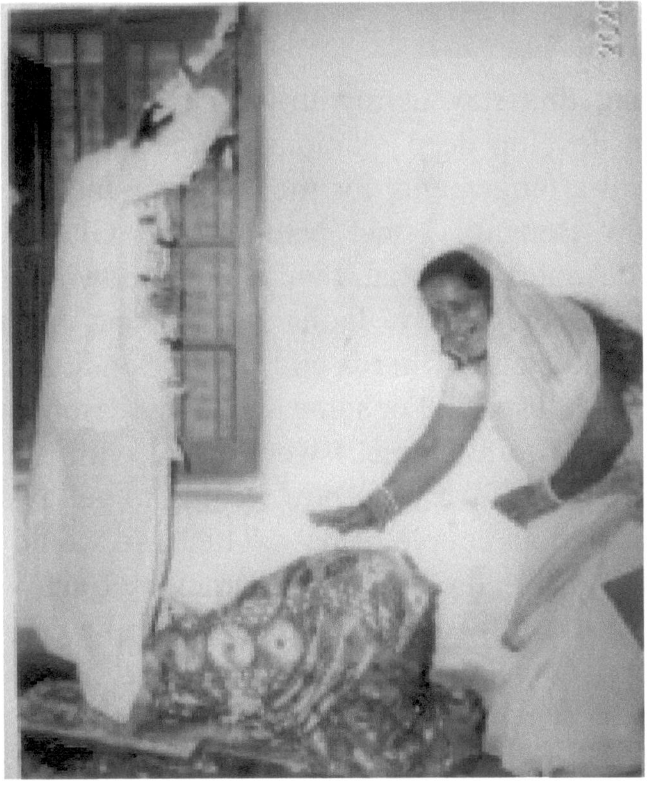

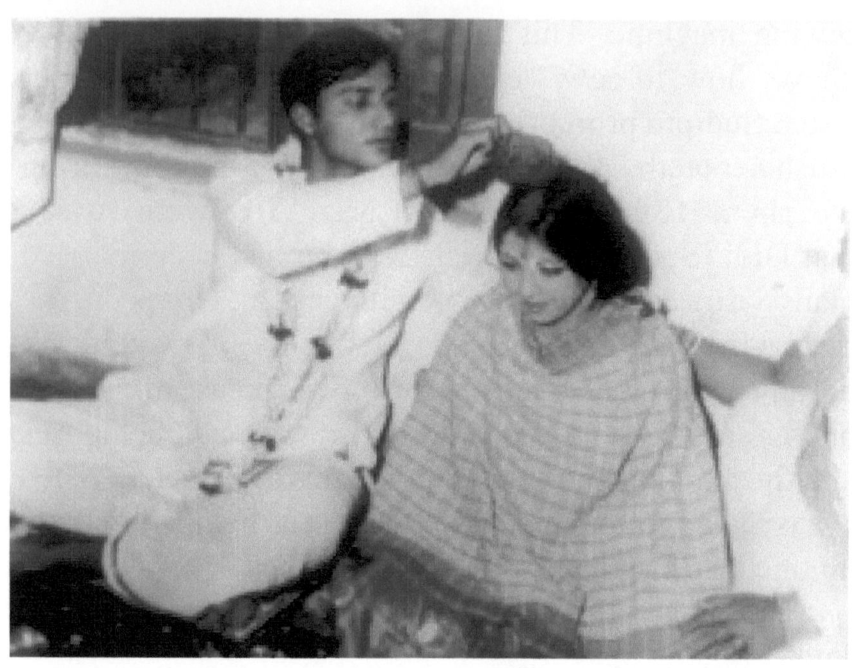

During this stay at my in-laws for about a week, I did not develop deep relationships as the family was busy with arrangements for the wedding and also I did not know Bengali. I met Nau-ma and Gita di, who I liked, but apart from that, I only got to know immediate members of the family. Jaitha Moshai and Jathai Ma, Babu da and Boudi, Chorda and Choto Boudi, and Mejo Boudi were all sweet. For some unknown reason, Sudipto would not go to a temple. I went inside with Ma while he stood outside. We were now itching to get away and had kept aside a couple of days which we would spend by ourselves. So, on our return journey by train, we first stopped in Delhi with Dada, where we had a ceremony, then stopped overnight in Chandigarh and then went off to Chamba (I remember having a bad throat and fever) before we went to Shimla to join our duties.

With my parents on the way back to Shimla

Meanwhile, Sudipto had a prize posting to NDA. It was a prize posting since he had done so well in his courses he topped the Young Officers Course too. However, Daddy said that at least for the first year of our married life, we should spend together. I offered to leave my job, but my Chief Secretary said no, not so soon as I may regret it. Sudipto did not want to interfere as he felt that if he encouraged me to leave, I might blame him, but if he encouraged me to stay, I might think he was after the perks of my job. He preferred to ask for a change in posting, and he got an inconsequential posting in Shimla in the Territorial Army HQs, as that was the only vacancy. And so, we started our married life in Shimla.

The surprising element at work was that my Chief Secretary had changed. Mr. Tochwang, the next senior officer became CS as Mr. Sharma did not get the expected extension. When I went to the office on the first day, he asked me if he should give me a change as mine was a key post. I said sure, as I would have been happy with a lighter job at this time. But when he said that my loyalties were with Mr. U N Sharma, I told him that there would never be any conflict in my loyalties. I also invited him home for a welcome dinner with Mr. U N Sharma, whom I invited for a farewell dinner. We did not have drawing room chairs, so we sat on trunks and whatever seating arrangement we had. I had learnt never to be embarrassed about your home. I continued as JS personnel with the additional charge of Home.

After marriage, most couples get invited to parties and we did too. So, I was always tired: heavy work, late night parties and moving around even on weekends kept me exhausted. Let me tell you about one of our first parties at the house of DIG CID. But before this, I have to recount one incident before our marriage that led to a kind of *pre-nuptial agreement* (or so says Sudipto). We were sitting at a restaurant at Oberoi Clarks and he ordered rum and coke which is his favourite drink. We were chatting in the warm and congenial atmosphere when I knocked his drink over and it fell on his clothes. I looked so embarrassed, and as I said very sorry, he smiled and said, "minor point". I was relieved but asked, "will you continue to say minor point rest of your life when I am so clumsy?" He replied in the affirmative but asked me never to count his drinks. He said that his regimental officer, Maj Sandhu's wife, Ruby, said that led to a lot of bickering. I said OK but don't get drunk. He said yes, but what if I feel like getting drunk?

I said that he should not get drunk in public. I agreed that if he wanted the company to drink, I would drink with him. Now about this party at the DIG's house. It was a few minutes' walk from our house, and we left at one past 8 (Sudipto commented we were late, but we were the first to arrive as the time given was 8). Apart from some officers who trailed in, some German girls were at the party wearing short dresses. And oh, I forgot to mention that an emergency had been declared by Indira Gandhi and fundamental rights suspended. On this day, there was news that the press had been gagged. After a few drinks, a heated discussion on the emergency started; the host was trying to calm people down as he was DIG (CID). Sudipto felt very strongly about freedom of the press and when there was an uproar against Sanjay Gandhi, who seemed to be orchestrating this, he said, "Sanjay Gandhi should be shot," and I tried to calm him down. "No one will shoot him", I said and he replied, "I will shoot him, and I will become a martyr". There was pin drop silence. I was also in charge of Law & Order as Joint Secretary (Home). Anyway, the conversation settled down and I did not say anything that night. Next morning, I talked to him and while he insisted that he was not drunk and I agreed, though he was very close to it, he promised that this situation would not occur again and he has kept his word, I still don't count his drinks and he does not get drunk.

We had a small flat and a young boy to cook for us. Daddy had sent beds with Sudipto, but we still did not have decent seating in the drawing room. So, I had put trunks covered with blankets, bedcovers or sheets and we sat on them. And we were so happy. I had long office hours, while Sudipto would finish by lunch. He walked to HQ Western Command from Chota Shimla every day and then back home. He picked up lunch from home and brought it to the office which we ate together (though late) and then he went home again and came and picked me up around 6 or 7. Sometimes he suggested a movie and we would walk to the Mall and back. Vehicles are not allowed in the Mall but even where they were allowed, we could not go as we had no vehicle.

Shimla is a popular tourist destination, and many summer events happen. We went to Hotel Oberoi Clarke's that summer and danced. We got the best couple prize on the dance floor; he got a bottle of whisky while I got a travelling iron! Gender issue, I thought even then: men can drink and women get to iron!

It's worth mentioning that there were a lot of monkeys and the first sofa set we ordered from money given by friends and relatives at our wedding was torn by monkeys as the truck driver left the sofas outside for us to put inside on return from the office.

We had a young man working for us, Dilawar Singh. One day when we came back from work, we could not find him in the flat. Looking around, finally, he emerged from the kitchen store. He said that monkeys had come into the flat and he had locked himself up there to remain safe. Ironically, some months later, I helped him to join the Himachal Police!

Two months into our marriage, I was expecting. I was nauseous and had missed my periods. Sudipto was keen on a child. I was ok, so we took no precautions. Also,

I was over 28 when I got married. My first pregnancy was quite difficult, right from backache to itching and tingling in the stomach. Actually, it's surprising that I don't now remember all my discomforts. I remember Sudipto always had a supportive hand on my back to help me climb slopes while going and coming from the office. Meanwhile, we were allotted a better house, Mansfield Estate, and that too, the Ground Floor, with blooming hydrangeas. Others were trying to grab the flat, so I was advised to shift on a Sunday while I really wanted to have some repairs and painting done before shifting. I remember there were no cupboards, so Sudipto tied a rope on which we hung my clothes which we carried on hangers. There was a large bedroom, a veranda that we converted into a sunroom for our daughter, a guest room, a drawing, and a dining room. After a year, Mr. Attar Singh got charge of Secretary Personnel (there was none earlier) and moved to the first floor with his family.

Sudipto had resigned from the army once earlier when he was at Binnaguri; it had been rejected. He decided to try again, giving normal reasons, only son, needed by the family, etc. and my father met the then Chief of Army Staff, Gen Raina, to request him to help. Gen Raina was also from the Kumaon regiment, like Daddy. Gen Raina, after he saw Sudipto's record told my father that he had the makings of a Chief of Army Staff. When Daddy said he wanted to leave, Gen Raina replied, "He doesn't know his mind." When Sudipto heard this, he said that no one asked him if he knew his mind when he joined RIMC at the age of 12 yrs Sudipto topped in the NDA entrance exam, and I proudly wear his gold medal as a pendant. My

Chief Secretary had also served in the Army and called and told General Raina, "You have so many Captains, this girl has only one husband!" but General Raina was not to be moved. So, his resignation was rejected.

Sudipto felt he should give it a final try; else, he would start preparing for the Staff College entrance examination. Doing Staff College was essential to progress, career-wise, in the Army. Meanwhile, we were in Delhi and with a batch-mate, Kiran Bedi, who said she could help and referred him to Mr. O.P. Arora, PS to Jagjivan Ram (Defence Minister). He met Mr. Arora, who assured him that the resignation would be approved.

He suggested, based on another officer's case whose resignation had been accepted, that I should give him a divorce notice, the reason being since we were in different services and could not be posted together. I should say that Sudipto had promised to leave the Army after our wedding. He had tried, but his resignation had been rejected, so I wanted a divorce. I was a bit scared, but Sudipto, who otherwise is always correct, was willing to go ahead. I was, in any case, worried that a person who is getting a bit disillusioned with the Army would find civil so ruthless and competitive. Will he be able even to tolerate the corruption around? What if he regrets it? But Sudipto was firm." "Don't think of what I may feel after 10 yrs. I want it now; that's what matters!" So, we went ahead. We first went to the Chief Justice of HP and told him the problem. He was very understanding, handled the divorce notice himself, and kept the file in his room. We did not want people gossiping that our marriage was breaking up. I was also trying not to be superstitious.

My in-laws visited a few times. I was happy that Sudipto's elder sister Bonya Didi came with her husband and son, Tukun. So did Tinku, his younger sister for whom I developed a special affinity. Ma was having problems like any mother-in-law, accepting that her son loved someone else so much. Also, she was unhappy that traditionally the girl goes to the boy's house but here we were settled in the north rather than the east. Sudipto handled this very well. Once she wrote to him in Bangla that for a child, his mother comes after God, but he had given that place to his wife. Sudipto replied so aptly that mother was in her place, wife in her place and God in his place; he said he had no confusion in his mind and we should also dispel any such illusions in our minds. Ma and I soon became best friends and always enjoyed chatting. I realised that our circumstances apart, we were quite alike!! Baba, meanwhile, was simple and happy to read fiction or anything around and doze off; he loved food and his drink too, though he did not have it regularly.

Meanwhile, I was in the eighth month of pregnancy and took maternity leave for 3 months, the ninth, tenth, and eleventh months. I had a vehicle to go to Chandigarh, but Sudipto wanted to take his scooter for transportation to Chandigarh and as we were about to start, he suggested I sit behind him. I was reluctant as I thought so many jerks might not be safe, but I brushed that aside. I went on a scooter behind Sudipto while my baggage went by the vehicle.

We settled down for about a month of leisure before the baby came. I don't know how this time passed but

it was relaxed and nice. We booked tickets for a movie, Chhoti si Baat, starring Amol Palekar and Vidya Sinha.

That day, the 16th of Dec 1976, I started having some pains, but it is not easy to distinguish early labour pains from gastric issues. In any case, I had registered in PGI, where I was going for check-ups. My friends advised me not to rush to the hospital as the first delivery takes a long time. So, we all went to see the movie with my suitcase packed in the dicky if we had to rush. My Daddy was worried, but Sudipto asked me to squeeze his hand when the pain came and kept timing it. We came home after the movie and went to bed. The next morning, we went to PGI; still not sure if these were labour pains, but my father was worried and agitated. The doctor confirmed the labour pains and put me in the labour room. It was a very difficult labour and Mitali was born at 11.30 pm on 17th Dec 1976. I was put in a ward as rooms were not readily available. A long difficult labour, unsympathetic

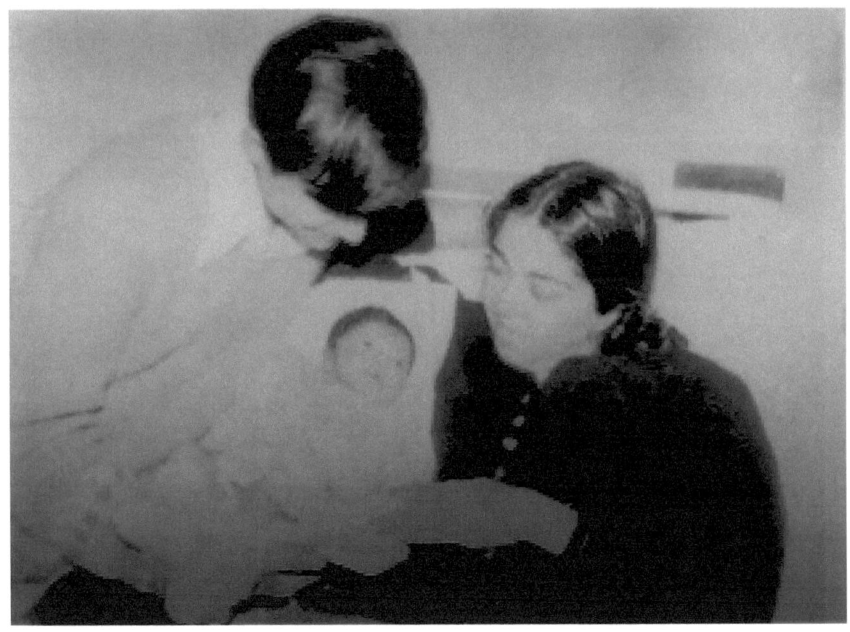

staff and stitches made it so difficult that I think Sudipto made up his mind that I would not go through it again.

That was not all. While at home, with my husband and mother looking after me well, the Chief Secretary summoned me in early January for a Cabinet meeting which was discussing reservations, especially for backward classes, which I seemed to have developed an expertise for; he said he had already sent a car to

pick me up and that the car would bring me back at night. Sudipto came with me; I was very weak and he was protective. I was breastfeeding, and my parents were left looking after the baby for one night. However, I could not go back and that one night became a week.

The Cabinet meeting was about reservations to be given to backward classes and reviewing the overall reservations as according to the Supreme Court ruling, reservations could not exceed 50 percent. This is to enable general category candidates to get jobs and retain recruitment by merit. The cabinet meeting went on till the evening and while the discussion continued, the group promoting this reservation went on strike and were shouting slogans outside the Secretariat. They blocked all traffic and a lathi charge took place. The meeting was postponed to the next day and the time sought to consult Courts through Secretary Law and a reference made to Govt. of India. I could not go back. We had home and clothes there, but what I could not explain to the senior officers (we were constrained in talking about these things) that since I was breastfeeding, our daughter was crying in Chandigarh and my parents were struggling with her. I had acute pain in my breasts. I would go to washrooms and extract milk from my breasts every few hours, but the problem did not settle down even after I used a breast pump and in addition to feeling terrible about throwing away milk which belonged to my daughter, I developed a high fever. The doctor had to give me injections to stop the milk. My mother proposed to bring our daughter to Shimla to drop her, but the nanny I had taken on was from March; she was over 60 and, although she had been a nurse in British times, she found it difficult to come in this cold to Shimla. Anyway, we begged and pleaded and she (Dwarko) came after a week. So, Mummy brought our daughter, called by different nick-names to Shimla.

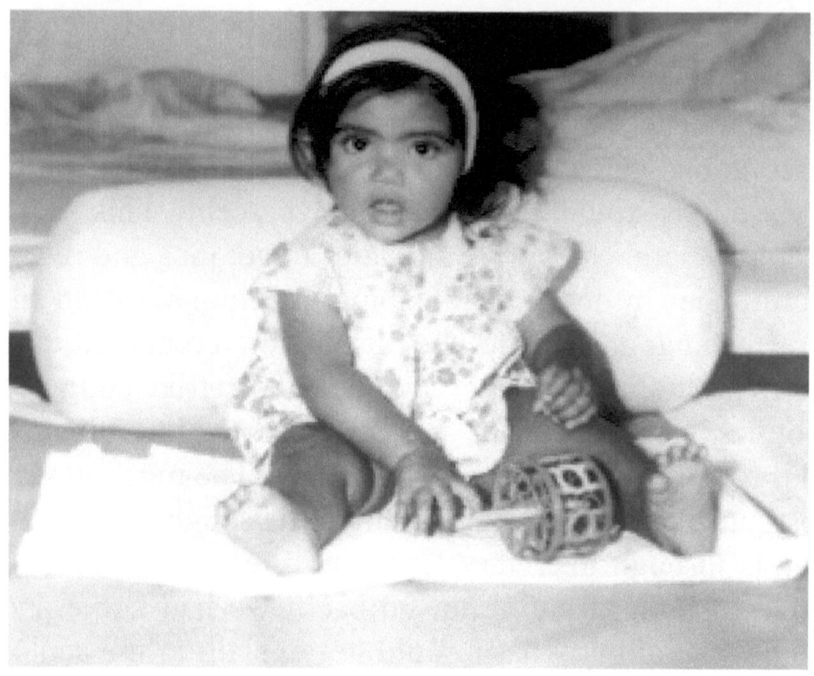

We did not agree on any name; Ma had proposed 'Sunanda' as both our names started with Su, but we did not like that. We were looking for a name which would have a similar pronunciation in Bengali as well as Punjabi. We also wanted it to be musical and have a good meaning. After a few months, we settled on Mitali, which meant a good friend as well as a companion. Dwarko stayed with us for more than 6 years! There is no provision for maternity leave to be carried forward so this unutilised leave was a sacrifice. I did not resent it as we were all together again, but my health was affected as I had not recovered after childbirth.

Mitali cried a lot as a baby, especially in the evenings, and we learnt it was probably colic, and Sudipto, with an abundance of patience, just rocked her. She slept with us. Between 6 PM and 9 AM, I breastfed her. At that time, there was no method of storing breast milk. Sudipto spent his afternoons at home with Mita now. Dwarko would just be with Mita, and even her food and tea had to be brought to her. We thought that she did not do much, but if she was on leave for a day, we found it very difficult to manage. We realised her value, even more, when one of our dissatisfied employees came to our house one day with a knife in his hand when Sudipto and I were away

at work, threatening to kidnap Mita. Dwarko stood like a rock at the door and would not let him into the house. The man eventually went away. It was indeed very brave of a frail old woman, and for some time, she could not talk, as she was suffering from shock.

Sudipto now started planning his future in case his resignation was accepted. I suggested he complete his graduation, as even some of the candidates coming for Class 4 posts had a Masters degree. We found out that though cadets passing out of NDA were given a graduate degree, at that time it was only equivalent to BA Part 1.

So, he still had to do Part 2 and Part 3. Then we found out that Punjabi University allowed Defence Service Officers from the NDA to appear directly in the final BA exam. When we tried to register for the exam, we found that the last date was over, but a friend Kumkum was working in Punjabi University and we managed to pay the late fees in time and so Sudipto was set. He's brilliant, but I helped a bit with European history. His examination in Patiala was quite amusing. For the English Literature paper, he was the only one who raised his hand to do the paper in English, the rest in Punjabi. Punjabi language was a compulsory subject, but then again, Army officers could

do a paper on Punjab History and Culture instead. His optional subject was Military Training. The result came later and of course as expected he topped the university.

One day as I got out of Chief Secretary's room to come down the stairs, we got a telegram from a batch-mate, Gopal Pillai (husband of Sudha, who was with me at army attachment), who was undersecretary in the Defence services. It said, "resignation accepted." In a typical filmi style, I tumbled down the stairs and came home in tears and pain. Cold and hot water fermentation, ointments, and crepe bandage settled it, and I was in the office the next day. Sudipto was very happy, but I was worried about his future. He had no job in hand and did not want to accept favours from my colleagues who suggested some companies he could work for. He told me if he took a favour, he won't be able to look in the eyes of his boss, who would think that he came on his wife's recommendation. I did suggest he try for IAS, but that was not to be, and I think this is a mistake we made. He would have had a totally different and satisfying life despite the problems. The next day, Dr. Parmar, our ex-CM, had invited us for tea and we walked there with a limp. When we came back, my foot was swollen; hence, after an X-ray the next day in Snowdon, my foot was in plaster. I remained home for two days while Sudipto prepared to look for a job in Delhi. My brother Sawraj was then working in Delhi, so he went and stayed with him; in a hurry to get back as I had a broken leg. I, however, started going to the office on crutches and was provided with transportation and a room on the ground floor. I was very lonely without Sudipto but Mitali occupied my evenings.

Sudipto went around looking for a job and, in a walk-in interview, said yes as he liked the boss, I asked him whether he was interviewing the boss and he replied both ways!! This was Methodex and they sold office equipment including photocopiers. He took time for a week to join in order to spend some time at home. As he left Shimla, he wrote this poem.

Because We Love Us

The lights of Shimla recede
Into a misty nothingness
Faint flickering spots of brightness
In an intense murky gloom
The state of my mind
My life being cause self existence

Concentrated in these spots
Fading away as the bus moves on and away
Am I going away from you
To seek my future
Uncertain, unsure, unsteady steps being taken
Is it worth it? The pain, the separation, the wrenching of
Two hearts, bodies and soul
Which are one?
All in pursuance of a hope
Hope - the thread of life
That makes us move on
As the spots of light
Disappear completely in the murk
Hope - because we love us.

...Sudipto Mukherjee

Marriage, though a meeting of souls, assumes new responsibilities along with all the joy and shows you a whole new world!

❐

Chapter 7
Deputy Commissioner Solan (1979-1981)

Doing a tenure as a Deputy Commissioner/District Magistrate is a milestone in an IAS officer's career

I was to be responsible for a District. It is very important for an IAS officer to be DC and handle the responsibilities of running the district administration. Govt. of India requires 3 years of field experience to consider an officer for a posting to the Central Government. I had done one year as an SDM and had to do two more as DC. With Sudipto and me in different professions, our future would be in Delhi. Sudipto suggested I first take a posting which would help me as DC. DC looks after all developmental work and I did not have much knowledge of agriculture, horticulture, animal husbandry, etc., so I requested to be posted as Jt. APC (Joint Agricultural Production Commissioner), with Mr. Anang Pal, a seasoned officer, as the Commissioner and my boss. When you are in Personnel, it is easy to choose your next posting. I learnt a lot there as I prepared to be the first woman DC of HP. There was another lady officer, Sarla Gopal, who had been a DC during the time of Punjab Statehood before

Himachal became a separate State. After Himachal attained statehood no woman had been given charge of a District apart from brief temporary periods when the male DC may have been away on leave.

Postings were to come soon, and I took leave for a week and went to Dhanbad, where Ma and Baba stayed. Ma had a sister in Dhanbad, so they had a house in Dhanbad and stayed there. I had requested for Nahan District as I could really do a lot of developmental work there. Sudipto would come to Shimla by night bus every weekend and I wanted to be as close as possible to the plains. We had 6-day weeks those days, except for the second Saturday, which was a holiday. On my return from Dhanbad, Sudipto met me in Kalka, where I was to get off the train and told me I had been posted as DC, Solan. I reached Shimla and was told to join at once. I went to call on the Chief Minister, and he asked me to give a press interview, as I had been avoiding it. I left within a day without taking my baggage in the hope that I would join my new position and then come back to pack and collect my baggage, but once I joined, there was no going back. My household staff packed my bags and furniture and after a few days, Dwarko and Mitali arrived with my baggage.

I joined as DC Solan on 1st June. Solan lies on NH5, the road connecting Shimla to the foothills. Shimla is known as the queen of hill stations and the capital of HP. The shortest route to Shimla from Delhi was via NH5, passing through Solan. In the absence of an airport at Shimla, Ministers, Governors, and all dignitaries would

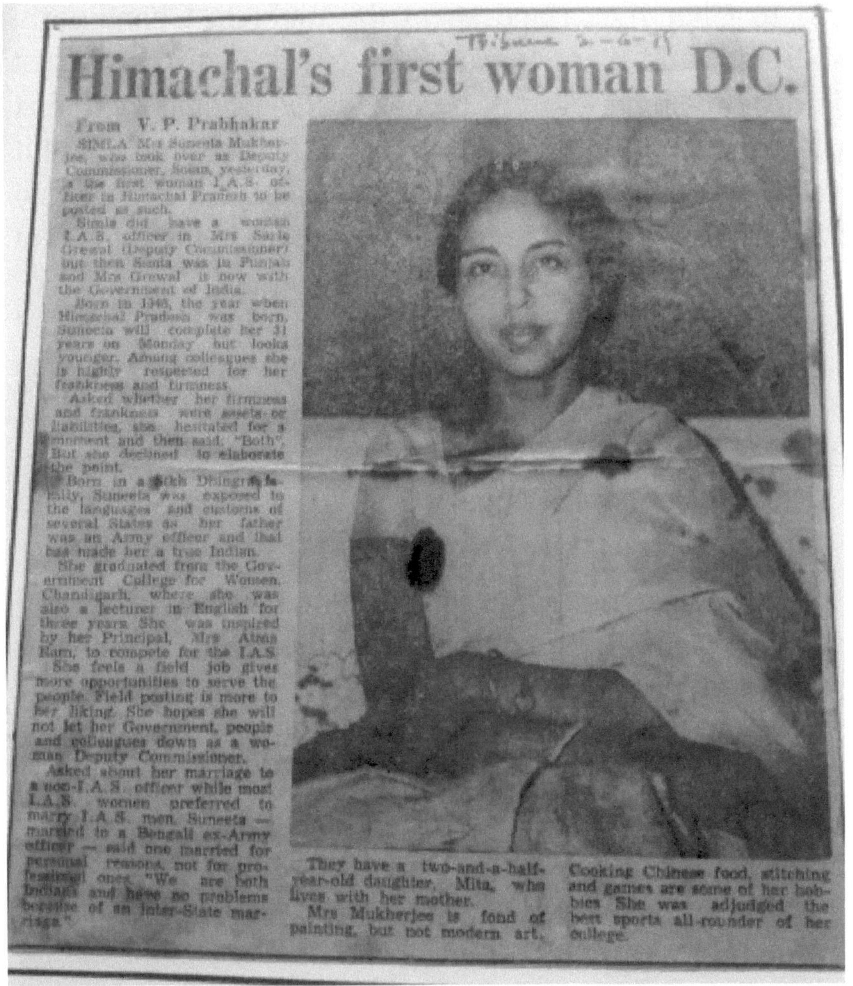

Himachal's first woman D.C.

From V. P. Prabhakar

SIMLA: Mrs Suneeta Mukherjee, who took over as Deputy Commissioner, Solan, yesterday, is the first woman I.A.S. officer in Himachal Pradesh to be posted as such.

Simla did have a woman I.A.S. officer in Mrs Sarla Grewal (Deputy Commissioner) but then Simla was in Punjab and Mrs Grewal is now with the Government of India.

Born in 1948, the year when Himachal Pradesh was born, Suneeta will complete her 31 years on Monday but looks younger. Among colleagues she is highly respected for her frankness and firmness.

Asked whether her firmness and frankness were assets or liabilities, she hesitated for a moment and then said, "Both". But she declined to elaborate the point.

Born in a Sikh Dhingra family, Suneeta was exposed to the languages and customs of several States as her father was an Army officer and that has made her a true Indian.

She graduated from the Government College for Women, Chandigarh, where she was also a lecturer in English for three years. She was inspired by her Principal, Mrs Atma Ram, to compete for the I.A.S.

She feels a field job gives more opportunities to serve the people. Field posting is more to her liking. She hopes she will not let her Government, people and colleagues down as a woman Deputy Commissioner.

Asked about her marriage to a non-I.A.S. officer while most I.A.S. women preferred to marry I.A.S. men, Suneeta — married to a Bengali ex-Army officer — said one married for personal reasons, not for professional ones. "We are both Indians and have no problems because of an Inter-State marriage."

They have a two-and-a-half-year-old daughter, Mita, who lives with her mother.

Mrs Mukherjee is fond of painting, but not modern art.

Cooking Chinese food, stitching and games are some of her hobbies. She was adjudged the best sports all-rounder of her college.

drive to Shimla. The tradition was that the DC would accompany these VIPs from the border of their District, which meant for Solan from Parwanoo to near Shimla. This is one reason that I did not want to do Solan District, as a lot of time goes into VIP escorting. Not that it is not useful as one can get to discuss and get clarity on issues from the Ministers, as sometimes you get to sit in the same car. On 4th June, my birthday, I escorted our

CM to Chandigarh and spent the night in Chandigarh. Sudipto came there too and bought a small cake. Just before the shops closed, he asked me what I wanted; I asked for a cotton saree, as I wore silks in Shimla, and it was little hot in Solan. He bought two sarees and also an overnighter, a small suitcase to travel. This meant a lot to me, and I treasured and wore the sarees almost every week. I was already being threatened with being posted out as the local Janta Dal politicians wanted their own choice of DC. So, at the earliest opportunity, I asked the CM, Mr. Shanta Kumar, if this was true. He laughed, so I felt a bit settled. I was back at work in the morning and Sudipto went back to Delhi to his job.

Sudipto had now kind of completed his probation and was posted as branch manager of Methodex in Chandigarh and had a nice office cum residence in Sector 16, and was now 2 hours or less from Solan, a big improvement from

the Delhi-Shimla distance he had had to travel earlier. Sudipto would come every weekend on his scooter and spend time with Mitali, as my weekends were uncertain. I tried to be home, but the Governor often spent weekends in Parwanu and I had to be there. Members of the public came to meet the Governor and he needed to check facts and clarify issues before giving instructions.

There were also other duties which turned up on weekends and there were only a few weekends one could be home. In addition, after a few months, I was given charge of DC Nahan. Though it was an additional charge, sometimes I had to stay overnight. Dwarko started sleeping in Mitali's room when I was not there. Though Dwarko was very good at her job and responsible, I realise now Mitali would have been happier with a younger girl who would have played with her and not just disciplined her. This has made a permanent impression on Mitali's life and now she does not work much professionally so that she can spend all the time with her daughter. And this remains an area where I have regrets. Of course, I could not have taken a break from my job or could not have had less commitment and nor could I leave her with my parents and in-laws, but I should have maybe tried out a younger girl along with Dwarko.

Solan was a newly created district and did not have a designated house for the DC. My predecessor had converted a PWD Rest House into the DC's residence, where we stayed. Situated on the main road, it was noisy and easily approachable by the general public. One night some people barged in, despite there being a guard, to complain that the petrol pump was not selling the fuel at laid down prices. In any case, being on the national highway with heavy trucks driving down the road all night was disturbed and I had been asked to look for a more permanent DC residence. I started to look for an alternate accommodation, with the approval of the Government as, in any case, this was a temp residence by converting a rest house.

I found almost a palatial house a bit on the outskirts in a quiet area but at a very attractive price: 1.75 lakhs for 5 bighas of land and a lovely house, but by the time it was approved, I had finished one and a half years of my tenure and did not have much longer to stay. The trees on this land of 5 bighas on which the house was situated were valued at a higher price than what we were paying. The owners had settled abroad, were selling this house, and were happy that the DCs would stay there. Thus, even though I did not stay here for long, this was a kind of gift from me to my successors. For me staying in the Guest House was not without its advantage. Next to my house lived a couple, Mr. and Mrs. Amarjit Dua, who had no child and often in the evening, they came over

Mitali as a small child during a prize distribution function in her school

Mitali dressed up as a Himachali girl on a new year eve

and spent time with Mitali; they joked and laughed and played with her and she was happy. Mr. Dua has now passed away, but we are in touch with Mrs. Dua till date. Soon I put Mitali in a play school there, she went without grumbling, but I wondered if she was happy. One day they called me for the prize distribution in their school and Mitali cried as she got no prize and saw me giving prizes to so many. However she was soon laughing when she saw me become serious wondering what I should do.

I wanted to give her a brother or sister as I thought it would be good for her to have someone to play with, but my husband said that he did not want to see me go through another difficult pregnancy and hence he said absolutely no.

Now about my work. The BJP Govt. had just announced the Antodaya Scheme. This meant that in every village the 5 poorest families would be identified, and attempts would be made for their upliftment. A no. of suitable schemes had been identified at Govt. level in which the grant was 50 percent and the loan would be 50 percent. This was done because people often do not value absolutely free things, and that's why the component of the loan was introduced. While the panchayats were to select these poorest five families, it was the DC through the SDMs and other staff like tehsildars and patwaris and maybe BDOs that these 5 poorest families were to be verified and the poorest selected. The success would be in uplifting these families above the poverty level. This scheme was to be inaugurated in Solan on 2nd Oct, Gandhi's birthday; I joined in June. We were told to cover 20 percent of Antodaya families. In my monthly staff meeting with all staff, we agreed to

The local MLA handing over mules to the beneficiaries

cover 100 percent of the families as we thought it was better to go through a detailed process once rather than over and over again. We were often in the field identifying and talking to families and deciding on which scheme would be suitable for and be accepted by the individual beneficiaries. The schemes that were relevant to them were keeping cows or goats, or getting a sewing machine, and so on. For the elderly, without any support from children, there was a provision of an old age pension. From July to Sept., we were immersed in this.

By mid-Sept, I informed the Govt. of our intention to cover 100 percent of families though ultimately it came to 98 percent as we could not convince a couple of the poorest families to participate in the scheme. I went and met all the beneficiaries during the selection and also later, but basically, the SDMs were in-charge of their subdivisions, and I allowed them independence, and they had a sense of ownership and pride. On 2nd Oct., each SDM sat with his group of beneficiaries and the panchayat leaders with a sense of pride and achievement written large on their face.

However, the Government was surprised and did not believe that it was possible to cover so many families in such a short time and sent the APC (Agricultural Production commissioner) a few days earlier to enquire how correct our selection was. There must have been, as there always are, complaints from those who did not get selected or the political leaders on the ground who want to benefit their party men or their friends. Mr. Anang Pal (may his soul rest in peace) did not tell me anything but he was in the field conducting his enquiries.

Presenting our progress to Mr. Anang Pal

The beneficiaries are in front row and the public at the back

I also did not try to find out what he was doing as I was sure of our work. On 2nd Oct, the Chief Minister, Mr. Shanta Kumar, came for the function. Mr. Anang Pal and the CM had been hustled together, and I was concerned but brushed it aside as I had done my best. Mr. Shanta Kumar went to the dais to speak and his first sentence made me hold my breath.

Mr. Shanta Kumar said that he had had great hopes from this DC (that was me) and that he had thought I would fulfil my duties. He then looked at me and I looked down, a bit scared at what was coming. Then he said that this DC had not done her duty. Oh, God! I thought, what is coming next! But then he said, "what she has done is actually a prayer, far beyond the scope of her duties". I finally let out my breath and had tears in my eyes as he

CM Shanta Kumar talking to the officers and beneficiaries

went on with his speech. Recently, I went to Palampur and went to call on him after more than 40 years, as my sister-in-law was buying land there, and he remembered this day and event. I had now established myself, and after that, though people and politicians may have had differences with me, they did not doubt my leadership in the district.

I had the good fortune of having a CJM, Mr. K C Sood, who was very supportive and an SE Electricity, Mr. Ramji Das, with whom I also had a long-term friendship after this. My staff, despite small failings, was excellent. Mr. Kashyap, my SDM, Mr. Nainta, my GA and later SDM Nalagarh, Jogishwar Singh SDM Nalagarh and then DC Kinnaur (now somewhere in Switzerland).

With Mr. Anang Pal and Mrs. Shanta Kumar as they leaving

Parthosarthy Mitra, my probationer (who later became Chief secretary), S S Ghuman my staff officer, and Mr. Jaiswal, my DDPO. It is rare to have such an interdepartmental supportive team and I gained a lot from it.

This does not mean there were no staff issues. Let me tell you about my Tehsildar at Kasauli, Mr. Mahajan, quite a regal man fond of his drinks and well established and shall I say entrenched with all his contacts. When he learnt, I was posted to Solan, he tried to get my posting cancelled as he had heard I was very tough. My brother had also set up a small ancillary in Parwanu for Purolators and I knew he took a small amount of money from him for his peon's uniform. However, I had promised not to bring that up. When I continued

With My SDM Jogeshwar Singh during a field visit

to get some complaints against him, I advised him to be careful. I saw he was not progressing in his work and often looked drunk. He was located at Kasauli, about half an hour from the main road, so I decided to make surprise visits to his office. On my first visit, I got a bottle of liquor from his drawer during morning hours. On the second visit, I still smelt liquor on his breath, but he denied having taken any. I asked him to open his mouth, and when the smell was stronger, he burst out in tears, saying he had gotten the dental treatment done. I felt guilty seeing his tears and sat down with him and over a cup of tea, I heard that all his aberrations were because of the previous Dhanics service not being added to his HP service, which would affect his pension drastically. I took his relevant papers and details, and he promised not to ever drink in the office or during office hours. I sent a request to the Personnel Department where I had worked and followed up there. When I was leaving the district in 1981, he was in tears again, and my husband said to him," Why are you crying? This is probably the last you will see of her but think of me, I have to spend all my life with her, but I am not crying" the Tehsildar laughed and cried together and touched our feet, saying that he was crying in gratitude as his service records had been rectified.

Work went on as usual, Revenue work, Interdepartmental and coordination work and administrative work. But

Playing a TT match at Nehru Yuva Kendra

the heaviest work was VIP duty. I also worked for the upliftment for women and provided aid for the formation of cooperative societies where they could get loans for handicrafts and take some assistance in marketing. I took off time to attend to the youth through the Nehru Yuva Society and once in a while went and played table tennis with them.

There are always people outside DC office and residence seeking help and I tried to help whoever I could. My in-laws visited twice, and my sister-in-law Prachee (we fondly call her Tinku) also spent time with me after they left. I had always covered my head in front of my in-laws but did not do so in Solan as I was always rushing around. I asked my mother-in-law if it was okay, and she said of course; she added that she felt very proud of me when she saw so many men listening to me or following me for instructions. Slowly my mother-in-law and I were to realise that both of us were very similar, education and job apart. Someone has rightly said that often a man marries someone who reminds him of his mother, and Ma and I were like friends till she left for her heavenly abode in 2010.

We also took our share of a brief holiday to Goa. Mummy seeing how little time Sudipto and I spent together, suggested that we leave Mitali with her, but we took Mita along and here we thought we would give her undivided attention, but I don't know why she was stubborn like a teenager and wanted only coke, no milk please and kept spilling her milk. We did not know how to be a parent, we thought then and I continue to struggle about giving her the best motherly support.

Himachal is a peaceful State and does not have many law and order problems. However, one day over a policy matter decided in Shimla, the people of Solan blocked the main road. Vehicular traffic came to a stand-still, leading to a lot of inconvenience to travellers. The SDM spoke to the local leaders but to no avail, so he consulted me. He would have to order a lathi charge by the police. I suggested tear gas first, and we alerted the police. I personally went to the room of the SP (Superintendent of Police - Mr. Ashwini Kumar), who was from Sudipto's school (RIMC) and used to say he was a great admirer of Sudipto, who was his senior. The blockage was on the main road just outside my office and the police joined us there. The SPs or Dy SP did not join us, though when I went to his room to call him he said he would join me, but he never came. I stood a little further away from SDM as he was in charge, and I stayed there for moral support but was not visible to the public. After tear gas, the SDM ordered lathi charge, "Charge, Charge!" he said, but the police disappeared from the scene one by one. I was worried about a possible enquiry later, but God saved us and the crowd disappeared, opening the blockage. When I went to my room and called my immediate boss, Mr. SM Kanwar, the Divisional Commissioner, to apprise him of the situation, he said that I should have called him before the lathi charge was ordered. I said, "Sir, should I have told them to hold on while I go to my boss and seek instructions" He laughed; he was a good soul. In another instance, when the Govt. ordered the arrest of specific people for hoarding (on political grounds), I told him that my conscience did not allow me to do targeted political arrests. He drove down from Shimla and signed the papers without holding them against me.

Coming back to the road block that got cleared at Solan; some of those who were blocking the road in Solan drove to Dharampur, a small settlement down the road towards Kalka, and blocked the road there. I was on the road for something else when I saw this blockage and, with God's grace, managed to convince the few truck drivers to open the blockage and talk to me. Dilip Kumar, our veteran film actor, was on the road, stuck in the road block on his way from Shimla, and scheduled to stop over at Chandigarh for the night. We met him over dinner at the house of a retired Army Officer that evening in Solan, and he said that he had not thought that this young lady, meaning me, would be able to open the road block. He had thus driven back to Solan and was spending the night there. He was overwhelmingly complimentary, saying I was his 'Didi for life". We have not met again!

I tried to have some social life for officers and their families by all of us joining a local club. We had Holi celebrations where Mitali cried because she was not happy with the colours. Life was settling down a bit when Mr. T. N. Kaul came to Solan. He was a very senior Indian Civil Services officer and was close to Mrs. Indira Gandhi, the then Prime Minister of India. He called from the Circuit House saying he wanted to meet me and can he come to my office. I replied that I would go to the Circuit House and call on him. I was surprised, wondering why he wanted to see me. Well, he said, Mrs. Gandhi had lost her private secretary and wanted me to join her. I was taken aback and told him I am an apolitical person and would not be suitable for the job and he said that I would learn soon. I came back full of doubts and was sure that I would not go. However, Mr. Kaul went to Shimla and met the then Chief secretary Mr. Pandey, and the CM, Mr. Ram Lal Thakur and made the request to them; I was under pressure to go. I have always been keen on staying in a good house, and to me, the only attraction of it all was that I would get a good house and easy admission for Mitali in one of the best Schools when I moved to Delhi (i.e., Govt. of India). It would also have been a very high-profile post, something many civil servants can only dream of, but I had no desire to go. Then God intervened and something momentous in my life happened at this time. I started getting the early signs of pregnancy and when Sudipto asked me what I wanted to do on New Year's Eve in 1980, I said that I would like to go to a gynecologist in

Shimla. So, we went to Dr. Ahluwalia in Rippon hospital. I was worried as I had gone on a field visit about a fortnight earlier, where I had to walk 15 kms one way to get to the village. No other DC till then had ever visited the village. Most officers of the district administration under my charge, e.g., horticulture and agriculture, fisheries, civil supplies, tehsildar, and the SHO, went with me. But a night before our trip, my breast had swollen and I had an abscess, it was hurting and I did not know what to do. Mrs. Dua, our ever-helpful neighbour, came to see me and put local herbs including Tumeric, in Atta, heated it, and put it on my breast. The abscess burst at night and I was not so uncomfortable. It was a 24 hrs. trip and there were no washrooms or rest houses on the way. I had started a course of strong antibiotics before leaving; this was what was worrying me. What could be the effect of the antibiotics I had taken in case I was pregnant? I wondered. Sudipto, of course, kept saying he had not done anything but later remembered when we had spent time together in Parwanu and we had not taken enough precautions.

There was no pregnancy kit available there, so Dr. Ahluwalia examined me and confirmed the pregnancy. As regards the effect of the antibiotics, she asked me to consult Dr. Dhall in PGI.

Meanwhile, I sent a hand-written note to Mr. T N Kaul in an inland letter explaining that I had just discovered that I was pregnant and hence would be unable to join.

I was now impatient to talk to Dr. Dhall and booked a call to the PGI exchange and asked for Dr. Dhall. The exchange asked me which Dhall and I said the gynecologist and was put through to the home no. A lady picked up and asked the same question, "Which Dr. Dhall do you want to speak to?" I asked if there were more than one and she answered yes, there are three. On this, I said that I would like to speak to the gynecologist in PGI and she answered that all three were gynecologists in PGI. I took a long breath and asked, "Are you one of them?" and when she answered in the affirmative, I heaved a sigh of relief and told her that she was the person I wished to speak to. But she would not answer my question on the phone and asked me to come to see her in PGI.

So, I went to Chandigarh. After she examined me, she counselled me. She told me that I was not an uneducated person coming from a village and that I should have had a planned pregnancy. I was exposing myself to the possibility of having a deformed child and I would not only ruin our life but also subject the child to disabilities all his/her life. She advised me to abort the child and assured me that I would not regret it. However, I said I would have to think about it before taking a decision and I would come back later; she said in that case she would have to do it under general anesthesia. I am so scared of anesthesia and hospitals and, most of all, injections but I said I will not decide now as my whole being was rebelling against it. But I was sure that due to my own desire to have another child, I would not risk bringing a deformed child into this world. Sudipto dropped me back to Solan. I was now sure that I had to go for termination of this pregnancy though my heart was crying all the time. Anyway, mechanically I asked my Chief Secretary for

1 week's leave to attend my brother Sawraj's wedding. He approved one day along with the weekend. So, I went to meet him in the Circuit House and when he said that weddings were done in a day, I told him that I had another problem. I said that I was in the family way, and he asked what I meant. I said that I was expecting and he frowned and asked me why I let that happen so I told him that it was not planned. And he scowled and asked me why I let such unplanned things happen. At that time, I found it very awkward to discuss such subjects. He said, "How can you let that happen? You are the DC. That's why we don't give Districts to women". I left in disgust, but he approved my leave application.

So, I went to Chandigarh on leave. We booked the procedure, which was to be done in the operation theatre in PGI. We went without eating, Sudipto driving me to the hospital, I had tears running down my eyes. He kept asking me to talk to him and I said there was nothing to talk about; then why are you crying, he asked? I said because it was raining, so he stopped the car and asked me again. I was sobbing, saying that I didn't want the abortion, so Sudipto said that we could easily stop it. But what if the child is deformed, I asked. He replied that the child would not be deformed. He guaranteed me. I was so relieved that I hugged him and cried even more but then composed myself. We went to PGI; Dr. Dhall was in the operation theatre in her surgeon's clothes and the first thing she told us was that we were late. Sudipto explained to her my dilemma and our course of action, and she said that we should go to the PGI library and look at the research which dealt with the impact of taking these medicines during pregnancy. We went to the library and saw that there was nothing that we could not handle. Oh, we were so happy, and I felt I was flying. My parents saw me bouncing back and were surprised but also happy. Hats off to Sudipto, I thought!

After Sawraj's marriage and meeting his wife Indira (called Indu), who was to be an asset in our family, I left for Solan. The environment in those days was such that I did not want to tell anyone about my pregnancy. It was not something one could talk about, and somehow people then did not see the DC as a woman who could get pregnant, that was my feeling. So, I thought I would go on long leave before I started showing. But I was too concerned about possible comments on my leave. However, one incident happened which strengthened my resolve to go on leave.

One Saturday evening, I got information that a bus had gone down the hill. This meant injuries and possibly deaths. I called the SP, who did not pick up the phone. I called the police station but did not get a great response. My SDM, however, was responsive, and I told him I would reach the site and that he should join me there. Sudipto came with me, it was raining and going down was slippery. With Sudipto's support, I avoided slipping in many places. I was already nauseous but seeing the gory site of dead and injured victims was terrible. After giving necessary guidance, basically how to identify dead or unconscious, inform relatives, and move the injured to hospitals, I came back. We struggled with

how to handle the bodies of those we could not identify. I realised that this trip down and back had drained me and that I did have to leave soon as I was not going to be able to do all this.

I then thought I would go on leave once I could not wear sweaters and shawls any longer, around March. However, around that time, a search was initiated to find a suitable piece of land to build an airport which would serve Shimla. I found some land in Arki district bordering Shimla, Inauguration was to be on HP day 7th April at the site, so I applied for long leave from 10th April. But I still had to meet the Chief Secretary and explain to him that I did not undergo an abortion and now wanted to go on long leave. He was fed up and asked me to speak to the Chief Minister myself. I spoke to the CM on Holi; he was reasonable and readily agreed to my leave. Now I started to complete whatever was pending and also started telling friends and colleagues I was leaving as I had an important personal assignment.

My farewell was very touching. Sudipto, with his strong principles, drove up in his car to pick me up. Normally the office car would have dropped me as Chandigarh almost borders Solan district, which ends in Parwanu. You pass Panchkula and you are in Chandigarh. The staff decorated my vehicle with flowers, but the surprise element was that the CJM and XEN Electricity, as well as officials of other departments, drove to Chandigarh to see me off. I remember Sudipto asking Mr. Kashyap, my SDM, why he was coming all the way to Chandigarh, to which he replied that he was coming to see off his sister. There was a tearful farewell, but I was also happy as I was going home and felt that we would have some time with Mitali before the baby came.

A befitting experience which I would treasure for life. The nuggets of learning and the joy of giving and serving enlivens my whole being even now!

❐

Chapter 8

DDA, PGIMER Chandigarh (1981-1982)

Our son Abu (Rajat) is born

I had the wonderful opportunity of spending quality time in Chandigarh during my long pre-maternity leave. Sudipto had a nice house in Sector 16. It was an office come residence and enough for us. Dwarko had come with us, and Bachittar, a boy from Nurpur, came and worked with us, cooking and doing other odd jobs. Mitali (called Mita) went to school, and our neighbours were Mr. Singh and his wife, Palli. Mr. Singh's family-owned Aroma hotel, a well-established hotel in Chandigarh. They had 3 daughters. Mrs. Singh had had a son a year earlier, but he had died in the first month with jaundice and now she was expecting again. We were due around the same time. My parents lived in Chandigarh and this was my hometown and I could meet my friends. I also joined dancing classes and took some singing lessons. We would go to PGI for check-ups. I was not having issues like I did during the first pregnancy. I was happy and looking forward to this peaceful period and then childbirth. We had bought a second-hand Fiat car and we also had a scooter. At times I would take the car out for a drive.

Thus, from May 1981 to July 1981, I had a lovely relaxed period. In July, my parents went to Deolali, where my brother Haramrit was posted and while my due date was towards the end of August, I did forewarn them that a second child normally comes earlier than expected. Meanwhile, there was an epidemic-like situation of conjunctivitis and I kept requesting Sudipto to be very very careful. I also asked Sawraj and Indu to be careful. Dimple, our Pomeranian, had been very sick with skin disease and it came to a stage when she was getting injections every day. The vet told us that it was not safe to have her in the house with a baby arriving soon. We knew our priorities, but she had also been like a baby to us. One morning when we got up, she was gone as if she was giving us a solution to our problem. We were sad but understood that this was the best solution then. On the 8th of August, Sudipto and I were on a scooter (the car battery was down) in Sector 16 market and saw some African boys (students) knock a rickshaw-walla over and try to run away. The rickshaw-walla had got injured and his rickshaw was damaged. Sudipto asked them to take care of his medical needs and also the repairs of his rickshaw. We also realised that they did not have a driving license. So, Sudipto held on to them and asked me to drive the scooter and get the police. I hesitated due to my condition, but he added in Hindi that I could pretend to go but come back soon. I took a round and came back; by then, they had agreed to pay the rickshaw driver for treatment and repair of the rickshaw. We came home and Sudipto started complaining of itching eyes. Sawraj had already been suffering with conjunctivitis for the last two days. We had a fitful sleep that night, getting up repeatedly and finally at 4 or 5 am in the morning. I felt that my water bag had leaked. I woke up Sudipto, who could hardly open his eyes. My suitcase was already packed; we called Dr. Kamala Dhall, my obstetrician, who also had conjunctivitis, as did her husband. OMG, I thought, my parents are also not here; I felt very alone. Dr. Dhall called the labor room and I went there, but there was no bed. I was asked to share a small bed and as more patients came, told to go home and come back when contractions started. I went home, but Dr. Kamala Dhall told me on the phone to go back again. I was wondering who to turn to for help and remembered Mrs. Dua in Solan. She had said that I should call her for any need, so we called her and she and her husband came in the afternoon. However, Sudipto refused to go home and Mrs. Dua and Sudipto stayed there at night, sleeping on the floor of the hospital corridor.

In the labor room, I was on the bed with another lady and her child and so could not even move or shout. I could feel that my cervix had dilated and I was almost ready for delivery. The pains were not too bad and I was not crying or screaming. In the labor room, there are generally younger doctors only (residents), and a male doctor was passing. I clutched at his hand; he looked at me and was about to dismiss me. I said, "Doctor, this is my second child and I know it's coming, please attend to me,' so he stopped and examined me there itself. He said, 'You are right but delivery beds are not vacant". I was exasperated, so he added, ok, you'll deliver here. Luckily a delivery bed was vacated and I had an easy delivery. But the tough part was now to come.

Given that I had taken strong antibiotics and there was a chance that the baby could have a problem, and with the background of an abortion having been suggested and not carried out based upon Sudipto's guarantee that nothing would go wrong, I wanted the pediatrician to examine the child before I left. Sudipto tried but could not get me a room in the private ward. It was a Sunday and the pediatrician did not come, so I decided to stay on a bed with another mother and child. Sudipto and Mrs. Dua slept on the floor outside. I managed to walk to them briefly and talk to them. I stayed awake all night and the pediatrician came late. When he saw the baby he was surprised that I was worried, he said that the baby was fine and I could go home. Sudipto stood in the queue to pay the dues and it took forever as the counter guy went to have tea just when his turn came. I carried the baby home in the afternoon; he was less than a day old. When we reached home, Mitali was impatient to see him and hold him. She pronounced that his name would be Abu as another neighborhood child was Abu. Somehow, we managed an early dinner and then Abu slept on a baby cot in Mrs. Dua's room since Sudipto had conjunctivitis. The drill was not to have Abu infected, so we would wash our hands before going to him. We slept soundly that night as we had not slept the previous night. In the morning, we woke up with the same thought, how is Abu?! He didn't cry all night. We rushed to his room; I went in and saw that Mrs. Dua was also checking whether he was breathing. We heaved a sigh of relief. I breastfed him. He was a happy baby, didn't cry even if he was hungry just made some sounds to attract attention. May he always be happy I would say.

Meanwhile, my neighbour Pali's son, who was born even before Abu, had jaundice and similar symptoms that the earlier baby had and this baby also left for his heavenly abode. So now we were looking carefully at Abu. His skin was yellowish and I took him daily to the casualty for examination, and after a long wait, they'd tell me to go and come again the next day. It was tiring and often nerve-wracking. Sudipto was down with malaria now, bitten probably when he slept on the veranda and my dad would drive me. I wanted to show Abu to Dr. Narang, who was a neo-natal specialist but could never get beyond the junior doctors. So, one day when I was very worried, I tried to walk past the guard, who ran after me with his stick, but I reached the doctor's room with Abu. When the doctor asked me who I was, my answer was, 'a mother

who wants you to see her baby.' He said he had to go for a lecture for an hour and I said that I had waited so long, I'll wait another hour. He came after 2 hours or more, and in those days, we did not carry water as we do now. I was feeding the child but very thirsty myself. I waited patiently, thirsty and tired, refusing to leave till I saw the doctor. After the doctor saw him, he recommended taking out blood from his groin to check; this painful procedure happened the next morning and was nerve-wracking. Anyway, Abu recovered without any interventions but was under observation for about a week after this.

I now had recurring severe headaches and read an article in the Readers Digest that in such cases, there is a possibility of a brain tumor. After my recent experience in PGI, I did not want to go there, so I went to Dr. Chuttani, who, after retirement, had opened CMC (Chandigarh

My brother Sawraj feeding the first grain to Abu

Medical Center). Dr. Chuttani had been the Director of PGI and had also served with my father in the Second World War. I paid the fees and the junior doctor wrote my history and, at the end, wrote that the patient suspected a brain tumor. Dr. Chuttani smiled and told me that I did not have a brain tumor but a migraine and I should take diazepam and sleep in a dark room after I went home and think about what is bothering me and the solutions. I did that and realised that one issue was Abu's health and the second issue was that I now wanted to be here with family support when Abu was small. I did not want to go through the same experience as when Mitali was a baby. With a full-time job, I needed family support when the baby was small. So, the next day, I went to see the Chief Commissioner of Chandigarh, Mr. B. S. Sarao, to ask him if there was a possible post for me in Chandigarh. He told me that the only post for an IAS officer from another cadre was Deputy Director Administration in PGI which was a Govt. of India, Health Ministry post to which no IAS officer wanted to be posted. I asked why not and he said that IAS officers don't want to report to a doctor. This did not worry me, I said, and he said he would write to Secretary, Health, Govt. of India, Dr. Sidhu, and suggested that I should meet him.

The die was cast and so I called Secretary, Health and got an appointment. Some friend was going to Delhi by car and I took a lift and was in the office by 11 am. I was again leaving a baby I was breast feeding. I intended to be back by 5 or 6 pm, but no one would let me go into Nirman Bhawan as visiting hours were 3 to 4. His PS would not put me through, and when he did at 3 pm, Dr. Siddhu said he had a meeting soon and could give me just about 3 minutes. I said unhappily that I would take 2 minutes. I think I took one. He said if my record was good, which he would check, he would recommend my case to the Minister. Anyway, to cut the story short, I got the post of DDA, PGI. The Deputy Medical Superintendent was upset, thinking that he did not give me a room when Abu was delivered and now, I may not be nice to him, but I reassured him.

Dr. I C Pathak had taken over as the Director of PGI recently. He was new to the job and wanted to do things carefully. He had not even heard about me and was unsure about me. The Administrative Officer of PGI had held additional charge of the DDA's post till then. Since a DDA was joining for the first time, there was no office room, no phone, no PA, or any kind of assistance earmarked for the DDA. So, I found ways to solve the problems I took his approval for an office and a telephone and made the Committee Officer, Mr. Dutta, my PA, in addition to his work. I found that his support meant a great to me. The administrative staff was not used to supervision, and there were no Recruitment and Promotion Rules for any post. Adhoc promotions were the norm. There was no seniority list for all the staff, including doctors. When I asked for a file and did not get it, I went to the office and found staff missing as they took friends and relatives to the Hospital to be able to jump the queues. I met with the senior staff and they gave me deadlines when they would give me data on the date of joining of each staff so we could make a draft seniority list. A Senior Assistant and Deputy Superintendent gave me a date two months away and said that I should not ask them in between. They were never in their rooms and whenever I asked, they would say, 'don't worry, you will get your list'. The Employee's Union was very close to Mr. Shankaranand, the Health Minister, and I was told not to disturb them and let sleeping dogs lie. Everything was an issue, such as house allotments. Thank God we had Dr. B K Sharma, a brilliant physician, as Head of Dept. of Medicine, in the House Allotment Committee.

An enquiry had taken place in the Engineering Department. One Sunday, when we were clearing papers in the office, the Director asked me to go to Delhi to get some papers signed by the Minister; these papers were related to the termination of the Superintending Engineer and to bring the file back by hand. I was reluctant and Dr. Pathak was surprised, so I told him that I had an abscess and was feverish. He asked me to show him and I said no, he said that he was a doctor and I said that I saw

Dr. Amrit Tiwari, Dr. B. K. Sharma, me and Dr. I. C. Pathak (L-R)

him as my boss only! So, Dr. Kamala Dhall was called to attend to me. Meanwhile, Abu was also running a high temperature, and Dr. Narang was requested to go to my home and check on Abu while I was on my way to Delhi. I returned home at about 2 AM and placed the file under the carpet in my drawing room. No one had found out, at least not from me, but as I reached the office, I saw that the SE had placed a stay order from Court on my table!

I would work till late setting procedures in place, drafting rules etc. I would be tired and sleepy and as soon as I reached home, I'd be ready to sleep. I would breast feed and eat and then was sleeping even while

With the Union Health Minister Dr. Shankaranand and Dr. Pathak, Director PGI

feeding. In the mornings, I would feed Abu, have breakfast and want to rush to the office quickly and all this made Sudipto say, "You go to the office first of all, come last back last of all and then go to sleep. If you come home to feed Abu and sleep, we'll bring him for his feed to your office and put a bed for you to sleep there". I had to do many things myself as I got very little support from the office, so I spent long hours and also carried files home. When the deadline for submitting the seniority list came, the Senior Assistant, Banwari Lal, got admitted to the emergency with a chest ache. I did not know what to make of it, I thought that maybe he was so stressed that he had developed angina. A meeting of the Standing Committee on Finance (SFC) was going on in the board room to be followed by the Governing body (GB) meeting. For these meetings, the Secretary of Health comes from Govt. of India with other officials and chairs the SFC, while the Minister from the Centre chairs the Governing Body meeting. Between the two meetings, there is lunch, and at this time, I drafted and got SFC minutes approved and signed, which then went for approval to GB. During lunch, I whispered to Dr. Pathak that Banwari Lal was in casualty and he looked at me and said I'll go and see him. I was so tense, wondering if he had a heart problem, but I also wondered whether he was faking it. Dr. Pathak was back very soon; he looked at me and said, "I've discharged him". I was startled! "What if he gets an attack later?" I said. 'He'll be fine', was Dr. Pathak's reply.

Mr. Shankaranand, Union Health Minister, with the Employees Union

I was suffering from low blood pressure and also a bad throat. I had had a throat problem ever since my tonsils were removed when I was three years old. My throat only got okay with homeopathy, with medicines dispensed by Dr. Mohan, who was introduced to me by Sudha. A long-term problem solved so easily and effectively.

Meanwhile, my maternal uncle, S Santokh Singh Narula, visited us and stayed for dinner. He is very fond of his drink and after a few drinks with Sudipto, his uncle said, "So you are well settled in Chandigarh?" Sudipto's answer surprised me. "We are well stuck and not well settled," he said. I didn't say anything that night but asked him the next morning what he meant and he said that he had not seen himself selling office equipment after leaving the army. He wanted to do something more fruitful and when I asked what he would do, he replied that he would apply and then see what he got. I had got this PGI posting and was in my hometown bringing up our children. But I realised that we also needed to look after his career, so I said that he should look for what he could get. He went for interviews in the next two months and came back with an offer to work for Far East Computers in Malaysia, as yet India had not opened the market to computers and he wanted to do the latest thing. So, we went to meet Dr. Pathak. "You will get a substitute," I told him, "But Sudipto won't". He laughed; I promised him that I would not leave till a substitute as good or better than me was found. He reluctantly asked me to get approval from Dr. Siddhu.

My search for a substitute led me to Sudha Sharma, Income Tax 1970 batch. Everyone talked about how she always wanted to be posted in Chandigarh and I heard she was again under orders of transfer from Chandigarh. I had first met her as Veena Jain's (now Veena Chottray)

Sudha and me

friend. She was very charming and always immaculately dressed. She asked me why I thought that a PGI posting would be good for her. I answered that she would gain experience and enjoy the post and have an excellent boss. I introduced her to Dr. Pathak and to Dr. Siddhu and they all approved.

Banwari, the superintendent who had faked a heartache, said during my farewell that those who never worked during office hours now worked even at night for me. The seniority lists had been circulated. The first draft of the recruitment rules was ready and the institution of DDA was well established in PGI. Sudipto left for Malaysia in Sept 1982, and I left my charge on the 4th of December and Sudha joined on the 5th. I spent exactly a year in PGI but developed a lifelong relationship with that Institute and, of course, with my boss and some others in the Institute.

Life has its own plans and often we reap a great harvest without expecting it. PGI was my first posting in health and I specialised in health after this. I got a close friend for life in Sudha Sharma! Abu(Rajat) is an adorable kid and we were so glad that we kept him! Our life would not have been the same without him.

❒

Chapter 9

Malaysia

(1982-1984)

Family time during leave and preparation for Ph.D.

And so, in December 1982, I was off to Kuala Lumpur with Mitali and Abu (Rajat). Sudipto had gone a few months earlier and I was following on after settling my official and personal issues. To get a passport, we had to have a formal name for Abu and I accepted Rajat as suggested by Ma. My parents came with us to Delhi to see us off. We bid a tearful farewell to Dwarko, who now had an old pension, which assured her of some regular income. My Mother was very worried about whether I would be able to look after the kids and a household on my own. However, when she saw that I told Abu to pee only in his portable pot and he started doing so, she said now she was confident that I would be able to look after the kids.

Sudipto was beginning his career in computers and he did not have a family posting, but he was doing his best to ensure we were comfortable. He met us at Singapore airport, and when Abu refused to go to him as he did not recognise him, he felt hurt but soon we were home and happy. We rented a small cottage, a kind of outhouse with a small lawn and moved away from the multi-storied flat Sudipto had rented. It was off Jalan Bangsar in a green and nice small area. Bangsar market was within walking distance, as were some basic medical shops and Bukit Bintang, a very popular mall.

Mitali joined the British school, so in the morning, after Mitali and Sudipto had left, Abu would try to help me clean the house, and I cooked; Sudipto always did the dishes at night; he would say that the day's tension went off as he did the dishes. On holidays, he sent me shopping while he looked after the house and kids and tried his hand at cooking. Sudipto tried to lighten my work by assigning tasks to everyone and when Abu got the lighter ones, such as dusting (he was only 2 years old), he protested, saying he would do the dishes and ironing; I think he too was trying to shoulder manly responsibilities that he

The family at Bukit Bintang

saw his dad doing. I now quote this when I talk of gender: how my two-year son told me not to give him lighter duties and heavier ones to his sister. This has resulted in his being super at cooking and managing house today.

We had to be careful about money: One-third of the salary went to school fees, one-third to house rent and we managed on the leftover one-third. We got some money from India too, and we bought a TV after two months and a sewing machine soon after that. I then began to buy lovely materials and sew dresses not only for Mitali but also for my nieces. This gave me something constructive to do. I still have that sewing machine. We got new gadgets such as a rice cooker; we would put the rice to cook and then come back for dinner and find hot rice waiting. It seemed such a luxury!

Within the first year, we all travelled to India and met our parents and friends. I met my guide for my PhD too. In fact, I visited India often and Sudipto did not try to restrict me as he saw how I longed to go back. I took lots of gifts for family and friends and once took things to sell to make up part of the fare. I realised that an

At our friend Ashok and Leena's house for dinner

IAS officer could not just get a job anywhere and I could only get a job as a sales girl or something in Malaysia, so I did not try. Once I tried to stitch clothes for others which Sudipto did not like and hence stopped it. The good thing was that I was also getting my salary in India as I was on study leave and could use that. We got visitors from India friends, some relatives as well as some service colleagues and could look after them too.

Sudipto had an Indian boss who was not very nice. An example was that he asked Sudipto to travel on Diwali for an assignment which could have been given to a bachelor. When I protested, Sudipto told me we would celebrate Diwali on his return which we did. Slowly we managed to get used to the place. However, one lasting damage was that Mitali was discriminated against in her school because of her skin colour and it has taken her many years to get over that. She says she was called 'brownie' and 'chocolate stick' but never told us then. Meanwhile, before going to Kuala Lumpur, I had registered for my Ph.D. The subject acceptable to the Govt. was "Recruitment and Promotion Policies in HP". I had preferred to study a subject like Co-operative Societies. So, on weekends I also started going to a library and writing. My guide was Professor Satya from Public Administration in Punjab University, a learned and systematic academician. I would type a chapter and send to him and discuss it during my visit. I would then rewrite and post it again. Computers were not in vogue in India yet.

Bukit Bintang was a happening mall near our house. We did not have malls and escalators in India yet and we

A memorable holiday at Penang

all loved the music, colours, lights and glamour of the malls in Malaysia. Similarly, a small holiday place which thrilled me was Genting Heights. We had a memorable holiday in Penang, a world-renowned exotic holiday destination. Known as the Pearl of the Orient, we still remember its soft sandy beaches and the fact that Abu called the ocean a "huge bugging pool."

The best part of Malaysia though, was that we were together and doing everything as a family. We loved to see the kids growing up and Mitali looked after Abu very gently and he was a very sweet kid though naughty. One morning I was at the neighbour's house having coffee after I saw off Sudipto and Mita. I had left Abu sleeping at home; however, he woke up and put a few of my dressing table stuff at the front door grill. When I came and asked him what he had done, he told me in his broken speech that since I left him alone, he had put everything as far outside as he could get. He also told me that if I

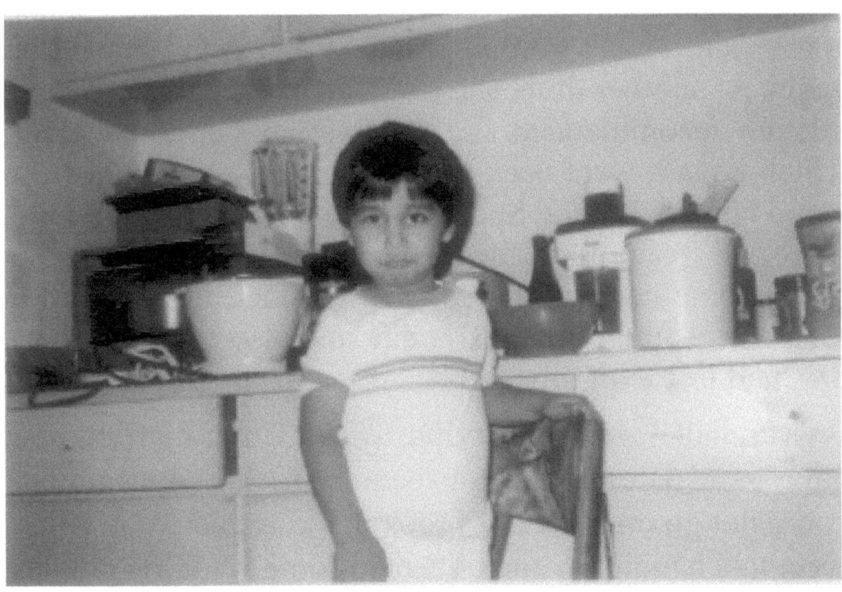

did go out again, leaving him behind, he would break all the bottles. He then curled his underlip so cutely, as he always did when he was about to cry.

Another Indian couple who came at the same time as us were Ashok Desai and his wife Leena, who was based in Singapore; they are very nice people and we are in touch with them even today. Our experiment to buy a video camera and a VCR flopped the first time. After a great deal of planning, Sudipto went to Singapore to buy it, as it was cheaper in Singapore, even after taking into account conversion and airfare. However, after he came back, the camera would not work, and the VCR stopped working as Abu playfully put a coin in it, causing a short circuit. Incidents which were frustrating at the time, but which now we can look back upon as fond memories.

We had a bizarre incident. Mitali's panties were full of blood and there was no sign of injury. Although this happened only once, we were worried and went to India (PGI Chandigarh) as she had to have a gynae exam under anesthesia. Thank god all was fine and it did not occur again. At another time, she had a constant bad throat and doctors recommended the removal of her tonsils, for which I again went back to India with the kids. I always loved going back and Sudipto never complained. I would cook and freeze food for him before I went, but he also learnt some cooking for himself. In fact, he went on a long diet, eating one meal a day and also running every day, and lost a lot of weight.

Ma and Baba were trying to get Tinku married and gave us a date along with details of the boy. Sudipto could not go on leave, so I took the kids and went. I first went to Chandigarh and collected some wedding clothes

Mitali

and jewellery. However, before I left, rather on the day I arrived, Daddy had a mild heart attack but advised me to carry on to Dhanbad as he was not in danger. I reached Dhanbad and learnt that Tinku had not said yes, but the guy was travelling from Calcutta and the train was passing through Dhanbad, so we went in search of the boy on a night train, waking up sleeping passengers but did not find him. I realised that the marriage was not going to take place. In fact, even Baba had lost interest as Tinku was not keen and also his only brother's daughter's (Rashmi) marriage had got fixed and he was now looking forward to going there.

We thus all went to Calcutta for Rashmi's marriage. By now, Ma and I were good friends. Abu was drinking powder milk on which the kids had a little feast, and we were awake all night after the marriage in all our fineries. Ma and I joked and spoke the same language, but we managed to attend the function. Sudipto had some issues at that time and was very unhappy that I attended this wedding, but in the long run, it was good as after some years, all differences were settled and everyone was close again.

I had taken two years' leave and was to return soon. We decided that when Mitali's school closed in K.L., we would take her school leaving certificate and leave the kids in Dhanbad until I got a house in Shimla and was ready to receive them. So I undertook another trip to India and left the children with Ma and Baba, where they shared their lives and experienced a semi-urban area; Abu would walk to the milkman and see the cows being milked,

Abu and Mita with their grandparents at Rashmi's wedding in Calcutta

picking his way gingerly on the streets, avoiding the cow dung. They also celebrated some Bengali festivals with them. Ma and Baba took them to school, though only for a couple of months, and Tinku looked after them bringing joy to their lives.

While I was DC, I had visited Sanawar for a prize distribution function and taken Mitali along. The Principal, Mr. Somi Das, suggested she came to Snawar at age 8 (she was less than 4 then) and I said no, but she wanted to go and something the Principal said also softened my stand, He said, "You don't realise how difficult it is to be children of successful parents!" We had started feeling that we needed to handle Mitali better and thought she needed a change and maybe this was the answer. She was very stubborn with us, sometimes like a teenager, even at age 2. We also realised that we had not been great parents and she may have a chance to blossom in Sanawar. Sudipto always felt that children must go to the hostel and learn to be independent and so we were all looking forward to Sanawar, me with some apprehension.

I came on the transfer of residence, and so brought a TV, VCR and everything I wanted to. Sudipto had a three-year contract, so would follow a year later. We had the lovely experience of our nice family staying together in Kuala Lumpur from 1981 end to 1983 end.

A break mid-career helps you reflect, put together what is scattered and plan for your future. I was happy at first working and lazing at home, but soon got restless and started exploring books and libraries for my Ph.D. I also started sewing after we bought a sewing machine.

This posting shaped Sudipto's future as he was trained in computers and gave us time together along with allowing me the pleasure of being a housewife and mother.

❐

Chapter 10

MD HPSEDC

(1984-1987)

New learnings, back to professional development

In my office

When I had about one and a half months of leave left, I got a telegram from the Chief Secretary (C. S.) HP saying that I should rush back to Shimla to join the post of MD Tourist Corporation, a post verbally offered to me earlier, but which had somehow always gone away. I rushed to prepone my entire programme and did my shopping, packing, goodbyes etc. and in a fortnight reached Shimla where I stayed in the claustrophobic P.W.D. rest house. which is next to the Secretariat. I went with great excitement to the CS early morning only to learn that an officer with political favour had got the Tourism Corporation orders in his favour and my orders had been cancelled. I was now posted as MD State Electronics Development Corporation (HPSEDC). I rushed to the CS to say that firstly I did not know anything about electronics and secondly, if I was to be posted in Electronics, they should have informed me, so I did not have to rush back. However, the CS, Mr. P. K. Mattoo, dismissed everything I said; he said that I should hire GMs who are familiar with the intricacies of electronics and added that the Govt. needed me as a manager and he was sure I would do well. With my husband overseas and kids in Dhanbad, I did not look forward to anything, at least not a cold winter with no house in sight in Shimla.

The worst was yet to come. The charge of the Electronics Corporation was with Mr. S. K. Alok, who was also Commissioner cum Secretary of Finance. I went to call on him and learnt that he ran the Corporation from the Finance Secretary's office and that there was not even an office for me and there was a complicated procedure to get a new office such as advertise, get tenders, have P.W.D. undertake an assessment of the building, take it to a Committee of Secretaries of Industries, Finance and MIDC. I asked how much budget we had. He replied that they had a token budget of Rs. 2 lakhs, which had been spent on foreign travel that he and the Secretary Industries had undertaken. He also told me that he had no intention of handing overcharge yet and that this much of privilege he was entitled to, having served in HP for over 20 years. He was awaiting his posting to Govt. of

India and would only leave after that. He was a son of the soil and very close to the CM and so the CS would also not intervene. Why did I rush back? I wondered. If you are recalled from leave, as per Govt. rules, you are paid the return fare, but I did not ask for it as I did not think they would pay a fare from a foreign country. February can be very bad in Shimla, and I did not have a personal or official vehicle, no house, no office, and no staff. I went a fortnight to Chandigarh and, without introducing myself professionally, attended one or two short courses with the Electronics Development Corporation in Punjab and learnt the basics. One of the courses was on multi-layered circuit boards and I wanted to understand the basic concepts and not make a fool of myself.

Meanwhile, I had requested for an advertisement for the office and it was done, and a committee was formed for assessment of suitability and rent. I went back and we ended up choosing the incumbents house for an office off Cart Road but towards the Secretariat. I was allotted a Brockhurst Cottage and moved in with the furniture we had kept in store. My predecessor had also selected one GM, though left it for me to finalise. He was not very qualified but had a good experience and was very hardworking, "he will be very loyal to you", I was told, tell me his weakness too", I asked," he will trouble everyone else but be useful for you." The posts of GM Technical and GM Administration and Finance were advertised and Mr. K. K. Dhar and Mr. N. K. Goyal selected. A small budget was allotted in the supplementary budget as the financial year ends in March. I sat with the assistant and ensured the

My two GMs Mr. Goyal and K. K. Dhar

supplementary allotment and allotment for next year. We bought an office car too.

Towards the end of March, I went to Chandigarh to get the kids who Ma and Baba had brought to Chandigarh. I remember how they ran in and out of the house, screaming with excitement. Seeing them run around screaming and laughing endlessly on meeting their cousins in Chandigarh, Ma commented that she had never seen the kids so happy.

We settled in our Brockhurst Cottage. I had my cupboards made and a sunroom ready for the kids getting cupboards in every house I lived in was my weakness. Avay and Neerja Shukla and Sarojni and Ashok Thakur were our neighbours, and Abu made good friends with their children. Abu joined his first school there and did nursery and KG in Shimla. Mitali was getting to be eight and I asked her again if she really wanted to go to Snawar and she said yes. In Snawar, in the first year or two, the children stay in a dormitory, so they are together and not lonely. We collected all her hostel requirements and were getting ready to go to the boarding school. Mitali was cool and seemed to be looking forward to it, even though I was sad and not too sure. I undertook to tell Mitali about the birds and bees. Since she did not know anything from before, she asked many questions and I answered them with a straight face. Basically, I wanted to tell her about menstruation, but we went on to sex and childbirth. The latter was touched on very briefly. Actually, I thought we had gone a bit far, but when she came home after a month, she asked me why I did not tell her about hymen! I see she is now very communicative with her daughter on these subjects from the very beginning. So, Mitali went to Sanawar. None of us cried in front of each other, as we waved bye and promised to come after a month. However, I sobbed later and I think she did too.

Mitali often had a cold and had a flowing nose. She had a lot of ayurvedic treatment. Sometimes she took antibiotics too. I hoped the change to Sanawar would improve her health, but that was not to be; she tells me now that she was always made fun of as she had her nose flowing most of the time and called the flow from her nostrils "Ganga Jamuna". The warden had her daughter in the same class, and the warden was also not nice to her. Sometimes I wish I could put the clock back and sort it out with her warden. Another thing that upset her enormously at that time was that the daughter of Sudipto's boss took admission in the School and the hostel and since her parents were abroad, I was allowed to bring her home once a month. Sudipto's boss in Kuala Lumpur also admitted his daughter in Sanwar at the same time and she did not get along with Mitali here. I had to refuse to take the girl home with Mitali and he withdrew her from school and I suppose Sudipto bore his wrath quietly, but I had no option. All my life I have tried to do what is best for Mitali and keep her happy but I don't know how far I have succeeded.

I was getting to know my job. We identified electronic industries which could be set up in HP. The geographical area which was selected for the Electronics Complex to come up was a hillock in Shogi and I did not believe the industry would come to an isolated hillock with no existing infrastructure, but land development was with MIDC, so I let it be, but I got approval that the industry would have the option to come up in other areas too. I also managed to get approval later from my Board to construct some sheds in Chambagnat, Solan, which would enable the industrialists to start while they constructed their bigger buildings. This was a good move as Usha Electronics started here, as did HFCL. We applied for licences to Govt. of India and got a few, such as cordless phones, some critical electronic components, fibre optics cabling etc. Shiwalik Bimetal Controls also came to the nearby area of Chambaghat. We would then advertise for the industry to come and set it up as a joint venture. Initially, 51 per cent had to be the State Govt. share, but this was gradually relaxed. So, when we ventured into a project, I was the first MD of the new company till we disinvested and handed it over to the new MD. Everything was controlled by the Board, which was chaired by Chief Minister Raja Virbhadar Singh, who was honest, forthright and hardworking. The Secretary Industries, Secretary Finance and Govt. of India officials were on my Board too, while Chief Secretary was part ofthe General Body.

We were moving at a fast pace. However, I needed to sort out what were the expectations the Board had from us. The Board and the General Body did not see eye to eye too. My Secretary and Minister, who represented the Board, felt that our role was promotional, while in the AGM, I was firmly told that the Corporation should not run at a loss. And they did not sit together and sort it out. I realised that I had to resolve the problem and I proposed to be the technical arm of the Govt. in giving advice and procuring electronic goods, but I charged a commission

My expanded office staff

from the vendor without allowing an increase in their supply prices. We also set up a Data Processing Centre with CMC (Computer Maintenance Corporation of GOI) and started processing Board Examination results.

I met many industrialists and we had a lot of discussions, but the main issues were that neither the raw material nor markets were in HP, so why should industry come to HP? But we had a dust-free and cool environment and electronic components were not heavy and it was felt that the electronic industry could succeed here. The first electronics industry to get established was Cosmo Ferrites of J K Sanghania in Jabli. It was wonderful to see that the locals got employment there. A few small electronic units came up specifically for components, and then, Mr. Nahata set up a telecom equipment manufacturing unit, which later became well known and popular as "Himachal Electronics or HFCL'. Mr. Nahata is closely working with the Jio group now. I encouraged them to appoint Deepak Malhotra as MD; he held a PhD from the USA and his thesis was related to the product they wanted to manufacture. I was the first MD of Himachal Futuristic before I handed over to Deepak Malhotra as MD. They set up their factory in Chambaghat. We were excited about setting up a unit for cordless phones from day 1, but that did not materialise as it was now open to the private sector and imports were also soon allowed. From being a unique product, it was now readily available and had therefore lost its charm. Also the economics did not work out as the phones being imported were cheap and we had expensive technology. We had set up "Himachal Wireless" and handed it over to P K Shandel and Manu Chhabria, but it was never set up and the unit went to Westons. They also lost interest. A very prestigious project was planned with Marconi for manufacturing electronic components for guns on tanks. The MD was a tough German Jew and came with a big team and gave us drafts to sign left and right but all this was new to me and I would sit with Mr. Goyal and a PA (Roshan from Solan) and struggle. We finally hired Ashok Vij, a CA who knew company law, as a consultant to help us with the terms and agreements. We sat till late night working. Goyal often slept in the office itself. True to his reputation, he did not get along with other staff nor CMC but was extremely hardworking and useful. Mr. O. P. Yadav, Secretary, enjoyed his drinks and life in general and often asked me why I worked so hard. When I said that I was paid to work, he turned around and said, "you would pay to work!" The first Board meeting with Marconi was held in their private jet as we flew from London to their factory site, and minutes were drafted, typed and signed in a private aircraft of Marconi while travelling with them from London to Scotland to see their unit. I took the Chief Secretary and Finance Secretary along just to be sure we didn't make mistakes.

But alas though the project was signed, it could not materialise as the proposed component was to be used in Bofors Guns, which fell into problems. Similarly, the huge project of fibre optics of GEC did not come through as the CMD, Dr. R S Mamak, left the post and the country and his successor did not honour the agreed terms and wanted free land etc., and we were not willing for the same. In any case, he too resigned his post very soon; by then, I had left.

Signing the Marconi Project. Behind me is Chief Sec. P K Matoo and on his left Finance Sec. S M Kanwar. To my left is ED Marconi

I learnt to raise funds too. UNIDO agreed to fund a trip abroad for product and technology identification. Not only did my Board members join the bandwagon, but Govt. officers in the Corporation too spoke to the CS and the CM to go with UNIDO funding I had raised, so we went in 2 groups: Goyal, Mohinder Lal (Director Industries), Deepak and Mr. Balraj Bhanot from GOI and me on the first trip and MIDC, Dhar, Hansa Gupta on the second trip. This was the first time Goyal was going abroad and I was excited for him, but just before the aircraft started, he asked me if he should get off the plane. He indulged in a lot of dramatics. Once when I had been reprimanding him for not being nice to CMC, our partner, he threatened to jump off the second floor of the office! So, I was used to his drama. Our trip was not as great as I thought it would be, especially as it included X-mas time and everyone was busy. And at the end of the very last trip from Amsterdam to Delhi my newly bought handbag, which had all 4 tickets, my passport and other colleagues' foreign currency in it, was stolen. Getting a new one-time passport from The Hague was a nightmare and KLM would not take us without tickets, but fortunately Air India obliged, which was very comforting. The best was Sudipto, who said that money lost cannot be redeemed; let us not lose our peace of mind over it. I took a loan of 40,000 from GPF and returned the cash I was carrying in my purse for the other guys.

With Mitali gone to the boarding school and Sudipto in Malaysia and me going to the office, Abu was very lonely, and for the first time ever I saw him crying and so I got him a dog, a sweet Pomeranian. He was going to school and also made friends with the neighbours' colleagues' kids. He went to school in Shimla and I enjoyed the way he learnt Hindi Ra oh d Road, he would say. Ma and Baba came and visited. Tinku had gone to the USA and did her Master's in education. We would go at least once a month to Snawar to meet Mitali. Abu was finally settled and happy.

Sudipto was to stay a year after I left and I was adamant he would come back" why did we get married if we were to stay separately?" I asked. Till now, he was on contract and had his compensation fixed, but now he would have been able to get great and lucrative jobs, but we wanted him back. So, on his visit to us, he saw an advertisement for Tata Unisys and applied and sure as ever, he got the job with HQs in Delhi. So things were working out, HP being a small place, sometimes some petty comments were passed and it was clear to us that we should plan our future in Delhi so I already started sounding out my seniors that I would leave HP and go on deputation to Delhi. The CM said that I should stay for at least one more year and now I was halfway through that year. Sudipto finally came on TR again and settled down in Delhi, He took a house on rent in Jangpura and we started planning to move Abu to a new school there for the new term in April. Even though my deputation was not yet assured, Abu went to Delhi for an interview in DPS Vasant Vihar along with Sudipto and sought admission in KG. Sudipto went for the interview with him and though Abu could not spell "apple", he knew the phonetics and the teacher was pleased with that. He would go by school bus from home, and I think the strong bonding with his dad took place here. I often went to Delhi for meetings, but after Sudipto came, people felt that I went there because my husband was there, so Sudipto and Abu would drive to Shimla by car for the weekend and sometimes we would bring Mitali as well. It was too hectic for him and I again renewed my request to go to GOI for a posting.

On one weekend, I left on Saturday morning to pick up Mitali and go to Chandigarh and Sudipto left early morning with Abu to come to Chandigarh as we were starting construction of our house in Panchkula and the foundation was to be laid. On the way, Abu went to sleep and Sudipto tried to recline Abu's seat to make him comfortable. With his eyes off the road, he went for a spin and the car overturned 2 or three times. Abu was unconscious and a milkman on a motorbike took them to a hospital in Karnal. From there, Sudipto rang Daddy and Daddy somehow informed me and also the Director PGI (Dr. Pathak), who very kindly sent Dr. Jaswant Rai to Karnal in an ambulance to get them to PGI. By the time I reached PGI, the doctors had brought Sudipto and Abu, who had recovered consciousness to PGI. They were admitted there. Mummy and Daddy came. In the evening, I sent everyone away and we settled down in the room. Sudipto had broken ribs and Abu had a broken leg which was now set and in plaster and also raised. When we were about to sleep after a hard day, I was told to take Abu for a head scan as he had some head injury; I had no help and wheeled him with the raised leg in a trolley around midnight. Anyway, all was fine in the end, but remembering that day even now sends shivers down my spine. I stayed in PGI for a few days but started going to Shimla in the morning and coming back in the evening. They were in the hospital for almost a month and during that time I also went to Germany for finalising and signing a deal; though I was only there for 2 nights, I felt terrible leaving them in hospital and going. Sudipto went back to work to Delhi. And Abu had to put his leg up for another month and he spent this time with my parents, quite happy with them and his cousins.

The official front also did not look bright. The CM had handed over all the Board duties to the Minister, and I was having problems with the Minister. He was first asking me for minor things, e.g. when I went abroad, he asked for a solar calculator which was ok but when JK Synthetics came and were setting up their unit in Shogi, he postponed the Board Meeting till I would get him a Maruti car, I told him that I did not even take a box of sweets from J K Synthetics, how can he think I'll get him a car; so he just postponed the Board Meeting. I went to the CM's house and requested for a transfer to Govt. of India, but the CM refused. I told him to take over the Board and when he asked why I just said that I was not getting along with the Minister, he then took me by surprise and said, "I'll change your Minister". This left me speechless and I went back, my eyes full of tears, However the Minister was not changed and J K Synthetics never set up.

I continued to work, but my heart was on moving now, I again requested CM for a deputation and he finally forwarded my name to GOI. I explained to him the situation with my daughter in Sanawar and my son and husband in Delhi. We were running three households, and financially and personally, it was very taxing, especially after the accident. I told him that I could not continue like this. So, CM agreed but did not expect me to get selected soon. Meanwhile, I was going abroad for some negotiations and technology identification, and he encouraged me to go when I suggested that my successor could go. He did not expect my deputation to get through soon. On the way to Delhi, I made up my mind to visit AIIMS and meet the Director, as I learnt the Deputy Director (Adm) post was vacant. So I called and took an appointment with Dr. Sneh Bhargava and went to AIIMS at 11 am to meet her, only to learn she was in the Selection Committee and would only be available in the evening. So, I went back in the evening and changed my evening meetings, I told her that I was interested in the DDA post in AIIMS and if she approved. Actually, my appointment with the EO was at 2 pm, and I had already made a request. She asked me why I thought that I was suitable and I said I had done DDA PGI. Oh, she scoffed, "that's a pigmy institution". I tried, unsuccessfully, to tell her about the challenges there, but she was not convinced. I then added that I had looked after a District and she said, "big deal, all IAS officers do a District". I did not then explain that no IAS lady officer had done a district in HP. I was feeling disappointed, but when I rang my Dad and told him, he said that I would be better off in a regular Ministry. I did not agree as apart from the job, I was also looking for a quick allotment of a good house so the kids could be comfortable. I had met Mita in Snawar before coming to Delhi and she said if we were all going to Delhi, she would like to study there too so, we would all stay together again. Anyway, after what Dr. Bhargava said, I called the appointments Secretary (EO) and left a message for him that I was not interested in AIIMS any longer as the Director was not keen.

There were no easy communication channels then, and when I returned to India in 10 days, I was shocked to learn that my orders for deputation as DDA AIIMS had already been issued. I drove to Shimla and as soon as I reached the office, I got a call from Dr. Bhargava asking me when I was joining. I could not help but say I was not expecting this after my meeting with her and she said that she made enquiries and learnt that I was the right person and wanted me to join at once. I told her that I needed a house as soon as I joined and she agreed, so in a rush again, I joined my new post as DDA AIIMS in July 1987.

Learnings: I belonged to a service family and had not got to know or worked with industrialists. I enjoyed the experience and the fact that I could run a corporation in profit. This was also my first brush with a request for corruption and I chose to leave as I could not handle it. This also taught me to give priority to family, so I really fought to be posted in Govt. of India so the family could be together.

❒

Chapter 11

DDA, AIIMS (1987-1990)

AIIMS had a totally different set of challenges, far greater than PGI Chandigarh and very different from any other previous posting

In August 1987, I reached AIIMS with Sudipto in the afternoon in an exhausted state; leaving your State on a posting out and packing up and surrendering your house can be quite tiring, as before you leave, you try and finish up everything you can. This was definitely a new beginning of kinds and in more ways than one as one is also leaving one's cadre and going to the Centre.

We were put in the guest house and invited for an early dinner at Dr. Sneh Bhargav's house that night. A few other doctors were there: Dr. P N Tandon and Dr. Lalit Nath are the two prominent ones I remember. Dr. Tandon a well-known neurosurgeon, and Prof Nath of community medicine. The evening started with easy conversations, I was going to join the next morning and we talked about the Institute, its working and I was told about an extension of AIIMS activities in the field in Najabgarh. They all seemed relaxed and friendly. I asked

Dr. Bhargava about my house allotment, but she asked me to go slow, stay in the guest house for a while and she would try to allocate soonest. I was taken aback and I reminded her next morning that I have a son lying in bed with his leg tied up, away from me for 3 months and I needed to get him home. She suggested that I got him to the guest house or we could put him in the hospital. I was aghast, why would I put him in hospital when he does not need to be there, I wondered. I was not going to put him in a hospital because I did not have a house. I reminded her that getting a house was a condition of my joining; the problem was that no house was earmarked for the DDA and the doctors felt that I should queue up like them. However, since mine was a tenure of 3 years, I would likely be posted out before I got a house. Dr. Bhargava was, however, a person of her word, and in less than a month, I had a house C2 /29 and I moved the family in. We had 2 servant quarters and Savitri and Kamala shifted in with their families and looked after us and our home.

Working in AIIMS, Ravi, a batchmate commented, while coming to my room, was like being in a control room: there were 3 or 4 phones in the room, external and internal, a hotline and exchange extensions too; one or the other phone was always ringing and my poor sole PA was always struggling with one of the extensions in her room and this continued even after my PA got extra help. One was always involved in some problem-solving or VIPs visit and rushing to join discussions or meetings or for spot resolution. A Minister once slapped a resident doctor and they went on strike as the Director and I struggled to get an apology. Sometimes tired doctors were shouted at and they refused to work; the system of resident doctors is such that they often work more than 24 hours. One night someone was raped in a lift; other times, it was the students creating a ruckus because they found no ice cream in the canteen at night or on another day when the canteen was just shut as the boys on duty had met with an accident. Almost every night, we were called out and by the time I would change from my nightie to some regular clothes, Dr. Sneh Bhargava would already be on the site. To reach early, I started sleeping in salwar kameez and then after I got a call, I could just slip into my slippers and reach with Dr. Bhargava. The work was so engrossing and overpowering that one could not think of anything else when at work. One day, soon after Abu came home, he had a high fever and I promised to go to the office and send Crocin; and then felt so terrible when I reached back home realising that I had completely forgotten about the medicine I could have killed myself for this. On another day, I saw him in a dry drain just outside the house, he was stuck and unable to get out, with the maid totally oblivious to it all. He had fallen in while, moving on his haunches, but the maid who was inside did not even know. I knew he would not really settle till he re-joined school, but somehow, he could not stand on his legs. His muscles had become weak, so he was not going to school. I took him to Dr. Dave, the head of the Orthopaedics Department in AIIMS, but in spite of physiotherapy and hydrotherapy, he did not recover. He would move while sitting on his bum, pushing himself with his hands. I thought that the only solution was to send him to school, where he would not be too conscious of his problem and start walking with other kids. We put him on a bus in AIIMS and the conductor, on our request, would put him in the classroom from where the teacher took over till he was brought back home in the same way. Sure enough as I had anticipated, he was walking in a few days and soon back to normal.

Mitali had also come home from Sanawar and I struggled hard to get her admission to another school. Mr. S Das, the Principal at Sanawar, was disappointed that she was leaving just when she was settling down, but I said that since she had asked to come to Delhi, I had to take her home. He said that it had to be Sardar Patel if she goes to Delhi. With great difficulty, I managed to speak to the Principal, who would not come online for long, and she allowed Mitali to take the entrance exam, after which she got admission.

On the official front, the first difficult file I was asked to handle was the computerisation of AIIMS patient records and other areas for which tenders had been floated to buy a mainframe along with software solutions. The two main contenders were CMC partnering with TCS and Tata Unisys, where my husband was working. I wrote on the file that since my husband worked in TUL, I would not handle the file. This was not acceptable to Dr. Bhargava, who could not trust anyone else, and when she insisted, it was clear that we could not place the order with TUL. We left them out of consideration. We placed our order with CMC and TCS, who were good. However, unfortunately, an undesirable person was later recruited to head the Computer section, which delayed and messed up the computerisation of AIIMS. This was done due to the insistence of an MP who chaired the selection committee and the Director agreed to this as he agreed to allow her to appoint the other faculty on merit. These were some of the insurmountable problems we faced.

AIIMS had a lot of surplus land, but it was occupied by Jhuggis. It was rumoured that the estate officer and the security officer were hand and glove with them. I pretended not to know any of such things and called them to work out a plan to vacate the land which belonged to AIIMS. We launched a plan to work with the DDA (Delhi Development Authority) and the Lt Gov to get land and resettle them. The process was started, but it would take up to one year. We also had some vacant land and plans were made to construct houses for faculty where we had a large piece of vacant land. Making plans and getting approvals from the Standing Finance Committee and the Governing body would take 3 months at least. Construction through Govt. agencies would take much longer, but at least we would have started this process and the process of getting the land vacated. But we had to also do something at once; our doctors had houses much below their entitlement and the juniors had no houses. Salaries then were very low and whilst we also began the salary revision exercise, we realised that housing was crucial. The doctors in AIIMS are very good and we did not want to lose them to the private hospitals coming up. So, between the Director Dr. Bhargava and me (we got along very well), we embarked on a plan to acquire the Asiad flats, which were now for sale. We had no money and could not expect a grant like 50 Cr for these houses. We thus started to get approval to take a loan from the bank. We took the approval of the planning commission (in a day) and the Finance Ministry, only to learn that the Act of Parliament under which AIIMS was formed does not provide for taking loans, so we began the process of amending the Act. Everything went hand in hand and the plan was that on 30 and 31 March, when the States surrendered funds which they could not use, we would take these grants and repay the loan, thus using the money in that very financial year for which the Govt. was always keen. Those of you who have worked in Govt. would realise how difficult this process would be, I even heard harsh words from the Ministry as I was rushing them. However I had the good fortune of working with two great Joint Secretaries, Mr. N. N. Vohra and Mr. Ravi Ahuja. Ultimately, we found complete support and the Cabinet approved the allotment of those houses to our doctors. After some additions (water tank and servants' quarters) the doctors moved in and are now extremely happy. As I write this, it seems like almost an impossible task, but at the time, the entire universe seemed to move to help us.

What happened to the land we were getting vacated was even more dramatic. We got alternate land a few km away for the jhuggi jhopri wallah and got the water and electricity connections there before asking the jhuggi wallah to shift. DDA was present during negotiations: LG had been supportive. On the Sunday when this activity was to be carried out, my private secretary, a lovely lady called Mrs. Khilnani, who is sadly no more, came to the office early along with me, leaving her son at my place. Many of us including the faculty made food, roti and vegetables for a few families and packed it for their dinner as they may not be able to cook on the first night; but there were sly smiles and I did not know what was coming. DDAs tractors were there but work to raise Jhuggies did not start and when I checked, I was told that the LG had granted a stay. I tried to contact LG frantically, but he went on a road trip, and we could not get through to him. Extremely frustrated, I called the Director who was abroad to offload my frustration. The LG later told me that the MP insisted that the jhuggi wallahs were not to be shifted. When I caught hold of the MP and told him that we were giving them better land, he replied that it was no use to him as that was not his constituency. Oh God, I thought, how am I going to handle this. I probed and probed and learnt that Dr. Nundy, our great gastroenterologist, had operated on the MP. And so, I pleaded with Dr. Nundy, who said that he never sought favours from patients, but I convinced him that this was not a personal favour but for the Institute. Finally, Dr. Bhargava also spoke to him, and we got the AIIMS land vacated. Sadly, these jhuggi wallahs sold the new land at high prices and I'm told most of them settled in jhuggies elsewhere, but I could not handle that. We restored AIIMS land, where many flats were built later on.

Office hours in AIIMS were from 9:00 am to 5:30 pm. I went around 8 to read the difficult files which needed undivided attention and was often there till 7:00 pm or 8:00 pm. Then, I went home and had dinner, talked to the children and reviewed a bit with the maid before going to sleep. Sudipto enrolled for an MBA in the evenings and he would drive from work in South Delhi to the

North Campus and come home after the maids had left and we had all finished dinner and gone to bed. I would sometimes sit with him at dinner but often had opened my files or, if too tired, was already in bed. Sudipto topped each semester. After he topped the first time, I said, "Oh you topped MBA in Delhi University?" and he replied, "no, it was Punjab university" jokingly. And then, in his last semester, despite the personal tragedy Baba passing away, he still topped. And that too with a full-time job and never ever faltering in his office and family responsibilities.

Sudipto Mukherjee topped MBA in Delhi University and received a Gold Medal from the President of India who was also the Chancellor while the Vice Chancellor looks on.

Mitali settled down in her school and had at least one close friend Vartika. Abu was doing well but Sudipto was talking of his going to boarding school too. Ma and Baba visited and Baba got his cataract surgery successfully done in AIIMS. My friend Promilla and Ranjit were posted in Delhi, as were KC, and it was good to catch up with old friends.

We used to take the kids for riding on weekends to Safdarjung Club. One day when they were riding and we were walking while waiting for them, a crow sat on Sudipto's head and flew away; he let out a yell and also said something has happened to Baba. I tried to reason, how can that be, but he said "I have never heard of this, but I know that this is an indication that something has happened to Baba". On reaching home, we learnt that Baba had had a heart attack and Sudipto rushed to Dhanbad and boarded Shatabdi, but the wrong one as it was going to Patna; he not only had no booking but did not eat anything and called me from Patna. By then, I received information that Baba had had another attack in hospital and had passed away. I left the kids with Dr. Usha Nayyar and went at once. So sad as it was sudden and as he was never sick, no one expected it. We had just sold a revolver we brought from Kuala Lumpur and the proceeds were used for his cremation and other functions. Sudipto stayed there for 14 days, following all rituals with my head shaven, and I went back with the kids for the final prayers on the 13th day. What we would not have given to have more time with him, but one thinks like this after the person leaves. So sad.

The Director did not want to get involved in or give advice on equipment. She was HOD in Radiology and I chaired the purchase committee. After a long negotiation, we bought the MRI without her advice, as she wanted to be absolutely impartial. We had completed the CTNS ('Cardio Thoracic and Neuro Sciences Centre') and we purchased equipment for the CTNS centre too, always a major role of the HOD and technical staff.

Basically my job was to ensure the smooth running of the hospital through the administrative staff, and engineering staff in close coordination with the heads of the different departments - the vastness of the operation cannot be imagined. There were teaching institutions too within AIIMS, e.g., the nursing college, graduation and post-graduation of medical staff and some post-graduation of non-medical staff too. The administrative staff was huge and there was an administrative block; I found most of the staff roamed around with their friends and relatives in the hospital and did not sit at their desks to work. So, I started sitting in the administrative block for half the day and

A dinner hosted at our house with some senior employees

doing my files there. It meant spending more time at work since the staff could easily access me for grievances, but on the whole, it worked better and we also livened up the place with cleaning, painting and putting up pictures. We started some games for the employees, such as badminton; I even won a prize though a shuttlecock hit my eye once and I was injured badly.

I introduced a cultural program, played with them and encouraged them to sing and dance to make up for the hard work. Thus, I could alternate my strictness in office work with some softer entertaining games and social get-togethers to build comradeship.

My parents also visited. The first visitors were Daddy and my brother's son for his tonsils operation, And then Mummy came often for an endoscopy as she had a hiatus hernia. She was always very brave. She would come by bus, take an auto and come to my office, meet me and go home, the next morning not eat anything, get

an endoscopy done and go back to Chandigarh by bus, always smiling and never making a big deal about it. My husband had told me after marriage that I should try to be more like my Mother; my kids adored her too.

The PhD students went on strike, wanting additional stipends which the Government would not agree to. We had orders from the Court that those on strike must not disturb patients and hospitals, but they did as this was the only way they could attract attention. This time their health was deteriorating as they were on hunger strike, and we had to force feed them so we called the police at night and with Sudipto and me in the hiding we saw the Security Officer do his duty while the students on strike were removed. We went to the High Court to get an injunction, as we did not want patients being disturbed. In Court, I found them represented by Kapil Sibbal, who was a famous lawyer (later a minister too) but was also my class fellow from senior model school. I walked across to him and asked him why he was on the opposite side and he said that I work for whoever can afford my fees. I requested him to fight for the general good, and he said he would charge us one lakh a hearing. I gave up!! Anyway. I took permission and spoke myself to further our case, and we won and got a stay: no slogan mongering within 500 yds of the hospital.

Issues became huge in AIIMS and every politician, even the small ones, knew some staff in AIIMS and things would get blown out of proportion. So I started calling staff home to get together to develop a better understanding. This built camaraderie and better working relationships.

I had met an IAS officer, Anupam Dhar, in Shimla who had returned from a UN assignment and as he told me about it, I got fascinated and determined to try for the UN. One of the first steps was getting my Ph.D. which I had started when I went to Kuala Lumpur on study leave and worked slowly on through the years: Collecting and analysing data and always sending my analysis and hypothesis (later changed to chapters) to my supervisor, who would correct and post back the originals. I planned to complete my thesis, but my life became more hectic; for a few months before taking leave, I used to get up at 3 AM and work till 6 AM when I got into first my household and then my office routine. This is because I was too tired at night and there was no other time. I finally took 15 days of leave and re-wrote the chapters on the computer, Sudipto helped me in this, and I submitted my thesis in Chandigarh, and later was called for an interview before my Doctorate was approved.

Meanwhile, Mitali was not keeping well. She would get a stomach ache and be in acute distress, vomiting, and in pain. All tests, including ultrasound, barium meal, etc led us nowhere and top doctors, including Dr. Nandi, would be sitting with her; she would be on a drip and often in hospital and the doctors were also at home with her, but it just could not be diagnosed. The astrologer Ms. Khan and Mr. Prem Sharma gave their own diagnosis and solutions to which we did not pay heed. Ma also got an acute stomach ache and they expected us to go and pick them up for treatment in AIIMS, but Sudipto could not go, so I just took a train and went one night and got them to Delhi. We did not have reservations but managed to get a shared berth. From the railway station itself, Ma went straight to the OT as I had already fixed everything with Dr. Nundy; she was out in 2 days minus her gall bladder. She gave me two bangles of hers to keep in case she died but since I said no, she just presented them to me which together we went afterwards and exchanged for a necklace and earrings as the bangles were too big for me.

Early on in my tenure, a DDA house was allotted to Sudipto in Sarita Vihar, which we were very happy with. Sudipto took a loan from HDFC to buy this house, and though it was on rent most of the time, he stayed in it after I left Delhi. In the end, we sold it when we bought our Palm Springs flat.

By the time I had spent 2 years in AIIMS the empanelment of our batch as Joint Secretary to Govt. of India had begun. This is the first time we had gone through a thorough selection. I was not worried, did not speak to anyone or check with anyone and almost forgot about it in my day-to-day work. The process is such that they do not publish a list but keep posting officers who

I am getting an award from the Director, Dr. Sneh Bhargava

are empanelled as Joint Sec. I never had time to keep in touch with who was posted, where and when, and I was not in a hurry to move. I had to complete what I started eg, Asiad flats and salary revisions, etc. However, when almost a year was over, an employee learnt about my batch being empanelled and tried to blackmail me, saying he knew my empanelment was on and that he would get the file released early if I give in to their demands which were most unreasonable. I then set an appointment with the establishment officer (EO) and went to see him. The EO took out a list of 72 batch and said that I was not there in the list, I said that was impossible as I had excellent records. He asked me if I had seen my records and I said that I had not but the officers often told me that they had given me outstanding etc. He laughed and said that I had been deceived and I said, but I know how I worked and he kind of sniggered. I was so fed up and sad that I got up and was dragging myself out when he said "wait". He had taken out another list, "you are in the first list," and I said what was the second list, he replied it was a review of leftover cases. He asked me why I had not checked earlier and I replied that he did not even like my checking today: I had faith in the system, so had waited. I found it difficult to do some knotty negotiations in the office after this and rushed home to find my husband waiting with two dozen roses!

The E.O. also said that I could only be posted in the Health Ministry and a post of JS Family Welfare and Health was vacant and that initiated my movement to the Health Ministry. which I joined with additional charge of AIIMS for about a month.

I had made great friends with Dr. Sneh Bhargava and Dr. Usha Nayyar (Dean), who became Mitali's Godmother and we are friends even today. I was satisfied with my tenure in AIIMS and was happy that I made such a difference. Before I left, there was a strike of the employees going on. Between Dr. Bhargava and me, we were a strong team and we thought alike, so the employees were shouting: "Ma Beti ki sarkar nahi chalegi". I also got a lot of opportunities to improve processes in AIIMS and improve the functioning of staff. I could help many sick people who came from HP, the CM's wife after the birth of her child, ex-Chief Secretary Mr. P K Matoo, and one of my bosses' wives are some examples of those who had surgery in AIIMS during my tenure. I always made Khichri at home and sent it to them in the hospital, which they greatly appreciated. An extremely satisfying tenure where the family stayed together for a few years, but would be separated after this. All four of us would never be living in the same station even though we spent a lot of holidays together.

With some of the employees

A very satisfying tenure, in spite of the long hours of work. An understanding with your boss helps you achieve wonders. Till date I marvel how we bought the Asiad houses with no money! And on the personal front we learnt that there may be some depth in astrology and its proposed solutions.

❐

Chapter 12

Joint Secretary, Health and Family Welfare (GOI) (1990-1992)

Seemed like a boring desk posting but that it was not

I was not looking forward to this posting. From AIIMS, you do not view the Ministry as supportive as they do not approve your proposals quickly enough and seem too bureaucratic to handle a living and pulsating Institute which needs immediate attention and responses. But I was told by the Establishment Officer that my choice was to go back to the State. So here I was spending half the day in the Ministry and half in AIIMS, as I did not want to withdraw my support to the Director without her getting a substitute. Many years later, I look back now at this tenure with great fondness, where I learnt a lot and which chartered my future. I was given charge of IEC (Information, Education, and Communication), NGO grants, Organised sector and Rural health for the entire Country in Family Welfare. I had a great boss, to begin with, Mr. Jaitley and good colleagues like Vineeta Rai, S B Mishra and later also Mr. R K Anand, Ajinder Ahluwalia, to name some of them.

I was to change house, and I was dreading it as I did not expect to get a nice house after the great C11 ground floor, we had in AIIMS. But most unexpectedly, we quite enjoyed the Pandara Road flat we got, and within a year, I got a better one (C2 in Bappa Nagar, near India Gate) and we were very happy there. The children went to school and Sudipto was not far apart from his office and went for evening classes doing his MBA at Delhi University. I went to the office at 8 and came back by 7 pm unless required to stay later. I enjoyed my job enormously. The artist in me enjoyed making small spots to advertise various methods of family planning. The Govt. sponsored condom was called Nirodh, and every time it was aired on TV, our son asked "what is Nirodh?" and I always told him to ask later and quietly eat his food. And I would remind my husband to talk to him about sexual matters. When he finally did, Sudipto said that Abu knew it all. He came to me several times saying that Abu is asking this and that, what all should

we tell him, he knows it all. Abu soon joined Doon School, where I expected him to blossom as he had great capability, but I thought I could not provide enough opportunity. We had to deposit forty thousand rupees which came from my GPF. After that, he came home 3 times a year on the school bus and we went to pick him up excited at his homecoming. Every month we went to meet him and take him out to eat Hostel food is never liked by anyone and my vegan vet today used to love butter chicken at that time. That was his request at every outing. Mitali had found her feet in the new school and began to blossom and I was glad I brought her home.

I chartered my nook in the office, and soon, IEC became a portfolio to envy. This was in contrast to when I joined, my colleagues sympathised with me for not getting a great portfolio; I was responsible for screening NGOs before a grant from any agency, routed through us, was released.

We handled NGO grants in our sector

In addition, the subcentres, the primary health care unit at the grass root level was in my charge though handled by the States. These were functional medical units under the supervision of the State Govt, but because funds go from the Centre, we needed to monitor many programmes such as vaccinations and family planning as they are executed through them. I looked after IEC, as mentioned earlier and through education (population education in schools), information (TV, Radio, and print media) and communication (all methods including folk songs and dances in the villages), we attempted to bring about a desired behaviour change in people. The purpose was to have planned families, avoid abortions which were often unsafe and have healthy children. The message of having a small planned family versus a large unplanned family was to take root. I had the cameraman with me wherever I went and took footage of ordinary people speaking on these issues, in fact my maid also acted to exemplify how the pill was giving no problems. During my tenure, we introduced two new contraceptive methods: 'no scalpel vasectomy' for men and the 'morning-after pill' for an unplanned sexual activity.

While I started doing this, I realised that the State media officers were being used by the Govts as media officers for VIPs, putting up a stage, giving press briefs, etc. So, I called a meeting of State media officers and talked to them. Some of them had lost interest as their duties were different. I had to take this up with Chief Secretaries and Secretaries of Health to reiterate and, in some places, redefine their duties. To revive their interest, I got funding from UNFPA and organised training in Udaipur and got the best trainers from John Hopkins to train them (I had been trained there). A year later, we had a review meeting at Munnar. I tried to take them to nice places to have exclusivity, develop self-esteem and make them feel they were important. We then started speaking the same language and things started improving in the state too, but of course, when you change things, you get some flak also!

We tried to revamp the NGO grants and systematise the procedures of grants and their execution and reporting. It was done with due consultation with others. The US Aid was a major grant agency.

I looked after the NGOs and the Organised sector with ILO as our partner and executing agency. There were programmes like one for fisherwomen on the coasts, for flower sellers in Chennai and for Bidi workers in a few States. Now the Bidi workers project had not started for a few years and no funds were released from the funding agency UNFPA. ILO, who was to execute it, said UNFPA is not sanctioning funds. I put a note up to my Secretary and suggested he should write to the ED of UNFPA, but he passed it back saying that I should write to her. Oh, I said," I am too junior", but our Secretary did not agree and I started looking for pictures of Dr. Sadik and finding out what she was like before writing to her. I finally wrote to her and she confirmed that they would release funds, but when the funds again did not come, I told her our counterpart funds would lapse on 31 March.

So she told me it would be done; however, the India office sniggered when I asked them. My friend Neelam was visiting from Canada and we were to go to Jaipur at the end of March and I was thinking of changing the dates as I thought it might be sanctioned, but the UNFPA representative checked with Director Asia and Pacific Division I also spoke to him: Mr. Rahim Sheikh and told me it was out of the question as even the first Committee it was to go to had not been called. So, I sent a message to Dr. Sadik and went to Jaipur with the kids and Neelam, but sure enough, I got a call on 30th March that the sanction had come and I rushed back to Delhi. Later I learnt that on seeing my mail, she called for the file and sanctioned it and told the director APD to get ex facto approvals "show me the law where ED cannot do it in anticipation," she said and they were quiet. Even after she had asked, the meetings had not been called and hence she took this course of action. This interaction with her was to bear fruits later, as you will learn.

At least at the time, we were Joint Secretaries, and most of the work was done at the JS level. So, we were very busy, which included travel to different States too and also foreign travel. The secretaries did more of policy making. My Secretary, retired soon and my new Secretary joined. I also got a Director who told me she was related to him and every time I advised her, she would take his name. Unfortunately, my boss did not like the success I was demonstrating through my work. I wondered what bothered him. One evening, soon after

I went home at 7 PM, he sent for me; there was no work or directions which was urgent; later, he commented on how ladies seemed to leave early compared to some other officers. So when I got a chance, I did tell him that I came to the office at 8 (I did not add that he came more around 11), did not take a lunch break except once a week (he went home for a lunch break every day, which I did not say), ate on my table as I worked, and left at 7 PM. I told him that it was not only to be with family, but I just could not work any longer because I was so tired. When he would give me a difficult task on Monday in the staff meetings, I could say next Monday it is done and he would not believe it. A classic example was of population clocks: we got these tall long clocks to be put up in different parts of Delhi through funding from UNFPA, which showed how many babies were born every second, then after one hour, the clock demonstrated how it added to the population. On one Monday, the Secretary suggested that we put one of them in Parliament. Mr. Shivraj Patil was the Speaker and I knew him from the days I was MD HPSEDC, as he was the State Minister for Electronics then. I called him and sent a letter and he replied in the affirmative. I sent the file to the Secretary and spoke to his PS, asking him to call me if he wanted to discuss but on Saturday, we will install it. It brought to the attention of our Parliamentarians how our population was increasing rapidly. When the action taken at the last meeting was being reviewed next Monday, I casually said done. And the Secretary was shocked, "done, he asked how

done" and "why did you not keep me informed etc., etc". I thought that I would be praised but instead was rebuked. I cry very easily but never cried in the office, but I was so sad. And then, one day, I got an invite to speak at the WHO conference in Chiang Mai. I was flattered as this was the first time I was being called as a resource person, and I had never met the organisers or interacted with WHO, but they had heard about my good work and called me. All letters, once you see them, were marked to whoever would deal with them, this one was marked to my PA; my Director used to go and sit with him and chat with him and would take the chance to look at all my papers and what I had written on the different files that came from home (I did not know she was doing that); it gave him a lot of tips on how to proceed with that letter; they had also asked me to write a resource paper for which I would be paid, so she asked him to check with them the subject and length of the paper. I would have remembered in due time and asked my PA to bring that letter to me, but I was surprised that in a couple of days, I was called by the Secretary to be reprimanded on why I had not checked with him. And he had a copy of the letter written by my PA. At that time, I did not know that it was my Director behind this, and naively, I was trying to protect my PA as well as my Director. However, when the Secretary told me that the Director had asked him to take action, I asked him to call her in my presence and he said that he does not want to embarrass her. He put his foot down and said that I cannot go to Chiang Mai as he could not spare me, I asked him if I could write the research paper and he hesitated but said he would review it. My leave was due, and I took 15 days leave and worked on the paper. My PA kept typing and retying and my Secretary could not add or delete a word! I got paid 500$ for it, though I did not get to go to present it. I split the amount with my PA, who helped me in typing, logistics, etc. (we deposit one-third with the Govt).

Though I did not go to Chiang Mai, I travelled abroad a few times for work. One of my first visits was a discussion cum training at John Hopkins, from which I benefitted enormously. Just before a visit to Indonesia, my parents were visiting and Mummy went to her brother's house, Uncle Santokh, where she broke her hip, actually she said it cracked while she was standing after which she fell. The surgery was to be done in AIIMS and Mummy kept saying I should carry on to with my schedule to Indonesia. It was too late to send someone else and my Bhabhi Sonu came to help out. The surgery was successful and though I was back in 3 or 4 days, Mummy told me not to go again when she is unwell like this. I regret going even today.

As you know Mitali had a stomach pain which did not go away in spite of all efforts and now she was to do class 12 and was admitted in AIIMS. I stayed with her overnight and sent a leave application for one day of casual leave. However around 10'o clock I got a call from my PA saying my casual leave was not sanctioned and I was asked to go for a press conference. I changed there in a saree which I was carrying, but just as I kissed her bye, she vomited. It went in my hair which I rinsed in the bathroom, but I arrived at the press conference in disarray. After the conference was over, the IEC officer of Delhi who was there asked me what was wrong and I told her how my daughter was in the hospital. She was a qualified astrologer, though a Muslim. She asked for Mitali's horoscope which we had not made, so she took the details and got one made. She suggested we put an emerald ring on Mitali's finger, but I did not give it much importance. During her class 12 exam, Sudipto and I sat outside the hall. She had already been given 2 baralgan injections for pain and since she was still belching, a diazepam was added, with the result that she was asleep on her desk and we asked the invigilator to wake her up. Her problem was to be solved through Miss Khan's astrology and emerald ring a bit later!

Rajiv Gandhi had been the PM since 1984. He had taken over after his mother's death, but now

Chandrashekhar was the PM with the support of Congress. When Congress withdrew support in 1991, we thought Rajiv Gandhi might take over, but that very day I met him in AIIMS at the outdoor clinic of Dr. Kakkar to whom I had taken my children with a bad throat Rajiv Gandhi had come for his own loss of voice. In whispers he had communicated indicating he was not taking over as PM and I said that I understood he would take over after elections.

That very evening, there was a function in Pragati Maidan. Every year from 14th Nov there is a mela there where States showcase and sell their wares and also sometimes neighbouring countries come and exhibit their products. The Ministry of Health and Family Welfare also has a building there through which we do advocacy on population issues, e.g., planned families, safe motherhood, preventing violence against women, prevention of HIV/AIDS, and adolescent health. I was called there as Chief Guest to give away prizes for the competition organised by Delhi Govt. Miss Khan was walking me back with other officers to the gate and they were discussing whether Rajiv Gandhi would take over as PM the next day, and Miss Khan said clearly that he would not be PM. I was walking ahead; I slowed down and asked her, "You mean there will be an election? "and she said that his days were over; actually, in Hindi she said "*unka suraj doob chuka hai*" and I asked how she came to that conclusion. She replied that she had seen his horoscope as part of her studies when she did astrology. Anyway, the next day elections were announced, and Sheshan, a strong bureaucrat known to be a great disciplinarian, was heading the Election Commission now. All the senior officers in Govt. were assigned one constituency to look after. Mine was Ranikhet in Uttrakhand, but Mr. R K Anand had Rajiv Gandhi's constituency, so we teased him. Rajiv Gandhi was quite popular so we used to tell Mr. Anand during our weekly lunch meetings that we were sure Rajiv Gandhi would win and that Mr. Anand would then be Cabinet Secretary, so we already decided our next postings which Mr. Anand would ensure. I told the lunch group about what Miss Khan had said and they all laughed. But soon, Rajiv Gandhi was blown up and all the Joint Secretaries now wanted to consult Miss Khan.

Meanwhile, Miss Khan had insisted that I try an emerald ring on Mitali after she got her horoscope made. I didn't know these stones at all and was hesitant. I was pursuing a UN posting and, for that, did a crash course of 3 months at weekends in French and also applied to a few places, but almost always, the candidates were already decided. I got selected in one place, ICOMP, an international NGO, and even got an offer from them, which I accepted but soon learnt that some other candidate had joined. No number of questions and emails helped and I could only scream in agony within myself. Miss Khan told me to wear a diamond and then this UN post will get settled and when I said I could not afford it and also did not believe it would help, she said she would get me one for Rs 8000 and I gave her a silly reply " If I could afford Rs 8000, I would buy a washing machine". My husband was worried about my disappointments and obsession. He felt that I might get into depression with all that was happening on the official front and in the future planning of my career.

I found that to avoid my writing a straightforward note, my director was marking things to the Secretary straight, writing Joint Sec (out), I may have only gone for an hour's meeting. I later learnt she did this in all her postings and got the boss posted out. I remember coming home and lying in a dark room with tears in my eyes; what am I to do if my boss and director are 'hands in glove'? To be fair my boss was not a bad character but could not tolerate me. One day his Private Secretary called me to his room and asked me to get him an appointment with a doctor in AIIMS, Dr. Mallvia; this doctor stuck to the rules and did not give preferential appointments but saw patients in turn. The PS of the Secretary called me to the Secretary's room and connected us to the doctor. I spoke to Dr. Mallvia, who not only gave an appointment but assured me he would see her. Many VIPs come to AIIMS and are seen out of turn, but Dr. Mallvia had his own principles and it was known that he kept Rajiv Gandhi, when he was the son of the Prime Minister, waiting for his turn on the bench outside. Now he gave us an appointment and promised to see the patient out of turn but mentioned that the Secretary should remind him about the appointment only being got through Suneeta Mukherjee. As soon as the phone was put down, the Secretary's face was red, and he threw a file on the table which hit the glass of water toward me, and I jumped aside. I asked him what was wrong and he said that he was not happy that they had to take my name when he had held many important senior positions.

These kinds of incidents continued. I did once talk to him and tell him he was so senior to me and I was at a junior level, I was trying to tell him not to feel threatened by me as he said that the press guys were praising me after a press conference. Anyway, after a fiasco over a file, I decided on Sudipto's advice to leave. There was a vacancy for the much-coveted post of Resident Commissioner and I decided to make the pitch for that. We have to revert to State after we complete 5 years, so about 5 months before I completed, I requested for repatriation to the State. The Secretary spoke to SB Mishra, the Senior Joint Sec, requesting me to stay on, but I said only if Secretary requests me personally, I will stay. He did not; as the file went to the Minister, he sent feelers to me asking me why I was going, but I maintained the official stand that my daughter is finishing class 12 next year and I need to be in Delhi and RC was the only opportunity. This got approved. The dye was cast but before I left I did meet the Secretary and told him in a diluted manner how miserable I was and gave him the example of taking my name for appointment with the doctor for his daughter and his throwing a file "Is my name so bad?" I asked him. His only answer was that I was very sensitive.

And thus my tenure as Joint Secretary Family Welfare came to an end. The Health Ministry was actually very active and my tenure was professionally very satisfying.

How does one work with a difficult boss? This was one of my learnings here. I also saw the vastness of the operations in Health and Family Welfare and how Centre and States work together. Since we worked with UNFPA, UNICEF, WHO, World bank etc, here a whole new world opened up for me.

❐

Chapter 13

Resident Commissioner HP (1992-1993)

I came back to my beloved State though remained in Delhi

Each State has a Bhawan with an office for the Resident Commissioner (RC) and staff and a residential complex with a restaurant in Delhi, ostensibly to liaise with GOI and follow up on State cases, attend meetings for State Govt. and represent State Govt. in different forums so that officers from State don't have to keep travelling to Delhi. However, this does not always happen as officers also like to travel to Delhi and to be fair, they know their case best. This is a nice relaxed posting, and generally, I could go a little early but come back after office hours. A very important responsibility is to look after the CM and the Governor, who one has to receive and see off and also attend to. The CM travels to Delhi twice or thrice a month and the Governor once a month approximately. Abu and Mita and also my parents enjoyed visiting me there. However, it's a coveted post, and some officers senior to me wanted to come there, but the CM made it clear that he had agreed to my request as next year, my daughter was to appear in class 12 and then entrance exams but some officers did not give up.

I've always enjoyed every job. When for a little while, I got posted as Secretary GAD in the State, I took great pride in uplifting and modernising the washrooms of the Secretariat. By now I was well accepted in the State; officers enjoyed having a cup of coffee and discussing their official and other matters with me. I take pride in the fact that during this time, I found a groom for one of my colleagues, I first met the boy, and then he met the girl, and after they liked each other, I fixed for the Registrar to come home and register their marriage. That day the Governor came unexpectedly and I begged to be excused and sent my Deputy RC, but all the cars went off. I remembered at the last minute that I had ordered a cake from the Bengali market and was to pick it up. No auto or cab would go so near, so I asked my son Abu to come, and we went on his bicycle, me sitting behind his bicycle in a Saree holding a cake, to her house where her sister was. Marriage formalities completed, they live happily and have a bright and handsome son.

My Deputy RC was not used to working or coming to the office at 10 and resented my being there, but I was cool and tried not to reprimand him. After some time, he moved out and Diljeet Singh, who we cherish even today, joined as my Deputy RC. We made a good team and he adopted a good strategy: he remained out of my reach when I was stressed.

My brother had taken premature retirement from the army and I and my husband supported his moving back to Daddy's Sector 8 house. However, the house was not built for three families and there was bound to be difficulties. So, though initially against it, Daddy sold the house and bought three houses - one for himself and two for my brothers. It must have been traumatic at the time, but it brought all the families closer; however, my parents missed the old house especially as they aged more and sometime had hallucinations. We however could never buy the old house again as prices had shot up steeply and we lacked resources.

I was grappling with Mitali's problems. She was in class 12 and had the first setback when she was told that she had to change from Maths to Home Science; she always felt Maths was her favourite subject and was heartbroken, but thanks to the teacher of Home Science began to enjoy it. However, her stomach aches would not let her be, and when one day Miss Khan came and sat with me, a batchmate who was Secretary, Health, in Rajasthan was there and when she talked of wearing an emerald, he said that he would send emeralds from Jaipur for our selection. However, when his representative came with a large no of emeralds for choice, Miss Khan rejected all of them. And then she arrived one day with an emerald ring and told me to pay her Rs 4000, which is the highly concessional price which she had paid. I hesitated again and she said if it does not work, she'll return double, i.e., Rs 8000. So, I called Sudipto with this proposal, expecting him to tell me that I'm not illiterate, so why am I going that way. However, he did not say that and said that there was no harm in trying this too. So, I took the ring and she gave me with instructions on how it was to be worn and on which day at what time to put it on which finger, but at home, Mitali started telling me that this was not scientific and why I was making her study science when I believed in all this. Anyway, we persuaded her to try this as scientific solutions had not worked and also by telling her that maybe there is a science behind this which we did not understand. Miss Khan assured us that while Mitali may have a minor stomach ache again but she will not need to be hospitalised. The ring worked like a miracle, and she never had to be hospitalised again, Years later, when Mitali was doing dentistry in Bombay, Miss Khan wanted to use that ring for herself and asked for it, but Mitali said that she had left it in her cupboard and when she checked much later, it was not to be found; anyway it had worked for Mitali.

I was applying for international posts and had not gotten any response from UNFPA and UNICEF. Dr. Sadik used to call me when she came to India, and along with Vineeta Rai, we would go for her saree shopping. Once I got selected in ICOMP and even after getting an appointment letter, someone else joined. Dr. Sadik heard of it as the head hunter sent a report to the Doners of ICOMP (UNFPA was one of them) and asked me how a person like me could allow this to happen to me. I told her I had no choice; I even called the Chairman who was travelling to Japan and he claimed that he knew nothing about it. She asked me why I did not apply to UNFPA, and I said that I had applied twice but not got a call. I applied again and so did Vineeta Rai and some others. Vineeta Rai got an appointment as a consultant, later called advisor, in our regional office in Kathmandu.

My parents had come a few months earlier, distraught and wanting to sell the sector 8 house. Their health was deteriorating, and Prem Sharma, who happened to be there, had suggested some remedies. One of them was to do Maha Mritunjay Jap many thousand times which could be and was subcontracted to a pandit. So, this was overcome to some extent, and in a few months Mummy and Indu came to my place suddenly one day after selling the sector 8 house, so relieved.

I applied for the post of Country Director of UNFPA and went to New York for an interview. I was studying hard, preparing day and night foolishly. I took a hotel, the Tudor hotel, just opposite UNFPA. The charges of the hotel were more than the daily subsistence allowance we would get, and the only reason I did this was to reach in time for an interview without being confused about the route. As I was going to the lift on my floor, there was a familiar voice and a lady shrieking, "who told you that I killed my child" and there I saw Prem Sharma doing an astrology consultation. We were surprised to see each other, and I asked him how he could afford this; he said that the hotel owner was a Himachali, and for 2 free consultations, he gave him a free hotel room and he was on an astrology consultation trip. I then realised that this man had travelled all over and had clients all over the world. Prem Sharma was absolutely sure that due to the alignment of the planets Shani and Rahu, I would succeed in the international posting, though after a lot of trials, and would travel a lot. I had 17 short interviews and one last long one with all departments. Except for the initial interactions in French, all went well. When I was leaving,

I was asked to stop for 2 days to meet Dr. Sadik; when I hesitated, they insisted and said it was good news. I reluctantly extended my leave by 2 days, changed flights and stayed on to meet Dr. Sadik. I wore a royal blue crepe saree and the moment I entered her room; she praised the saree and this happened every time we met. She had lovely sarees and also an eye for them and could mix her feminine traits quite easily with her strong overpowering professional personality. She saw my results and was very happy and read out comments of different people/departments who interviewed me and told me she was going to send me to Sri Lanka. She asked me why I was not excited and I mentioned the relations with India and SRL were sour after IPKF, and she said, "don't go to Jaffna and you will be fine". So, it was settled. She explained when I mentioned Bangladesh that with my interest in games, especially swimming, I would be better off in Sri Lanka than Bangladesh. She also said that in the beginning, I should do a smaller country with lesser problems. And I came back to India excited that I would soon join UNFPA and go and attend the international conference on population and development in October in Cairo.

Back home, I kept getting pressure from the other officers who wanted to come to my post. A peon in our office carried tales of the black magic being practiced there to oust me from my post. I did not believe in all this but started losing my direction sometimes and wondered if it was that, e.g. I could not reach the right place for my French interview! I loved my French teacher Shobhana married to an IPS officer and facing some problems, and she used to give me extra coaching, but I started faltering badly. Once I also boarded a wrong train and became nervous, and then came a catastrophe, I had got a call from Pt. Sukh Ram (Central minister, my association with him was from my probationary days in Mandi), he said that he had got a call from an important Godman, asking for me to vacate the post and that while he was not going to act on that, I had to be careful. I did not take this seriously and wondered why a Godman of highly placed VIPs was bothered about my post. However, when I went to receive Raja Virbhadra Singh at the airport, he told me that I had to move to Shimla. I joined my hands and before I could say anything, he said that I had to move as soon as my daughter had finished her exams. I told him that more critical was her medical entrance exam soon thereafter, but he just took hold of both my hands and said that they need me in Shimla. When I reminded him that I may be joining the UN soon, he said I must join in Shimla first. I was aghast and told Sudipto to come to this Godman's residence after work at 6.30 pm; I called his residence and made an appointment at 6.30 pm.

When we met the Godman, we were unprepared for what to say, but without mentioning any situation, I did say that I wanted to stay in Delhi for a few months due to my daughter's exams but was being asked to move. He looked at me and said I can see movement in your forehead; in so far as your daughter is concerned, bring her to me tomorrow morning. So, we took an appointment for the next day and left, but on the way back, both of us discussed how it was not wise to take Mitali to him. Thus, we came to the end of my tenure in Delhi and I decided to complete whatever was pending in a month and then move to Shimla.

We were in May, and I set my target to join HP in June, I had told CM about my joining the UN in a month or two, but he said "we'll cross that bridge when we come to it"; so I started winding up in Delhi. HP had been under President's rule 6 months earlier and the Advisor to HP Govt. was one Mr. P P Srivastava. He believed in Baba Nagpal ji in Chattarpur and while I accompanied him, I waited outside and did not go in. I had said that I will go and meet him one day as he kept saying that he is an Avtar of Ma. So, one of the things I was to do was to pay my respects to the Chattarpur Baba ji. Shobhna and I went one Sunday morning; there was a huge crowd outside, and everyone said that Baba ji was not seeing anyone as he was unwell. We waited and then asked the guard if he could take our card inside, but the guard laughed and said that they never took cards to Baba ji. Then as we were going, a volunteer came running to us as we neared our car and said that Baba ji was calling us. So, we were escorted in. Baba ji, a short guy on oxygen, garlanded us, gave us prasad and insisted we have breakfast. Breakfast was Idli sambar in an airconditioned room with a nice cup of coffee and cold water, and we were talking about how nice he was with us. Shobna asked me why I did not ask him about Shimla and I said that she should have asked about her husband, but we realised that Baba ji had already bid goodbye to us. However, as we washed our hands, we were told to go to Baba ji again. When we were taken to him, he asked us what we wanted to say; as though he had heard us, we told him of our problems. Then and till this day (he is no more now), I have always thought of him as a friend he was very knowledgeable, so I was able to discuss anything with him. He told me that I had to go to Shimla. It was my Karam Bhumi and that Mitali would get her due, and I could not hold on due to her preparations for entrance exams. At least I was clearer and started preparation in all earnest. I also always came and met him whenever I came to Delhi.

I enjoyed my HP posting in Delhi where Mitali finished her schooling and Rajat went to Doon school. Now I was preparing for an International posting. Preparation for international service was tough and the selection tricky but I made it. Meeting Baba Nagpal ji was a bonus.

❐

Chapter 14

Commissioner cum Secretary PWD HP

(1993-1994)

Going back to the state for a short period ... physically too. What was the purpose?

We drove in 2 cars to Chandigarh; one car was from HP, and one was our personal car, a Maruti. Sudipto drove the Maruti, and I sat with him along with the maid who was going for a short time with us. Ma and both children were in the Ambassador and coming behind us. We took a break in Karnal and soon after the break, a bus was overtaking us from behind and one appeared in front. To avoid the bus in front, the rear bus swirled into our car and the bus coming from the front also banged into us; we were literally crushed between the two buses. Our car was badly punched in, but miraculously we were not hurt. The GM Haryana Roadways and Secretary Transport Haryana were in a car close by and they stopped and assured us that they would get the car repaired. We managed to drive to Chandigarh in the damaged car from where they took it to repair. So, the journey back did not start well, and the next day we went to Shimla to join after a sleepless night with my parents.

I needed a house at once and the only vacant house was a little further away from the Secretariat, about 200 yards off the road downhill. No one wanted it as it was supposed to be haunted. It was also in a shabby condition as no one had lived there for a few years. I visited it, and with my posting as Sec PWD, I could quickly have the repair work done and after the bathrooms were functional, we quickly shifted there. Dwarko was with us and also her nephew, who I had helped get a job, was staying with us. Diana, our lovely dog, was with us and I was always scared if at night she went downhill as jackals and panthers sometimes came out. Mrs. Dua visited me here and we were happy with the idyllic green surroundings.

I was posted as Commissioner cum Secretary PWD and later given charge of water supply also. My Minister was Mr. Khachi, someone who was well read (he studied in St. Stephens) and knowledgeable. I felt I had only two or three months before I joined the UN but having come to my cadre, I must do some work. What will or can I do? I wondered, since all the works in PWD, like roads, bridges and buildings, take a few years to execute, what could I do in a short time which would make a difference and make my coming to Shimla worthwhile. I remembered that when I was in Personnel, I used to be aghast that most of the older staff in PWD was adhoc. This is because the officers who came from DHANICS (UT service) and were absorbed in HP never had their seniorities fixed, and so promotions were also adhoc. Now all confirmations and promotions did not only need department clearance but also had to go through the public service commission. Luckily, I knew the chairman of the public service commission Mr. Verma, he was from IPS and we had worked together when we were in personnel. I also had a good Joint Secretary, Ram Subhag Singh, and we could work well. My Minister was happy too. This would take day and night work for a few months. It meant completing ACRS (having them written if not there sometimes), collecting vigilance clearance certificates of past years, getting approval not only from the Minister but holding a formal DPCs and then issuing new seniority lists and inviting objections, if any, before the list was finalised. This had to be done for multiple categories of employees and everyone had to work very hard. It was a bit annoying that Public Accounts Committee (PAC) meetings were going on. They were chaired by Sat Mahajan. PACs point out discrepancies in the work of the department officers and in the works, and though those officers have changed, the incumbent has to answer. This is the time the politicians have solid grounds, e.g., audit objections and they pull up the officers. I had to go at least twice a week for one month and this took away from the time I had to regularise employees. Vidhan Sabha is far away from our office, and at least half a day was gone in the travel and meeting. Other works e.g. inspections of roads and bridges, came up, which I minimised, but one I enjoyed very much was the renovation of Chamunda Devi.

The legend is that when Lord Vishnu severed the burning body of Maa Sati into 51 pieces so that Lord Shiva would calm down and stop his Tandava, the pieces were scattered over various places in the Indian subcontinent. It is believed that Sati's feet fell at this place and is thus considered one of the most important of the 51 Shakti

Peetha. Our Minister Khachji was a devotee and called the Chhatarpur Babaji to visit Chintpurni. Since PWD was renovating it, I had to be there for any instructions. I was happy that I got an opportunity to meet Baba ji here. After I had gotten to know him, I had taken my parents there, my husband and children and whoever wanted to go. I always felt his warmth and friendship. He never took anything from me. Even when he came to HP, I took a shawl for him, but he gave it to my father as he said he does not take anything from his daughters. I told him that I don't believe in that and even when my Mother took gifts from me, he replied that my Mother was a Mother just in this life, but he had been my Mother for many lives!

Mitali was undecided about her future. She was preparing for the medical entrance, which she always wanted to do, but maybe it was also something that she thought we all expected and took it for granted. However, in between, she started thinking of hotel management and surprisingly filled in all forms (we were helping her with medical) and took the entrance exam on her own initiative. She even passed and got admission in Goa. Sudipto did not like the venue as he thought it was bohemian. I felt that it was not sustainable for her as so many people I met who had done hotel management shifted to other professions midway, but we gave in to her wish. However, she met some friends in the hotel industry who told her about the real life behind the glamour, which was not just sweat and hard work but also unpleasant work; so just before we paid the fees, she asked us to stop, she no longer wanted to do it. Meanwhile, she had joined St Bedes in Shimla so as to have something started while we awaited the results. She took up arts. However, when I returned from Una, she told me she had left college because she found the attitude of girls intolerable. They thought boys came from another planet, she said, and that they were always gaping at boys outside and thought the end purpose of life was marriage. I feel very bad now, but when I asked her that night what she wanted to do, she said maybe she should become a film star and I was harsh with her (which I regret even today). I told her she should qualify herself for a job and then do whatever she wants and that becoming an actress is not easy either. She later turned around and said that she did not know what to do and I should help her decide. So, I proposed that she does dental surgery, instead of medicine, as the working hours were more relaxed compared to a medical doctor and on the whole, it was easier. I also felt she was good with her hands and had nimble fingers and would do well. As an IAS officer, I did not find much chance of employability in Kuala Lumpur, but a dentist, I had thought then, if allowed to practice, could put up a chair anywhere. She also would not have to spend a large part of her life studying. She said, ok but remember, I'll blame you if you don't like it. I said that ok but first you better decide if you want to do it. As we progressed, she did not get admission in medical or dental in the general category. She wanted dental surgery and while I was trying in the North or in the South without a capitation fee, she made up her mind to go only to Bombay and study there. I took the help of Mr. Rajwade and she got admission in D. Y. Patil Dental College in Powai. However, a capitation fee of 7 lakhs was involved and this was after all the concessions. I asked my Father and he was unsure, understandably so, to let go of his old age savings. Sudha came to my rescue as they had just sold some land and I was expecting a UN posting and would be able to repay them. Mitali was excited. Bombay was calling and soon we got all the stuff she wanted and she began her study of dental surgery. We were all happy with this.

Sudipto was visiting Abu from Delhi. I too went one weekend. He seemed to have adjusted and was doing well in table tennis, but what I had imagined that with all opportunities, he would shine and blossom and be happy did not happen. He didn't talk to me about school though I encouraged him to talk. I was told he was unhappy with the ragging, but he did not talk about it. He was now focusing on doing veterinary surgery in London, for which Sudipto started looking at IB in India; it was in Mahendra in Poona and in Good Shepherd International school in Ooty, but there was no vacancy.

Mr. Khachi, my minister, said, when I took a stand on something, that he had considered me to be Joan of Arc, but I was stubborn. I turned around and told him that St Joan was burnt because she was stubborn. I worked very hard, thinking this is my last offering of my service to my cadre as I am going to move out soon and would never come back to that work. In this way, October had passed and I was supposed to attend the conference in October after joining the UN, I was glad in a way that my appointment had not come as I wanted to complete what I had started. However, in November I called New York and asked to speak to Director Asia and Pacific Division, Mr. Rahim Sheikh. The first thing he asked me was why I had not joined, and I said that I had not received the appointment letter. He told me he sent it in September and I asked at what address and he said India Office. I hadn't checked there, but when I did, they said that they had not received it either. So, I sent a formal representation and they began their process again and I agreed to join in December. I was first to go to New York for a briefing and then visit SRL, call on the Govt. get my house on rent, go back to my country, get my baggage and join.

I had completed confirmations and promotions of staff in PWD. I tried to do some for the additional charge given to me in public health, but neither was there enough time nor did the staff want to do it. I left it and wished the staff good luck as I was getting a bright and upright successor, Sujaya and was sure she would manage. I have never checked after leaving a post what happened after, and nor did I there.

So, we packed and Mitali was with us. She went ahead in a car to spend time with Mrs. Dua. Her cat, Cindy, and Diana was in the truck with Dwarko's nephew. The cat too had a chain. After crossing the Shimla barrier, when the truck had stopped at a traffic light, the cat ran away. I rushed, but we could not find her. However, when we went to Mrs. Dua's, Mitali went back to where the cat ran away and walked up and down the hills, calling her till she started mewing, and Mitali found her chain stranded in a bush. It is unbelievable but true! That was my last posting in Shimla successfully done. I requested to go on deputation to UNFPA and not resign from my service before knowing if I liked it, which was agreed to.

Back in Delhi, I found Sudipto not happy as he could see the whole family getting separated, I told him that if he did not like it, why didn't he tell me to stop and not go. He replied that he would never stand in my way of what I wanted to do and would only promote my well-being and not stand in the way. He did not give his passport to the India office for a visa or tickets. It was with Abu and Mitali that I went to Sri Lanka after my orientation and packing.

Could not understand why I had to go to HP for a few months bag and baggage. Later realised that it was my good fortune to be able to regularise all the adhoc PWD staff.

❐

Chapter 15

United Nations and Sri Lanka (1994-2000)

A new experience studded with roses and thorns

As I settled into my seat on the flight to New York, I thought of all the efforts that I had put in to getting into an international organization. It had been quite an eventful journey, with hope and disappointment ebbing and flowing, encouragement from some quarters, indifference from some, which may well have been cloaked expressions of jealousy or envy. However, here I was, travelling to the UNFPA HQs, with quite a busy agenda ahead. UNFPA is lodged in the Daily News building, an iconic building and a landmark in New York City. The Daily News building, 220 East 42nd Street, is situated in Turtle Bay and is an iconic skyscraper, just a couple of streets away from the main UN building on 44th street. It has a giant globe at the ground level, and there is always the hustle and bustle around with people moving to offices and boarding taxis, buses, and the subway. Grand Central Station where most trains come to and leave from NY city, as well as the outskirts and neighboring cities, is located about a km or less away and is within walking distance. UNICEF is also located in another building close by, as is the bank UNFCU.

I was to be briefed about Sri Lanka and the UNFPA program there, and I also had to meet some of my bosses. I also intended to take up, with Dr. Sadik, the level at which I was being recruited in the organization. I was given a P4 level, to which I had objected, but had been told by the HR folks that I should accept it or leave it. I accepted the offer but did record that I would like a review. Dr. Sadik was not happy with my representation, but I gave her my reasons: my qualifications and my work experience; later, I received a revised offer with a P5 level after I left.

My immediate boss, the Director of the Asia Pacific Division, Mr. Rahim Sheikh, invited me for lunch, but I was so jet-lagged I forgot all about it. I was then too embarrassed to face him but could not avoid that. I was full of energy and a strange excitement to begin work in New York, and I could not imagine how I could forget lunch with a boss with whom I was keen to establish a rapport and learn how the organisation would like me to function.

I completed all the paperwork, including getting my UN ID and my UN Laissez Passe made, and opened a bank account in UNFCU (United Nations Federal Credit Union), where my salary would be credited, and I came back to Sri Lanka. For some reason, the car for my airport pick-up did not turn up. The drive from the airport to the town is quite some distance, and I remember wondering if we were going in the right direction.

This was to be a short visit; I had to find a house, acclimatise with the programme and the staff and also call on officials of other UN agencies. I stayed at the Taj Samudra, which was just off the ocean and had a lovely view.

I went to the office the next day and met with the Resident Coordinator and the UNDP Representative, and of course, my office staff. Incidentally, as Country Director of Sri Lanka, I was also the non-resident Country Director of Maldives with the UNDP Representative and the Resident Coordinator, who was located in the Maldives and looked after any day-to-day needs when I was not there.

The UNFPA office in Sri Lanka part of the UN complex, was in a very nice single-storied house with a garden all around it. The staff consisted of an Asst. Representative, two secretaries, Shyama and Nandini, a financial assistant, and my driver, Arumuggam. It seemed a simple, straightforward office with a detailed programme.

I went around with a property dealer to see houses and selected a lovely house a few kms away from the office. It had an office, one large and one small bedroom and a large drawing and dining room and a lawn outside. It also had a very friendly IG of Police living next door and so I would be safe. I always wanted a large drawing and dining area for entertainment and socialising and two or three bedrooms.

I needed to open a bank account, but that was not possible as I was there for only five days. I could not understand why it was not possible, so I insisted, and though the account did get opened, I saw my staff look at me with some concern: they were probably thinking that I was going to be a difficult boss. I explained to them that I had to receive money from HQs, and I needed to furnish my account number; also, that the amount of foreign exchange allowed by the Govt. of India to be carried on one's person while travelling was severely limited and I needed funds in Sri Lanka.

I made two trips to India to get my belongings; the first time, I just brought some essentials, and on the next one, Mita and Abu also came along, as did Diana, our big black Doberman, and Dimple, the older but small Pomeranian and Cindy, Mitali's cat.

Pets are drugged and placed in cages for air travel. They are checked in along with normal baggage. Diana was a big dog and had been given almost twice the recommended dose. However, she was barking quite a lot, probably unused to being in a cage and seeing so many unknown people all around. The Sri Lankan manager suggested that we take her out on a leash for a while to calm her down. Abu took her out, and she promptly pulled and nudged very hard, barking loudly, and ran outside the airport. She presented quite a sight, a big black Doberman running and barking, and passengers at the airport rushing to keep out of her way and screaming; what a commotion it was! Diana looked for and found Sudipto, who had come to see us off, standing up on her hind legs, with her front legs on his chest/shoulders in a sort of a hug. Abu, meanwhile, had fallen on the floor and was complaining that he had hurt his shoulder. It was quite an event, and although one can look back and laugh, at that point of time, it was extremely unnerving.

The drama with our pets did not end there. Once we reached our home in Sri Lanka, Cindy the cat ran away. My home phone was out of order, and there were no mobiles those days. Sudipto called my neighbour, the IG, to find out if we all had reached safely, and he told Sudipto that his police officers were scouring the neighborhood looking for Cindy!

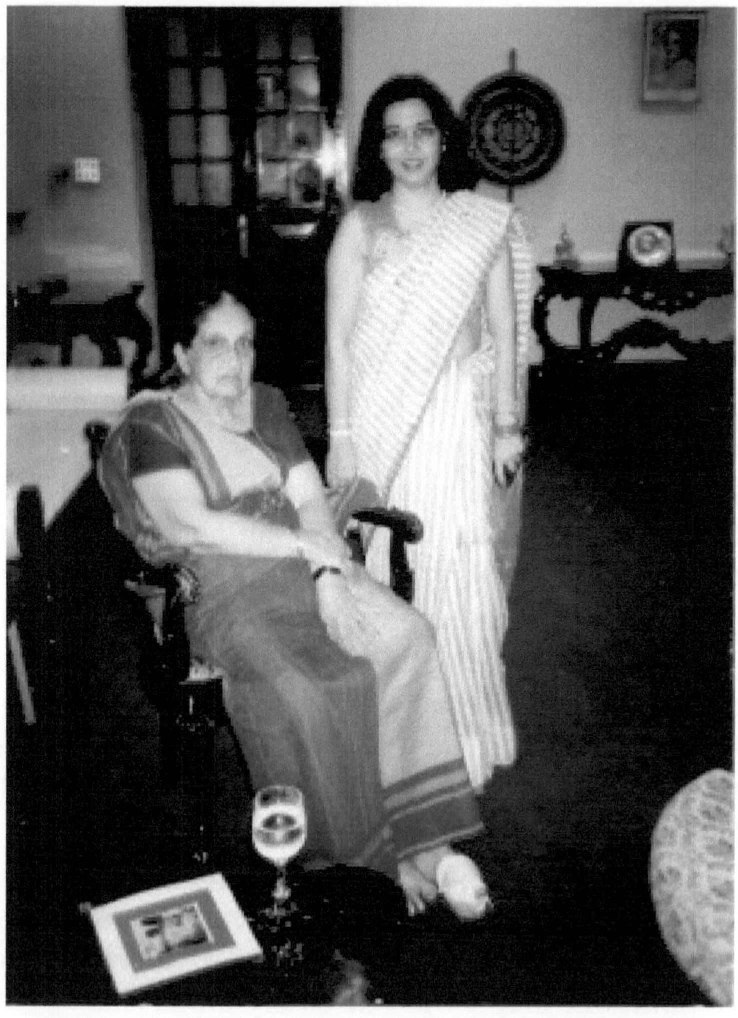

With the Prime Minister of Sri Lanka Mrs. Sirimavo Bandaranaike

Back at work, I called on the Foreign Minister to present my credentials and also called on the President and Prime Minister. Incidentally, the PM was Ms. Bandaranaike, who I had met on our college trip to Sri Lanka some 25 years ago.

Sri Lanka, officially the Democratic Socialist Republic of Sri Lanka, is a beautiful island country in South Asia, located in the Indian Ocean, southwest of the Bay of Bengal, and southeast of the Arabian Sea. It is geographically separated from the Indian subcontinent by the Gulf of Mannar and the Palk Straits. Sri Lanka had been struggling with internal conflict with the Tamils in the north, who were rebelling against the Government, demanding a separate state. In 1987 the Indian Army was sent to Sri Lanka to assist the Govt. in maintaining peace; the force was called the Indian Peacekeeping Force, and it was not successful. Not only did the mission fail, but the Indians also became very unpopular with the locals. I had been a little worried about this, but Dr. Sadik had told me that I would be fine as long as I avoided going to Jaffna.

The social parameters of Sri Lanka were much better than other South Asian Countries. Successive Governments had invested in education and health from the beginning of the century, which had borne rich dividends. In terms of social indicators, Sri Lanka ranked the highest amongst the South Asian Nations. With literacy levels at about 90%, a high life expectancy and low maternal mortality (58 per 100,000 as against 470 for India), Sri Lanka presented a dichotomy with its low levels of GDP and per capita income. The main religion in Sri Lanka is Buddhism followed by Hinduism, Islam and Christianity.

The Maldives, situated to the West of Sri Lanka, is an archipelago situated in the Indian Ocean and consists of about 2000 islands, of which less than 200 are habitable. Its total population is around 5,00,000. It is the world's lowest lying country and, on average, 1.5 meters above sea level. The Maldives had a hundred per cent Muslim population, but they were not conservative; women had equal opportunities and they went to school. There was no college there, and Male, the capital, was not more than 3 km from corner to corner, so we walked or sometimes I used a cycle. Taxis were also easily available at $1 from anywhere to anywhere.

With Mr. Maumoon Gayoom the President of Maldives

The main source of livelihood is tourism and fishing; there were no factories and very little agriculture or animal husbandry. Thus, almost all food items were imported, as were also clothing and other manufactured products. The Maldives had its own currency, but all payments were made in dollars. The first supermarket and the first parlour came up while I was there. For tourism, small islands had been converted into resorts. Each resort is a stand-alone entity, with nothing except a beautiful hotel, white sands and turquoise waters with coral reefs and palm trees. The islands inhabited by locals did not have any facilities for tourists; locals were not employed in the resorts as there was an attempt to keep the Muslim population away from the modern, sometimes half-clad tourists. In the resorts, we often found that housekeeping and other staff were Bangladeshi or Sri Lankan or Indian.

Visiting officials went to the resorts on weekends or even working days, though this was frowned on by the bosses as well as the Govt. So, I did not go to the resorts often. I took the family there once overnight. Towards the end of my tenure, at the invitation of the Government on their Independence Day, I did a scuba diving course in one of the resorts. Otherwise, I just went and worked in Male, though I did go a few times to the islands for work. The Maldives had a presidential form of Govt. and, at that time, did not have much police or army. In fact, the first traffic light was also put up when I was there.

Back home, Mitali was now in Dental college in New Bombay. She was not very happy with the hostel food. Abu was still in Doon school but would move out soon. When Sudipto's first Indian MD was retiring, he organized a get-together of the senior executives along with their families in the Leela Resort in Goa. So, Abu came from Dehradun, Mitali from her Dental College hostel in Bombay, and I from Sri Lanka. I spoke to Mitali's Dean and picked her up, and she was quite impressed by my arranging this and talks about it even today. In Goa, Sudipto told us that he had stopped smoking. I never asked him to stop, but we all knew that it was not good, and Mitali used to comment once in a while. It was remarkable that he stopped on his own, but he later said that we had not even noticed it.

While in Delhi, Sudipto had checked with me and from the proceeds of the house we sold in Panchkula for 18 lakhs, he bought a plot (all transactions in white) in Sushant Lok in Gurgaon. The construction of the house on this plot was contracted out and I sent my savings for this house for about a year or more.

Mitali soon got fed up with her hostel in Bombay. She said that she did not like the food and that every child has a right to have at least one parent stay with her. So, my husband sought a posting in Bombay and got it. He took a house on rent in Powai, and Mitali finished her dental education from there. Sudipto never looked back or thought he had done anything great by shifting his station of work where he was doing so well, in fact he grew to enjoy his work in Bombay too and moved from success to success. He moved up the ladder of MNCs very fast and became the Chief Executive of Electronics and Data Systems. Mitali loved Bombay and took up a job in Bombay. In fact, in India she belongs there, she says.

Abu had always wanted to be a vet, and as he got along, he wanted to study at the Royal College of Vet Sciences (RCVS) in London. The preferred academic level for entry into RCVS was the IB. IB was not so common in those days and only two schools in India offered it: the Mahindra World College and another one in Ooty. However, there was no vacancy in either of these schools and so Abu came to Sri Lanka and took admission in an overseas school. Here he learnt all about children's rights, but became a typical non-communicative adolescent. He enjoyed his school but was often out at night without my knowing where he was. On one occasion, I referred him to a counselor and after talking to Rajat, he wanted my husband too in a family meeting. We had hit the children a bit in their childhood and that had left a negative impact on him. So, I apologised to Rajat, and at least after that, he put it behind him. I sometimes discounted things as they were a part of adolescence, but it was difficult to cope with so many diverse issues at work and handle this too. Sudipto would say, 'you keep saying he is an adolescent; how long will it last?' One day I got a call from his class teacher to say that the next day she had scheduled a presentation by me on gender. Hey, I said, please give me some time and she replied that Rajat was told a week back. He was actually embarrassed and had not mentioned it. When his teacher introduced me, she said that though Rajat had the same surname, he was not related to me. As I talked about Reproductive Health and the responsibilities of adolescents, he was a bit embarrassed and told me later that I sounded like a feminist!

When I had gone on an official visit to Bangkok, he joined me for 2 or 3 days, and I took leave. He wanted a tattoo done on his arm, and I gave out my annoyance in Punjabi. I feel guilty about it, but recently he told me that it was good that I did not let him get it done. It was so good to have him with me during that period.

Just after I arrived in Sri Lanka, along with all Country Directors, I got a letter from HQs asking us to raise multi-bilateral funds, and there was a suggestion that we approach the European Commission. There was no EU office in Sri Lanka: Sri Lanka, as well as the Maldives, was covered by the EU office in India. I called the India office and learnt that the head of the division, Eric Muller, was passing through Sri Lanka in a few days. After checking with Eric Muller, it was suggested that I meet him at the airport, which I accepted, not knowing then that his flight arrived at 5 am on a Sunday morning. I had just been in Sri Lanka for a month or two and did not know enough about the country, so I stayed up the night to read up and prepare myself with various project ideas. I had already invited Vineeta Rai our regional advisor in the Maldives and she had drafted a programme for the Maldives, which included a daycare center and supporting activities of a mother NGO. I remember that when I was driving to the airport on the Sunday morning, I thought that a mad dog must have bitten me for me to have kept awake all night and now to be rushing to the airport at 5 am. However, Mr. Muller turned out to be a perfect gentleman. I learnt he was proceeding to Maldives, so I presented the Maldives project also to him. I had three project ideas and he asked me to combine them in one project and said he would fund it. He was not sure about Sri Lanka as it had good demographic indicators and would not qualify for funding. I came back and informed Mr. Farashuddin, the UNDP rep in Maldives on the phone. Since I did not reside in Maldives, he looked after our office when I was not there. I would have liked to have gone to ensure this, but I had some commitments in Sri Lanka, and also, Mr. Farashuddin did not encourage it. Mr. Muller later asked me to send a detailed project which I did, but when he asked me to go and present it in Brussels, I was hesitant. HQs. is always wary when we propose to travel and I was not sure that the funding would come through. Mr. Muller told me that Mr. Farashuddin had asked him to fund a UNDP project, and he had replied that a commitment was already made to UNFPA through me and that he would not go back on his word. I planned to visit EU HQs for a few hours to present the Maldives project on my way to NY when I went to present the Country Programme. This way, there would be no additional expenditure on travel.

When I went to New York to present the Country Program, I took a layover in Brussels. I left my baggage in the lockers at the airport, got into a saree and went to the EC office. I found this quite tedious and apart from not having large lockers to occupy my suitcase, I also had a large Noritake dinner set I was carrying for my boss. My audience for the presentation consisted of Mr. Muller and another staff member. I was not sure what to make of this. Was no one else required to approve? I asked him later if I could call his boss and he smiled and said that though I found it difficult to believe it, the project would be approved. He also said that he had more funds and was willing to give them to UNFPA if he had a good proposal. I mentioned this at Headquarters, and no one took me seriously as, over a period of time, their talks had not borne fruit.

Later I spoke to Dr. Sadik and she sent the Deputy ED to the EU, after which a regional programme was formulated for youth and adolescents. Headquarters was very happy with it as it was a multimillion-dollar regional project, and SRL was a part of this programme for adolescents. However, since it took two years to be formulated and sanctioned, they forgot that I had brought this whole idea on the table. As you have seen I got funding very easily from the EU but as I was to learn later, the EU reporting requirements were extremely cumbersome.

The landmark meeting in Cairo, the ICPD (International Conference on Population and Development) 1994, which I missed, was a watershed: while maintaining the core of UNFPA's mandate, it shifted the focus from family planning to reproductive health. While many of the critics thought it was mere rhetoric, time has proved it was not. This was especially significant for Sri Lanka. A careful perusal of the indicators showed that Sri Lanka had achieved 'replacement level of fertility', which was our goal in an FP programme; this was to have repercussions for our programme, as I will be telling you later. Thus, clearly, UNFPA would be hesitant to fund Family Planning commodities like contraceptives. The system in Sri Lanka had been that the government paid for half the contraceptives and UNFPA the other half. These were all procured by UNFPA Headquarters. The UNFPA Country Programme (CP) for the next five years was to be presented in 1995. The preparations included wide-ranging consultations, including the participation of UN officials from HQs, along with or through the country support team, which was then called the Regional Office (RO).and was located in Kathmandu. We did a joint review along with HQs and representatives of the RO and formulated a program which included contraceptives. The Sri Lankan Govt. was very vocal on the need for contraceptives, as it did not have the money to fund them. There were a lot of discussions with Dr. Vidyasagar, the retired MCH Chief, playing a major role, along with Dr Abeykoon, who headed the Population Division.

Sri Lanka indicators had a bit of a dichotomy: health and education indicators were high, but economic indicators were low. GDP and per capita income were also low and the Government was not in a position to fund contraceptives, so the team formulating the Country Program agreed to retain 50 percent funds for contraceptives.

I thought I had covered most flanks, but the day I reached HQs, I was presented with a notification just issued where countries were classified in A, B, and C categories in order of priority of UNFPA's latest mandate. Sri Lanka was category C, and the funds and staff were to be greatly reduced. I was aghast and at a loss on what to do. I thought I should partly redraft my program and presentation which I had so very carefully made, and did so, staying awake all night without help. The presentation was not done on PowerPoint, the software we got familiar with later, but with a fancy software was more difficult to operate, and I have no idea how I changed the presentation that night and went to present the next day without a wink of sleep. I was horrified at the idea of going back with a minimum fund to tide over the next five years and with a reduction in staff, as I really believed that Sri Lanka needed the funds to sustain the gains it had made.

For anything progressive, which would likely to be controversial, I had to first convince my staff, especially my programme officer, who had categorically stated after a presentation I made to the Resident Coordinator that women were chaste in Sri Lanka and there were no abortions. On the other hand, I had no evidence but could see from the large number of condoms strewn on the empty plots outside the Free Trade Zone complexes that there was protected sexual activity at night. Since the age of marriage was high, sexual activity was normal, and since unmarried youth did not always have a ready

Signing of the country program with senior govt. officials

supply of condoms, women often went for abortions that were well hidden at quiet backstreet abortion clinics. We had contracted the University of Colombo to do research and the findings were spectacular. The whole report was not yet out, but I had an abstract of the initial findings, which showed that the number of abortions was equal to the number of live births and it was clear to me that people were using abortion as an FP method. If funding for contraceptives was discontinued, the abortions in Sri Lanka would increase. I now redrafted my programme overnight and re-did my presentation to highlight this and made a desperate attempt to let the program in Sri Lanka continue at the level of funding it already had. I really believed that beneath an exterior replacement level of fertility and low MMR (54 while India was at 450), there were problems that needed to be addressed and making it category' C' would mean a small token funding and we would lose all the gains we had made.

While I was making a strong bid to continue the contraceptive supply, I was also proposing to make a shift to RH by setting up services for adolescent health in the existing setup to address STIs/HIV, AIDS.

I was disappointed that Dr. Sadik did not chair the meeting as she was out that day. Dr. Jyoti Singh chaired it, and the top brass of UNFPA was present when I made my presentation. Though everyone thought it was a fait accompli and I could not get additional funds as the decision had been taken by the board a few days back, I made a strong pitch and, with my arguments, managed to convince the august gathering about why Sri Lanka needed to be judged by a different yardstick. However, no change of decision could take place without Dr. Sadik, who was returning the day before I left. I asked her secretary for an appointment, but she said that Dr. Sadik had a chock-a-block schedule. At my insistence, she asked me to attend a farewell that Dr. Sadik was going to and talk to her for just one minute.

So, the next day, armed with brevity and a few focussed sentences, I barged into a farewell party and did not stay for more than 2 minutes and made my request to Dr. Sadik before I took my flight back. It was only after about a fortnight that we learnt that my request had been accepted and regular funding approved for UNFPA Sri Lanka. This made a great impact on my senior staff, and for some time, they took me a bit seriously.

Meanwhile, for the Maldives, I drafted the first Country Programme and set up a small comprehensive UNFPA office, and together we saw marvellous results! There was one programme officer in the Maldives office before I joined. I set up a small full-fledged office which worked under the guidance of the Resident Coordinator when I was not there, Mr. Farashuddin, who was replaced later by Mr. Narinder Kakkar; both were great in their own way, both were very supportive.

We set up a very effective program, though not large in terms of money, with tremendous results. We saw how within five years, the fertility rate went down from 4.6 in 1994 to 2.77 in 2000, with MMR coming down from 677 to 120 in the same period. Infant mortality rates also improved. About two years before I left, we hired the sitting President's daughter, Duniya, as our Project Officer. She was very good, and a few years later became a Minister in the Government.

I had gone for a meeting to Malaysia when my office in Sri Lanka got a call from my Mother to say that my Daddy had had a massive heart attack. He had had an attack previously when Tinku, my sister-in-law, was going to get married.

Daddy had a family history of cardiac arrests between 50 and 60 and his parents and brothers had all gone early. He had crossed the 60 barrier but went into a major cardiac arrest now. From Malaysia, I called headquarters for leave and my own office and tried calling my Mom, but no one was picking up the phone. I did not know how I would find him when I reached back and from the airport called and learnt that Sudha had helped in shifting him to PGI and he was recovering there. I heaved a sigh of relief when I saw that he was conscious in PGI and thanked the doctors. I'm sure Mummy found a lot of support in my visit, and I thanked God that I had chosen to work in PGI, albeit for one year only. Daddy soon sold the house and they moved from sector 8 where we grew up and all three of us got married. They bought houses in Sector 44 and 46, which my parents never considered their own even though they said that they were nice houses and everyone was much happier. There may be merit in families branching out on their own and my parents understood this, but they could never get over that house which was a kind of dream fulfilment for them. I thought I'd buy them the same house after retirement, but when I came home after retirement, the prices had risen so much that I had only one-tenth of the price the house was now worth.

Like India, Sri Lanka too had the colonial heritage of the British, so their systems were somewhat similar to the Indian Govt. The civil service officers of the Govt. viewed me as a counterpart and gave me all respect. I requested the Secretaries of various departments to be the Chairpersons of the steering committees of our projects and programmes so that they had some knowledge about our projects, programmes, and organisation.

In the initial days, some senior staff arrived late for a meeting in the Secretary of Health's room and sat down. She was surprised that the meeting had started without her and that it did not stop when she entered. I had only one predecessor and when I asked him later, he explained that he was a doctor in Holland and had come to Sri Lanka for one posting and worked on his own as he knew no other way and conducted the steering com meetings which he often attended. So, for her, it was a sea-change that things could happen without her presence. Maybe it also hurt her ego somewhat that I could reconstitute these committees at a higher level to ensure policy guidance and also monitor their implementation.

She would go off on personal visits during office hours, but I did not allow work to stop or slow down because of her absence. She was unmarried and that was one of the things that upset her, but nothing worked out even though we made a couple of attempts to find a match for her.

A particular incident I recall was about a Consultant, Mr. Dey. He was coming from Jamshedpur to conduct an advocacy campaign. However, his visit had not been authorised by headquarters as a secretary had not faxed all the papers in time to Headquarters.

Our family was going on a brief holiday and we were on our way to the airport when I found out about this. Our flight got delayed and I came back to the office to find my secretary crying. While I put in motion some messages to ensure Mr. Dey to come at the right time, my husband sat with the program officer and cheered her up. I briefly recorded this incident in the register which we both signed. Subsequent events would also be recorded by me but dispassionately and very briefly always giving her the benefit of doubt.

I tried to be very gentle but having worked in the IAS and not having been briefed on this aspect, that is,

Our office staff with Dr. Sadik, our office had expanded with multi bi funds and JPOs

to be very pleasant no matter what happened, took time to learn, but having said that I tried to be mild and not reprimand staff.

One day I asked Shyama, my Secretary, who was smart, efficient, and well-dressed, if she had a problem with me. She hesitated and then said: "I always wore the best sarees in the UN compound and now you are the one who is complimented". I brought many sarees for them whenever I went to India, but of course, I had a very large collection. The main problem probably was that I was an Indian and IPKF had not left a good reputation for Indians.

Meanwhile, the Programme Officers were to be made Assistant Reps and though I had recently promoted my Program Officer from level B to level C, she was the first one to be made Assistant Rep. I did whatever I could for her and for the other staff. I encouraged Shyama to become a Programme Officer in ILO, and when that materialised, Nandini got selected and promoted to become the Reps Secretary.

One day as I was talking to my secretary from outside the office, she asked me to hold on and put the phone down because a senior staff had come to her desk to talk to her. Later, I was shocked to learn what she had said. She had asked my secretary how she was calling an Indian "madam", "you cannot forget she is Indian when you take orders from her", etc., etc. I did talk to them gently later, telling them that in the UN, we don't work for or against nationalities; I also said that even their God Buddha was an Indian and that the sarees they wore were Indian and this comment on my being an Indian and not to listen to me because I am an Indian was totally uncalled for.

I sent my Assistant Rep on a training course to New York. After her course was over, she applied for a few days' leave which I agreed to. We had to appoint a goodwill ambassador, and the Govt. recommended Rosy Senanayake. I called and emailed my Program Officer to ask her views; she said it was okay, except that she had been married twice. Then she asked me if I could make her stay (leave period) in the New York office, official and I said I was not competent and would have to ask HQ, for which I need a justification. She was upset that I had not said yes straight away. Much later, when she met the new global head, she said in answer to a query about how is your country director, 'I wish she was as nice to us as she is to the country' without clarifying. She later told me she was upset that I was not converting her leave into official travel and that's why she said this. She said, "I would even say this about my mother". She thought it was a harmless comment, but it was mentioned in my PAD (Performance Appraisal Document), though she could not write it as she had not seen my work that year. But the result was that my promotion was held up for four years.

All this came later after Dr. Sadik retired. She was earlier nominated for ED of WHO and resigned her post to contest for the WHO post, but there was opposition due to her age and the vote of donor countries. She was, however, respected by all agencies and by UNFPA staff;

of course, she had our posts of UNFPA Country Directors changed to UNFPA Representatives which gave us more authority and converted our blue passports into red ones. Red passports are at the higher end of diplomatic passports and beget more respect and facilitation while travelling. We would still be Country Directors where we were not residents, e.g., in the Maldives.

I took ill one day and we found out on world population day that I had dengue. My efficient secretary Nandini had my clothes collected while I was at a function and called my husband, asking him to come. After the function, she informed me that I was to go to the hospital and that she had arranged everything. I am so scared of hospitals; I sent the blood report to Dr. B K Sharma of PGI, who said that I needed to be in the

With the Honorable Health Minister Nimal Siripala de Silva

hospital for observation and monitoring, and so I went to hospital. Sudipto came the next day, and thankfully my blood count settled down without any interventions and I went home in three days.

Meanwhile, I learnt that Mummy had become unconscious and her haemoglobin had dropped to 5 and she was admitted in PGI. I knew she would be well looked after, but I did want to go and see her and I was sure she was also expecting me. But within two days, I was due to leave for Turin. I just rerouted my ticket and went through Delhi. I went to PGI from the airport and found Dr. Sharma with my Mom, very annoyed about why I had travelled when I had been so sick. Anyway, he was satisfied after he had a quick blood test done for me in PGI.

We had been encouraged to apply for the post of Resident Coordinators and I went for the first competency exam held in Turin at the ILO training centre. It was a unique exam, more of psychological testing by a firm consisting of psychologists hired by UN Headquarters. So, staff members from all agencies at a level of P5 or above and recommended by the parent agency could take the exam. They gave us a laptop with internet access; we sat in or near the library and had access to books and friends on the phone. They gave question papers for three days, and one had to make a presentation during the interview. We were left alone, though there were cameras all around and all our activities were being recorded.

My baggage had not come and my contact lens solution was in the baggage. My specs were with me but they gave me a headache. However, I managed and guess what, I made it! I was the first person from another agency to pass the exam. Our son Rajat looked at me more respectfully as he heard all the congratulations pouring in, but it was a different story that I did not join that post.

My parents visited me briefly; Sudipto came with them. There was a slight problem at Chennai airport because my parent's passports did not have 'Emigration Clearance Not Required' stamped on them. But Sudipto talked to the officials there and given their age, they were allowed to board the aircraft. Their stay in Colombo was very brief as Sawraj recalled them. They had now sold the house and bought three houses: two in Sector 44 which was for them and for Sawraj and one in Sector 46 for Haramrit. I visited them as frequently as I could, for most flights were through Delhi when I was travelling, I would try and spend a day of the weekend there. Ma also came to visit, and we took her to a resort, and she wore a maxi for the first time in her life to get into the ocean! She would laugh a lot and chat with us. Manju and her son Raja also visited us, and so did Mrs. Atma Ram with another teacher of our time.

One of the last major things I did in Sri Lanka was to advocate with the Government to set up well women's clinics. These looked after a woman's needs other than pregnancy like R.T.I's, Prevention and early detection of breast and cervical cancer; adolescents were covered in another programme and could also be seen there. On one day of the week in the afternoon, the FP clinics, which had very little footfall, were converted into well women's clinics, and they have done well!

I had now done four years in Sri Lanka and should have moved out. Dr. Sadik was also to retire soon after many extensions. Abu was in his last year of school, where he would take his final IB exams. He applied to several Vet Colleges in the UK, including of course, his dream college, the RCVS, and also as a back-up, to a few universities in the US.

Mummy had a stroke and was in a coma in the military hospital and I was finding it difficult to leave the station. Sawraj was calling me, trying to tell me this was the end, but I was sure she would get out of it. The day I reached, I found Dr. B K Sharma in hospital with her and she had just regained consciousness and was on her way to recovery. She was a strong woman and made it back from illnesses so often that we did not believe or accept it when she finally left many years later.

I should have taken a posting out now; one should never overstay one's welcome. I was sponsored as UNDP Representative in Riyadh, but the country wanted a male Arabic-speaking RC; I also did not want to go to a remote country from where I could not visit my family often. My greatest concern was for my parents and my in-laws. I visited my mother-in-law at least thrice and my parents maybe six times but my visits were always very brief.

Mitali completed her dental surgery in Bombay and came for a few months during her holidays. She is very sensitive and used to have and perhaps sometime still continues to have nightmares. She felt there were ghosts in the house and I was ready to satisfy her. We called in a priest who prayed and threw holy water in the corners of the house to make the ghost go away; Mitali, in her innocence, said that she had expected the ghost to appear before disappearing.

Mitali took a fancy to acupuncture and did a full three month course with Dr. Jaya Sooriya and loved it. She was impressed how even paralysed women who came from overseas for treatment could walk when they left. Later she would do a project on helping children overcome their fear of the dentist's chair using acupuncture and presented this at an international conference in Delhi. Rajat also did a course later and practices acupuncture a bit on his furry friends and a bit on us.

We had a new global head and she worked for a couple of years in UNFPA before taking over. People knew about this and reached out to her, establishing friendships, but I was blissfully unaware, fully engrossed in my work in Sri Lanka and the Maldives. The previous head liked my work a lot and made no bones about it, I suppose this did not find favour with others and a loose jovial comment by USAID staff where they were praising me a lot during the discussion of a selection of ED was not quite appreciated by senior management.

I was offered the job of head of HRD, but I politely declined as Abu was in his final school year; also, I did not want to go to New York on a posting. The office is on 42nd street in Manhattan and I would only be able to rent a small flat close by and would not be able to afford domestic help. What would happen to Diana and all my crockery and clothes? Also, basically, I am more of a field person and do not like the desk job of a HQs posting. Dr. Sadik came to my rescue again and agreed that this was not the right time for me to come to HQs. However, headquarters insisted that I decide on whether I want to remain on secondment or get absorbed. I later learnt that it was because they were stopping permanent staff members and as they had already stated, future staff members had only two year contracts which were extendable. With tears flowing down my eyes, I sent in my resignation from the IAS and, since it did not get through easily, flew to India on leave and went to Shimla and met the CM and explained to him, who now recommended it. Saying some kind of a farewell to a service you loved was not easy, but I did not look back. It is great now to be in touch with my IAS colleagues!

I now wanted to move on; I had never stayed in a job so long. I requested Dr. Sadik for a UNFPA posting to Bangladesh, but she gave me Egypt as Bangladesh was not vacant. I went to Cairo for orientation, and called on the Govt. officials, looked at houses, and finalised one, only to be told by management they had got a call from Dr Sadik and Bangladesh was now vacant. I was to go back to Sri Lanka. UNFPA would withdraw the request to the Govt. in Egypt for my posting there. I no longer wanted to go to Bangladesh and had gone to Egypt and loved it, but management said they had promised Dr. Sadik and I should just accept it. So I went back to Sri Lanka, sad that my tenure was being extended till the approvals of the Bangladesh Govt. came.

Meanwhile, Abu had got admission in Boston University, and we were going to leave him there, so I took some leave. His acceptance from RCVS had not yet come, and we were not sure if it would, so we thought it best that he started his undergrad studies in the US. Actually, the acceptance did come through after his term had started: schools in the UK begin a couple of months later than those in the US, so the admission process is also delayed accordingly. We all took some time off and went to Boston, where my sister-in-law's son lived. We had a good time in Boston visiting the University campus. Rajat was sporting long hair and was a bit plump.

On one of our last evenings in town, we had dinner out, and Abu had some seafood inadvertently; he is allergic to seafood and avoided it. We dropped him at one of the many parties that freshers have in US colleges and went home. Late at night, Sudipto received a call from a hospital to come and fetch him. What had happened was that in the party, he had started to feel short of breath and broke out in rashes. He came out on the road and asked some people he met to take him to a hospital. They called an ambulance and he landed up in hospital. When we reached there, he had tubes sticking into him but was conscious. Thankfully he recovered quickly and also luckily Vanbreda covered his hospital charges which were like five thousand dollars for just a few hours.

I came back to Sri Lanka and Sudipto went back to Bombay. With the prospect of spending a few more months in Sri Lanka, I ventured to Jaffna. Surprisingly, there did not seem to be any threat and the people, as well as the local Govt, were warm and welcoming. The

Saying farewell to the President of Sri Lanka Mrs. Chandrika Bandaranaike Kumaratunga

demographic parameters and development in Jaffna were very good, better than the mainland and the administration seemed sincere. Soon after my visit, my Program Officer and Dr. Prasanna made a trip there so we could extend our programme to Jaffna too. Despite the war raging for many years, Jaffna's development had not receded, and the children were doing well in education, and literacy and health parameters were quite good.

In India, our idea of Sri Lanka is linked to the Ramayana, in which Ravan kidnaps Sita and keeps her in the Ashok Vatika. Some of the locations of the events of Ramayana can be seen in Sri Lanka.

Sudipto was going on an official visit to Bali and though he was always reluctant to take me on official trips, I went on this one. He flew to Bangkok from Mumbai, and I flew there from Colombo. From there we went together to Bali.

In Bali, we took a taxi to the marketplace, and at one point, we did not have change for the taxi, and a girl standing on the road paid for it. I do not know if it was a set-up, but she asked us to attend a presentation on timeshares, which we purchased for $5000. The first holiday we went on was to Tenerife.

Our travel to Tenerife was memorable. At first, Mitali lost her passport due to sheer carelessness. After a new one was made, we ran out of time to get the Schengen visa. Sudipto kind of cancelled the trip as he was off to Washington the next day on official work. I spoke to the French Ambassador in Sri Lanka, who rang up the French embassy in India and issued visas by hand after 5 PM. Later I made a quick trip to India to organise the rest; the children were using frequent flier miles of Air India. Sudipto flew to London from the US, the children from India by Air India, and I from Delhi by a different airline. Sudipto arrived first and was there at Heathrow when I disembarked. We both went to the terminal where the Air India flight had arrived, and Mita and Abu came out so late towards the end that we both had our fingers crossed that they had not missed the flight! We went to Madrid, and at the immigration queue, when Sudipto asked for all passports to fill up the form, Rajat realised that he had left it in the aircraft. I ran to the departing BA flight with security guards screaming, but I managed to get to the aircraft and retrieve his passport from the pocket in front of his seat.

At the resort in Tenerife, they asked us to deposit one passport and I gave mine. However, I forgot to take it back while checking out and realised it only when we had almost reached the airport for our return journey. There was no time to go back, but since I had my personal passport, I could use that to travel back. Later, I got my passport back through a diplomatic courier.

Soon the long-awaited clearance from Bangladesh came and I was off to join my posting in Bangladesh. I wanted to go there as apart from being close to India, it is from where my mother-in-law came from. She was born and brought up in Bangladesh. I also wanted to learn Bengali; though my husband had not insisted, and even my in-laws had stopped commenting about it, I was keen to learn the language. This is a big regret I have to date, the children would have spoken Bengali if I did. I'm not good at languages, but the best way to learn was to be in an environment where the language was spoken, so after I got the Bangladesh posting, I went there happily.

I got a lot of respect and recognition as I left, but the best thing was that everyone had now heard of UNFPA and what UNFPA does.

I had not realised in time that the way to work in your own country specially in the IAS was different from working in the UN, in another country. The learning was immense. It was gratifying that I made a name in the country as well as with my organisation.

❒

Chapter 16

Bangladesh (2000-2006)

The country of my mother-in-law's birth, gave me a lot of satisfaction and joy

There are about eight hundred Maulvis looking at me expectantly. All dressed in long flowing white robes, on their way to Mecca for Haj. I am on the dais and expected to make a speech. I do not know their language and am not fully familiar with their customs. I am not even supposed to be here.

Soon after I joined UNFPA in Bangladesh, the Minister for Religious Affairs asked for my presence at the Haj Departure Centre in Dhaka airport. The only connection we had with the maulvis was that UNFPA was training the maulvis on different aspects of gender. I wondered why I was required there. My Assistant Nurul Ameen insisted that I should go, so I went along with our Advocacy Assistant Asma Akhtar.

I repeatedly confirmed that I would not be required to speak; I would just sit in the audience. However, as soon as I entered and exchanged greetings with Salam-a-le-Koom, I was directed to the dais. I had covered my head but had no pins to keep my saree from slipping.

I heard the welcome speeches and my introduction, and suddenly I was asked to speak.

I kept looking for Nurul, but he was nowhere to be seen; later, he told me he had gone out for a smoke; Asma looked at me helplessly. I look at my audience, a mix of youthful and old and wizened faces, and try to wiggle out. I do not know Bangla; I have just arrived in your country, I said.

Urdu, Urdu, they cry out.

So I say, what I can say to all of you. *All of you are close to Allah and also close to the people: you have the earth and the heavens in your hands.* I manage to say this in Urdu. Marhaba, Marhaba! they cried out in unison. Marhaba is a form of appreciation. What I said came to me in a spur of the moment, I had not thought of it, and it came from my heart. Somehow, they also understood that and the Marhaba continued for a while.

What should I speak to you about? I asked. A young Maulvi stood up and suggested I speak on HIV Aids. My God, I thought, how am I going to cover this topic since it is primarily transmitted through unsafe sex and sex is so private that people do not even discuss it in their bedrooms? How can I talk about it with these religious leaders?

I reconfirmed with them if all, especially the elderly, wanted to know about it, and they said yes in chorus. So, in a somewhat restrained manner, I told them how it is transmitted, how it could be prevented, and so on.

That was a wonderful start, and from then, later in my tenure in Bangladesh, I could talk to them openly about

From L-R: Myself, Secretary Health Bangladesh, Executive Director UNFPA and the Prime Minister Begum Zia while presenting awards to the Maulvis

different issues in our mandate and usually convince them. Together, we addressed women's right to stand for elections, right to property, and most important, the right to safe motherhood and a life without violence. When Thoraiya, our Executive Director, came five years later and addressed a large conference, she said she was so overawed and could gather her wits only because the Prime Minister came half an hour late.

When I joined my office in Bangladesh, Begum Sheikh Hasina was the Prime Minister; in 2001, Begum Zia took over. While the former was favourably inclined to India and Indians, the latter was not. However, I had no problem with neither of them, and even the Indian High Commissioner was surprised at this. Bangladesh, or the People's Republic of Bangladesh, is the eighth most populous country in the world with a population of 1.62 Million, but in terms of land mass, it is only about 147570 km square and hence the world's most densely populated country. Initially a part of Bengal, it became part of Pakistan after independence as its population is mostly Muslim, but after the war in 1971, it became a constitutional republic and a unitary parliamentary democracy.

The Bangladesh office was well established. There were two Assistant Reps Nurul and Tahera, who had been there for perhaps twenty years. Before I came, I learnt that there were cupboards full of complaints in HQs about Bangladesh UNFPA. Janet was the Deputy Rep and had been posted here for about a year with Mr. Xu as the Representative. She was already averse to me as she had wanted to become the Rep and though promised by Mr. Nizammuddin, the Director of Asia and Pacific Division, it was not agreed upon by top management because of her limited experience and because, as per policy, the Deputy Rep could not become the Rep in the same station. However, I learnt of this five years later and wondered throughout what she had against me. Mr. S K Alok from my cadre had been posted here before and had told me there is very little work; he was also quite popular with the staff and they loved the sweets he got from India. I had learnt a bit of a lesson in Sri Lanka and was very gentle with the staff but ensured I did not become ineffective. I had a private secretary who was old and due to retire and could not meet my expectations at all, but I kept quiet. I had a good Finance Assistant in Rakib, though he was a bit wayward. Soon however I got Harun as my private secretary and he proved to be a big support.

We were housed in a UN building in the IDB Complex, and my house was far away in Baridhara. There were two suitable housing colonies for expats, Baridhara and Gulshan. Both were at a distance of around 5 kms from the office, but seemed very far because of the travel time: the roads were congested with traffic and jams were common.

I rented a house with four bedrooms, a large drawing and dining room, and a lawn. I wanted the lawn for my Doberman, Diana, who I was taking with me. There was a swimming pool on the rooftop, which I found was too expensive to maintain. The landlord provided me with a Buddhist boy who he said would do odd jobs and could also look after the security to a limited extent.

On the one hand I had a spectacular beginning with the religious leaders with headlines in the press, "The UNFPA representative says that the maulvis are close to Allah as well as to their brethren on earth," my luck with the maulvis continuing as I adopted different methods to convince them.

But on the other hand, I also had a terrible experience in the office.

There was a staff member who happened to be a Hindu who worked with Janet. He was a temporary staff member and was dealing with children's issues. He seemed a bit lost, and I mentioned that staff should try to come on time. He sought an appointment and talked to me about the plight of children with heavy bags and school books. Our agency did not really have a mandate on this, but he had also written to UNICEF. The next day Sudipto came with Ma to Dhaka. I was in the office and said I will come after the office. On my way back home, as I reached close to home, Mr. Das, who looked after commodities (mainly contraceptives) called me and asked me where I was and when I said that I was reaching home, he asked me to turn back and come to the office authoritatively. I said that my family had come, could it not wait until the next day? He said no and then told me that this guy had committed suicide by jumping off the office multi-storeyed building. It was as though the heavens had fallen; I could not imagine it. He was a Hindu, and Hindus sometimes felt persecuted in Bangladesh but not when Sheikh Hasina was there. I was his boss and also a Hindu. Various theories started floating around. He left a suicide note which said that he had cancer and was taking his life because he knew that the family would keep spending money to save him, but he would not survive and did not want to leave his family in debt. I just did not know what to do and cursed myself for not having sensed it. We also learnt that he was in depression and taking treatment on the side, but not claiming the cost from the office, so no one would know. This really quietened and sobered me, though I don't think my spirits can be low for too long.

My work in Bangladesh started with sobriety. What shaped my work were a few factors which of course changed as we went along. One major factor was that the USA stopped contributions to UNFPA as we were associated with contraceptives and abortions. We were not able to convince them that we were actually dealing with the prevention of abortions by providing various contraceptive methods and advocating planned pregnancies. The hardcore even considered a contraceptive as prevention of pregnancy and hence abortive. Republicans were in power and, on this pretext, they cut funding from UNFPA. UNFPA launched a campaign and requested people all over the world to donate $1 each and also asked representatives to raise multi-bi funds. Having acquired some experience in Sri Lanka in raising funds, this was one of my major tasks and also something I found exciting. You won't believe it, but by the end of my tenure, I had raised $100 million, out of which $40 million went to commodities and $60 million to programmes. But this had not been anticipated in the Country Program and so every time I sent information to HQs and sought their approval, they really had extra work, though they were happy with the funds. However, other agencies were envious, especially WHO.

A very special and unique feature of Bangladesh was the sector-wide approach adopted for health, which meant that all UN and allied agencies and actually multi and bilateral agencies worked together and coordinated their health programmes through the health forum. It was exciting and novel though it meant many hours of discussion. I attended a few times, but generally, Janet, who was very keen on this, went, and she even stood on my head and saw that I voted for her election much in advance of the due date! So whatever we did, we had to coordinate with the other agencies and keep them informed and, wherever possible, work together. There were many bilateral and multilateral agencies helping Bangladesh as it was receptive and one of the last newly formed countries.

Women's lives were not valued much as multiple marriages and remarriages were common. To address maternal mortality, women had to be brought to institutions for delivery or have deliveries assisted by trained birth attendants, for which no cadre existed. In this, I got support from the Govt. as well as the religious leaders for safe motherhood. However, we had to launch a huge advocacy effort with all relevant gatekeepers and also undertake a programme with the elected representatives. Mothers-in-law and husbands were important targets. I remember requesting a mother-in-law to get the delivery done in an institution as it was a high-risk pregnancy, and she insisted that she herself had children at home, and so should her daughter-in-law. I told her that she might die, and she said that was not a problem as the husband would marry again. I was aghast at this attitude, and we were determined to change this.

There were already 6 MCWCs (Maternal and Child Welfare Centres) in rural areas for which UNFPA had funded the building and equipment. These were run by Govt. and UNFPA collaborated with them. We decided to set up a few in urban areas. Since UNFPA had stopped funding buildings, we requested and got funding from ADB; we provided the equipment, and the Govt. provided the staff and ran the centres. Deliveries were done here, and Tahera, my Asst Rep, led this programme with a few NPPPs who were doctors: Jebun, Rowshan, Rafiq, and Aslam. Through these centres, we could address most of the high-risk cases located in their vicinity. However, we had to cover the entire country and for this, trained birth attendants were necessary, and there was no such cadre. It would take more than a decade to recruit and train midwives and create a cadre. It had been established repeatedly that with very few exceptions, Dais (traditional birth attendants) could not be trained; a lot of money had already been spent in trying to train them.

So I embarked on the journey of training the health workers who were in place in the field for delivering babies. It meant convincing the Govt. and all other agencies working in this area. WHO, initially hesitant, became enthused only to be a bit jerky later, since the trainers would be from the Ops and Gynae society and would also be the referral and support for these health workers if this was doable. I made it clear that the long-term solution was midwives, and we should not let women die giving birth till that became a reality 10 or 15 years later.

Dr. Wasim Zaman, Director Country Support Team (CS Team) with Dr. Saramma Mathai, Advisor and myself

My wonderful friend and brilliant Saramma Mathai, UNFPA Advisor for maternal health, supported us enormously, even though I don't think she understood fully my need to address the issue in the interim. This training was a grand success, and though I left, I did learn that an evaluation showed how many mothers were saved primarily due to the Obs and Gynae society taking keen interest and also supporting them. I was happy to see that during my tenure, these health workers felt empowered, began speaking in English, and used mobile phones to seek the support of the gynecologist, they were attached to. As a result of this and other efforts, MMR rates fell from 434 in 2000 to 280 in 2006 per 100,000 births.

Bangladesh has this unique feature and defies the theory that planned families and reduction of maternal mortality can only take place with the progress society makes in education and GDP. Improving educational levels and per capita income cannot be done in short periods, though several donors were working with the Govt. and civil society. Yet even without that, we made huge progress in contraceptive prevalence rates and maternal mortality with programmatic inputs and advocacy.

The fact that Bangladesh also had a colonial heritage and programme similar to ours helped a lot and I was able to invite Govt. officials and Ministers home and a lot of advocacy took place in informal settings. Let me mention a case with the Finance Minister. HIV/AIDs, though it had a low prevalence in Bangladesh, was present, but drugs for treatment were not allowed as there was the total denial by the Govt. of its presence. The World Bank representative was kind of reprimanded and no one dared to talk to the FM again on the subject as he was not allowing the medicines to be imported and was also very powerful in the Govt. The donors requested me to take this up, so I undertook the task. I visited his constituency and home place in Sylhet and interviewed positive cases (generally returnees from abroad) and made a presentation of the issue with these interviews too. I sought an appointment for half an hour; I did want to do this at lunch time as he was diabetic, and if he had not eaten, he would be in a bad mood. My appointment was at 3 PM and though I said that I would wait as he had still not eaten, he insisted that I do the presentation. I had worked hard but was still apprehensive, but by the time I finished, he approved all that I proposed! I got a round of applause from the donors in the next meeting.

However, as I continued to be successful, inter-agency rivalries grew. Agencies which were short of funds were not happy that I was taking most of them. They asked me to take a session on how to raise a multi-by. I did, and my main focus was on matching the mandate of the donor with the country's needs and also proving by performance. And for performance, we needed dedicated and motivated staff. I raised funds from DFID, EU, Danida, the Dutch, World Bank, the ADB etc. But for the last joint programme on safe motherhood we drafted for UNFPA, UNICEF and WHO, I had to wait till the last day of my tenure in Bangladesh for WHO to sign. I did pay the price of popularity, and WHO and even UNDP rep did not look kindly at me.

I could not have achieved anything without my staff. I talked of Janet, the Deputy Rep, Tahera and Nurul, Asst Reps (we just lost Nurul to Covid, may his soul rest in peace). We recruited a well-qualified finance officer who had pregnancy problems in the year she joined; despite my best support, she harboured grievances as she wanted me to handle her Finance Assistant, Rakib, who had some problems. She has done well for herself and moved to HQs. I hired Noor Mohammad for the Youth programme, while Mazhar was already there for monitoring, evaluation and handled population and development to some extent; Asma became the Advocacy Assistant, Das the Commodities Assistant and Jakaria the RH Assistant. Our star new face was Bushra, a doctor well established in the country, who joined us as a gender expert initially but also worked on our safe motherhood project. I was looking for an economist to be able to do a cost-benefit analysis of whatever we do. The economist was a Ph.D. in economics and had even worked with a Nobel prize winner in economics. He turned out to be very difficult and had already been thrown out by another UN agency, but he had hidden this fact when we selected him. All recruitments required HQs approvals, and it was a stringent process. So when we learnt about our economist having been thrown out of a UN agency, I wrote to HQs, and they terminated him though his probation was just over; we recruited Tauhid in his place, a young and I hoped a bright economist.

Let me tell you about what this economist did: he, along, with a temporary lady employee, sent a complaint to HQs that during a strike when we could not go to the

Thoraiya and me

office and worked from home, I called them to work and put their lives in danger. They forgot to mention that I called them home for work during office hours, their home was next to mine and that this area was peaceful. As you know, I was not in favor with headquarters so they ordered an enquiry, but I was not told anything. I was waiting for Abu (Rajat) to come home, and I got a call from my boss the day before, asking me to go to New York without giving me a reason. I asked him for an authorisation for a G4 visa, but he forgot to send it. With the position I had established with the bilateral agencies, I could get a visa without the authorisation and leave at night. I hoped Abu could go instead to Sudipto in Bombay, but Sudipto was also travelling, so I requested Abu to stay put, and I would come back at once. He was coming from the UK only for a week.

I went with a heavy heart and, without any papers, went straight from the airport in New York to the office and, leaving my baggage at the globe downstairs, went to my boss's room and asked him what this was about. He went away and brought the HR head to the room. The HR head showed me the complaint and I told him the case of the economist. He listened, checked his records and was satisfied and said I could go back any time. So I took the night flight back, arrived on a Friday, took the weekend off and went with Abu to Bhutan to spend some quality time with him. Though I was very tired, we trekked to Tigers Nest with some difficulty, and we went around and did some sightseeing in the fabulous country that is Bhutan.

Meanwhile an enquiry was ongoing in Sri Lanka about the next Rep who had to leave;. Mr. Howie, who headed the team, asked the staff and others who was their best Rep, and they named me. When I got some negative comments in my PAD (Performance Appraisal and Development) report, I asked them to give me a specific example or a copy of the complaint. I was told Dr. Sadik was the ED and she had retired. I did not turn around and ask her how my PAD for the period was written by someone who had not seen my work. I wrote to Dr. Sadik; she was aghast. My promotion, I learnt, had actually been approved a year back. The reason that it could not give it to me was that another Representative, Moushero, had gone to Court and won, and the senior post had to be given to him; I was told a year before this happend that I would get it next year since I was on top of the panel.

When Dr. Sadik got my letter about the PAD, she asked for a meeting with the bosses over lunch. Dr. Sadik later wrote to me that the moment she mentioned my name they were very annoyed and refused to discuss the case. I got a horrible mail to me asking me why I spoke to Dr. Sadik and I reminded them that it was they who directed me to her. There was a stalemate even though I was assured that I would get promoted next year. Now next year, this enquiry in Sri Lanka was going on. I asked to go for my Resident Coordinator posting as I had been selected there, but I was told that I needed to undergo training for that post. I enquired what training I needed, in response to which she appointed a company engaged in psychological assessments to determine my training needs.

So these company representatives were sent for the assessment. You must understand that Bangladesh was a very busy station, and I enjoyed my job very much, especially as I could see the results so easily. And the Govt. and donors and people, as well as religious leaders and elected leaders were ready to cooperate; it seemed the whole environment worked in unison to help in making healthy lives a reality, especially for women. So I was neither thinking nor following this up regularly. Also, in the face of this success in day-to-day work, my promotion often did not seem important, though the unfairness still hit me from time to time.

The team that came for an assessment of my training needs sent me a copy a few months later of the report that they sent to HQs. It was a super report, praising me no end, and as soon as HQs read it, it was asked to be withdrawn. But I had already printed a copy! So two years had passed now, and everyone who knew about it was advising me to go to Court; someone who knew a lawyer said that I could pay him from the amount I got as relief from Court, but I did not want to go to Court. I wondered what was wrong. How was I being judged so incorrectly? I even went through a past life therapy to address this and understood the prejudices a bit. In the third and fourth years of my stay in Bangladesh, I got involved in my own and my Father's medical issues but was assured every year that next year I would be promoted. The Executive Director came to Bangladesh only after I was promoted in the fifth year.

So I moved to the Grade of D1 from P5. It made only a little more than a $100 difference, and since I did not want to go to HQs, there was no other change but at least an issue set to rest in that my organization now realised that it was not my fault. This happened as Julie complained about a Nepalese Rep who was not in favour with headquarters and since he was not a regular staff member, his contract not renewed. Now Shamim (name changed) from HQ was sent as Representative, and before going, she asked me about the country. She had been a desk officer when I was Sri Lanka Rep. I had mentioned that Julie was a problem, but she did not take me seriously. When I met her a year later at a meeting, she said that she and Julie got on well, and I said that this was their honeymoon period. Meanwhile, when I met Julie, I told her that she should make sure that she should maintain good relations with Shamim, because if she complains against Shamim as well, people would think something was wrong with her and not with me or other reps. I explained to Julie that Shamim had worked in important positions and had more clout in HQs. Yet when I met Shamim next time at a meeting, maybe after a year, she was gloomy. When I asked her what had happened, she laughed and cried at the same time, saying that the honeymoon was over. She struggled with Julie and questioned me as to why I did not maintain records against her and why I did not report her. Since Shamim had been my Desk Officer, I asked her what she would have said if I had reported her. Would she not have said that I was to handle this on my own. I told her I had mentioned to Nizamuddin, the new Director for Asia and Pacific Division when he came to Sri Lanka, and he had said that all the old NPOs in Asia have some problems and we have to handle them. To cut a long story short, Lubra repeatedly wrote to HQ, and when she left, she was sad that no enquiry had been conducted.

Then came Anne (name changed), who was forewarned by HQ about Julie and given some guidance. So, after Julie started playing up, an enquiry was conducted by HQs in which her continuing misuse of the office vehicle was proven, and she was not allowed to enter the premises one day when she reached the gate. She, of course, filed a case against HQs and asked me to testify in her favour. I regretted saying that I did not testify against her either and since then, she has not spoken to me. It also became clear to people that I was not at fault.

Now about my health. I used to have kind of fainting spells even in Sri Lanka, and when I asked my cardiologist in India, Dr. K K Talwar, he told me to just sit when a spell like this happened, even if I was in the middle of the road. Once when in the Maldives, I could not hear from one ear. I got an MRI done, and it showed white spots on my skull. I sent this to AIIMS; they asked me to get admitted for a week for a detailed examination. I followed their advice, but the doctors did not do any intervention as they could not come to any definitive conclusion.

And after I joined Bangladesh, I started feeling more unwell, sometimes feeling like I was about to faint and often nausea and water coming into my mouth. The doctors wanted me to do an endoscopy, and I fixed an appointment, but Tahera persuaded me to do it in India. So, when travelling to Turkey, I routed myself through Delhi and took a day off. First, I met Dr. Talwar in AIIMS: he prescribed a halter which he fixed to monitor my heart. For my endoscopy, I went to Dr. D K Bhargava, who, after having retired from AIIMS, was now working in a private hospital. Sudipto came from Bombay and was with me. During the endoscopy, I felt I was slipping and told the doctor that I was going to faint. When I recovered, I was on oxygen; they had revived me and were so relieved when I opened my eyes.

I left the halter in AIIMS and was on my way to Turkey. At Dubai airport, I got a call from Dr. Talwar, which was very unusual because he had never called before, asking me where I was and to come back to AIIMS immediately. He reluctantly told me there was a problem with my heart and the halter showed a flattening of heartbeat for one minute and six seconds. I told him I would see him soon.

When I saw him on my next visit, he did some tests, including a tilt test which though a bit gross, was positive and a sure indicator of a problem in the heart. He recommended a pacemaker which needed to be implanted. I applied for leave after about six months as we were in the process of formulating a Country Programme, but my boss Nizam refused, saying that I was in great health. I had almost waited for six months before fixing the date but now leave was refused. However, when having lunch with Dr. Sadik, Nizam mentioned this to her. She asked for my reports, which Dr. Sadik took to her cardiologist, who confirmed that I indeed did need a pacemaker. Nizam apologised and asked me to go ahead. Nizam was a well wisher and a supportive boss.

I went to Delhi again, and when Dr. Talwar examined me, he said that I had responded well to the medicines and I could choose to continue with them. But he added a bit impishly that I would need to mend my pace or get a pacemaker. I asked him if there would be any adverse effects and he said that I would not be able to do an MRI but could do a CT scan. So I went ahead and got admitted, Sudipto, always wonderful, was by my side, and we had the pacemaker fitted. I was in ICU for a day or two, mostly sleeping, but ok. I was shifted to a private room when Sudipto got a call from Bombay and had to leave.

I called my parents and learnt my Daddy was in PGI and had undergone angiography and needed angioplasty. I was crazy; they had not told me as I was going in for a pacemaker, but my Mom wanted me to come to Chandigarh. Sudipto had gone to Bombay for a day or two, and I was not even carrying Indian money. I decided to take the evening Shatabdi train to Chandigarh. Sudipto made arrangements on the phone and asked one of his colleagues to arrange money for me at the railway station, and soon I was home. Mummy was stressed, so was Sawraj, and there was tension all around. I had left AIIMS without a proper discharge; I could not find Dr. Talwar, so I left a letter for him. We went to PGI the next day, and after buying all that was necessary for the angiography, Dr. Bedi started the procedure. However, after trying for some time, he was unsuccessful and said that the only option was bypass, but because of some operational problems this could not be done in PGI. I called Dr. Venugopal in AIIMS, who asked me to rush Daddy to Delhi and he would do the surgery. The doctors in Chandigarh said that for him to travel was risky, but Dr. Venugopal said that he would die if we didn't bring him to AIIMS. Director PGI sent an ambulance with a doctor (Dr. Sanjay Jain, then a young professional), and my Mother and brother came in the ambulance, and I travelled by train a few hours in advance. I had requested and hoped that a bed in Cardiac ICU would be vacant, but unfortunately, there were none. Dr. Talwar, always so mild and gentle, gave it to me for leaving the hospital without a proper discharge and put me through a comprehensive examination of the stitches, where the pacemaker had been installed.

Meanwhile, Dr. Venugopal, who was to operate on Daddy, felt that too many blood thinners were in his blood and wanted to wait 2-3 days, but within the day, Daddy started sinking, and so he was taken for surgery. However, a technician upset with the behaviour of some doctor, called for a strike in the hospital. The strike went ahead, and in some cases, patients under anaesthesia were dragged out by the technicians in trolleys. Somehow Daddy's surgery was done, but he took a long time to recover. Headquarters also did not like my combining sick leave for my pacemaker with the annual leave of about ten days that I took when Daddy's surgery was taking place. We had a VIP room, and all stayed there with friends, often bringing in food. Daddy recovered and lived up to over 94.

I got back to my regular duty. While Daddy was in the hospital, Mummy wanted to do some surgery on her knees, but that did not happen as she was also looking after Daddy. Abu returned after a joyous trip to Manali, which Sudipto had agreed to, as he wanted him to have a good time and Mita remained in Bombay as he did not want to trouble the kids.

Back in Bangladesh, I did not ever let my personal problems affect my work and got back with a renewed vigor. A very crucial thing we did in Bangladesh was to set up a Fistula treatment center. A Fistula is an abnormal connection that occurs between two neighboring parts of the body, often caused by injury, surgery, trauma or infection. Fistulas can cause urine and stool to leak, having a significant impact on health and quality of life. There were no formal studies, but there was anecdotal data on a large number of Fistulas in women in Bangladesh, as they marry at a young age and go through early and frequent childbirths. We asked Engender to do a study and meanwhile started interacting with HQs as well as some countries in Africa where incidence was high and treatment was available, all the while keeping the medical faculty in the loop.

In about a year, things were clearer. We identified lead doctors and went to Ethiopia, where there was demonstrated success in the treatment of Fistulas; our doctors were trained here in a kind of exchange program. Dhaka medical college was involved, and from my office, Tahera Ahmed, who was in charge of RH, took the lead. The hospital at Dhaka Medical College earmarked award for Fistula patients, and an operation theatre was reserved for a few days every week as these are long surgeries. It took over a year to put all this in place, and Tahera managed the programme very well with her NPPPS.

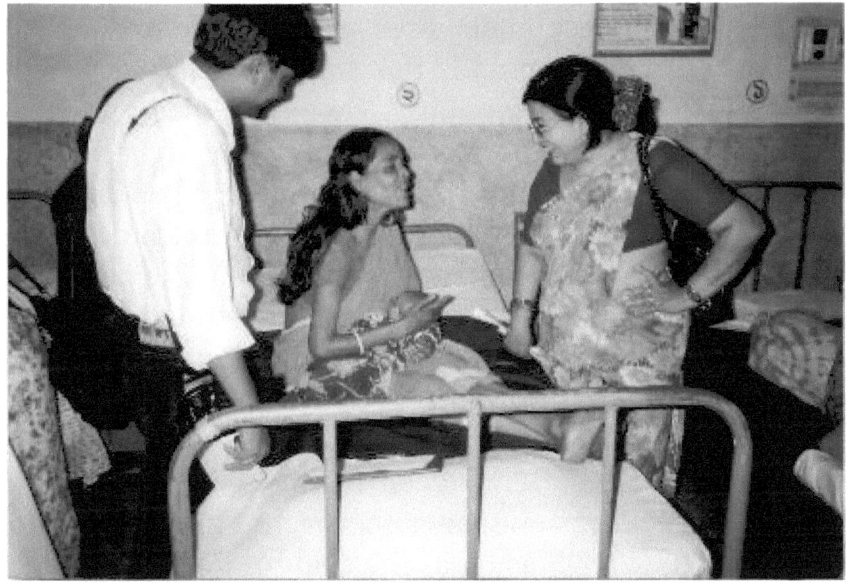

Women who had been suffering from Fistula, always had their urine and stools leaking, were smelly and had been shunned and discarded by their families. They started coming for treatment, and these unfortunate women could smile and see a ray of hope after a long time. They settled down, learning and practicing sewing and some handicrafts. Slowly they went through their day's routine and started looking happy as they felt encouraged seeing other women go through surgery and slowly recover. Meeting these women was very humbling, and even Thoraiya was in tears when she met them.

Another issue we addressed is the plateauing of TFR(Total Fertility Rate) which had palteuded inspite of increase in female literacy and in CPR. We got the doners interested as well as CST who led by Dr. Rafiq and Dr. Wasim Zaman helped us.

For support and advice, I found Mr. Towfique Elahi Chaudhry, who had been Secretary to the Govt. and was a friend of our Regional Director, Dr. Wasim Zaman, who was originally from the Pakistan Civil Services. We could consult him for anything. He also helped me with recruitment. Sometimes I used him as a sounding board, and my staff also began to rely on him. He had been a Minister during Sheikh Hasina's tenure as the Prime Minister and was put in prison when Begum Zia came to power. Another person who gave me unstinted support was Harun. He became my PA during the second half of my tenure. I was so grateful to have found someone reliable, but he was supportive also. The evening before my departure from Bangladesh for my next posting to Manila, the leading newspaper approached me to write an article on HIV/AIDS as I was the chair of the HIV/AIDS Theme Group in the country. My immediate response was not positive as I had no time, but Harun stayed up all night typing and retyping, and we had a fabulous article, which I read in the newspaper, when I got on the flight.

My Assistant Rep, Tahera, was a great colleague and a good professional, and we worked very well together;

her aid was sometimes critical. Bushra was brilliant and wonderful, but since she was emotionally attached to me, as I reminded her of her mother who had met with an untimely end, there was and is a lot of sensitivity. However, her support was invaluable. Noor, Asma, Jakaria, Tahmina, Das, Tina, Ruh Afsa and others were all great. We had a number of doctors working in projects called NPPPs and Doctors Aslam, Jebun, Roshan, Mizam and Rebecca were some of them.

HQs had shortlisted a company, MANFORD, to help us manage interpersonal or other problems which stand in the way of achieving excellence. I have to say that they were very good and helped my staff a lot. The Regional Director and RH Advisor Saramma was a great support too. Deepak Gupta joined our Regional Office, and his visits were also helpful; Sultan Aziz was the Asia Pacific Director. One never really knew how one stood with him, but I got along well with him.

With the expanded Bangladesh staff during Dr. Sultan's visit

I got a lot of support from the Head of the Govt. too. Sheikh Hasina was of course very supportive and Begum Zia, the PM for most of my tenure, was so appreciative; I think I first caught her attention when I recited a Bengali poem on gender by Kazi Nazrul Islam, their national poet:

Ei bishye ja kichu mahan….
Ardhek tar kariay se Nari arde tar kichu naar

I employed a tutor and took some Bengali lessons. I also tried to learn the dialect and correct pronunciations, and even in an English speech recited Bangla poetry, and people loved it. Once I was given an opportunity to address the Parliament, and I delivered a prepared speech in Bangla, and there was thunderous applause. Nazrul's poem, which I recited, was

Tajmiholer pathor dekhecho
Dekhecho ki tar pran
Ontore tar Momtaj nari
Bahirete Shah Jahan

Bangladesh is full of people I loved and got a lot of love in return. Two ladies I was fond of were Nashid Kamal and Najma Ahmed, who had very interesting personalities. I could go on and on about the people, but I better stop here.

On the personal front, Mitali was now enjoying working with Dr. Umrigar in Bombay, and I also went to get an implant there. She was happy but encouraged to go to the USA for further studies; she passed her National Boards, but just before the interviews, 9/11 happened. Everyone advised against her travel to the US, and she was upset and disturbed. We put her on a flight to

Boston, where Tukun (Didi's son) picked her up, took her for her interview and put her on a flight to Los Angeles, where Mrs. Ghumman received her. She chose to go to the University of South Pacific in San Francisco because she liked the weather there. Tinku helped her to find an apartment and settle down at SFO.

I visited her a few times; I would take a few days off when I went to New York. She graduated in 2004 and we all went for her graduation: Maa, Didi, Prosanto-da, Tinku, Santanu, Abu, Sudipto and I.

After this, she decided to do her residency in emergency dentistry in Fresno which she loved. She was now willing to get married and I interacted online with parents of boys working in California and started networking to find a suitable match. We laughed a lot, meeting boys every hour at Mrs. Ghumman's house near Los Angeles. We loved going to Mrs. Ghumman, and I started enjoying the slot machines. Sudipto and one of the guys we met for

Mita even got high on Sake one evening. But that was not to be as she met her lifelong partner Rudrajeet Samanta and though they had not yet decided to get married, I went and met his parents in Calcutta.

Rajat graduated in 2005 and we attended his graduation with great pride. He was the first South Asian to graduate from the Royal College of Vetenerary Surgeons, London with some distinction. He had achieved his dream and we were proud of him.

Ma visited me a few times. Ma was born and brought up in Mymensingh in Bangladesh, and with my NPP Jebun, we went around looking for the house and even found it, though the route of the river had changed. We went to the school she studied in, and she wanted to donate some money, but it was in terrible shape, and a small sum of money was of no use; they needed a lot. Ma and I had now become friends and could joke and talk about anything.

Sudipto was now heading the BPO arm of EDS and was not available to talk during my evening or night. Daytime I was busy, but when I called, he was sleeping or in the gym and even when I went to Bombay, he was sleeping or in the gym or the office. He had become a bit of a recluse, and even when Ma stayed with him, she said that he did not talk much.

When Mita went to the US, I gave up my huge bungalow to save some money and shifted to a two-bedroom flat. It had a huge dining and drawing room which I needed, but Diana's movements were restricted to our house and walking downstairs. She later developed a problem in her uterus, and I took her to Bombay to undergo surgery there, and that was another adventure.

The route of the Bangla Biman flight was Dhaka – Mumbai –Dubai. Diana's cage should have come with my checked-in baggage on the carousel, but it did not. I yelled out to Bangla Biman staff, but they said that the plane was already out of the dock and on its way to Dubai. I learnt that there were prawns on the flight and the temperature in the hold had to be colder than normal, so they covered Diana's cage with a thick cloth so she would not catch a cold. The men unloading the baggage missed her cage hidden under the tarpaulin. I almost screamed, and they said you don't worry, we will get her down when the flight stops in Mumbai on its way back. That was a ridiculous response. I started calling security and tried calling Delhi to talk to some colleagues in the police or at least pretended to; meanwhile, the aircraft turned around and thankfully offloaded Diana. Had she gone to Dubai and back, she may have been very sick or died in the cold without food or water.

Her surgery was another drama. Sudipto got it done by a Mumbai vet. Abu had met this vet and, in a way, approved of him. The vet called in a qualified surgeon, the surgery went off okay, and Diana came home. One evening, when the boy working at home took Diana out for a walk, she barked furiously at some street dogs, and her stitches came undone, and her intestines were almost hanging out of her stomach.

Sudipto's office was just next door, so he took Diana back to the vet at about 8 at night. There was no surgeon now, the vet's dentist doctor administered the anaesthesia, and the vet re-did the stitches. Abu later said that no matter how much effort went into the barking, the stitches should not have come undone.

Meanwhile, my talent for introducing two people into matrimony worked here too. I introduced the Vietnames Rep, to an Indian officer in the World Bank; they got along well and later married.

When I look back at my career, the tenure in Bangladesh was probably the most satisfying. The dialogue and understanding with religious leaders helped a great deal. I marvell that I could raise 100,000 dollars in multibit funds in all including the funds raised for contraceptives. It gave me a high that the political and administrative leaders of the country trusted me a great deal. Addressing fistulae was another high.

❐

Chapter 17
The Philippines (2006-2010)

I could not convince the Christian religious leaders but we did look after women's health and Govt. began to provide contraceptives thereby paving the way for the controversial and much awaited RH bill

The Philippines was the first foreign country I ever visited professionally (I had been to Sri Lanka on our college trip). In 1978 when I was joint APC, as part of the exchange programme, Germany sponsored a ticket for a lady officer to attend an International Women's conference in Manila and the Government of Himachal Pradesh suggested I should go, but I would have to fund my stay and other expenses there. We had no savings, but Sudipto, who is always very encouraging, suggested I use part of the house building loan we had taken out. My ticket gave me a stop in Bangkok while going and Hong Kong while coming back. I was fascinated by The Philippines and by the Filipino people. I loved the escalators and the huge malls. We did not yet have these in India. But what I loved the most was the people singing on the roads even while sweeping, the music everywhere in the offices and the Jippnies, which

With my staff in The Philippines

were a kind of auto rickshaw. At the conference, I gazed wide-eyed at the huge halls, the conference arrangements and the simultaneous translations. It was befitting then that my last posting before I retired, was in The Philippines. And this was suggested by Sudipto once the vacancies opened up in UNFPA.

The Philippines is an island country of Southeast Asia in the western Pacific Ocean. It is an archipelago consisting of some 7,100 islands and islets lying about 500 miles (800 km) off the coast of Vietnam. While a large majority of the population is Roman Catholic, Mindanao, a large island in the south east has a large Muslim population.

I did not have instant success or even any major success with the religious leaders there. I underestimated the rigidity and dogmatism of the Christian priests. Intoxicated as I was with my success with the Muslim religious leaders, I thought this would not be very difficult. However, in some parts of The Philippines, there were local orders banning contraceptives and sometimes action was taken against those who went to buy them and those who sold them. Divorce, too, was not legal, so though sometimes men and women left their partners and took other partners, they were not divorced, and marriages could only be annulled for strong reasons. Women were generally well educated, empowered and liberated. What was different was that often women did not want to get married but still wanted a child. They loved children and hence sometimes chose to have an agreement with a friend (with no bindings on either side) and conceived their babies.

I found that the words 'family planning' or 'contraceptives' were not mentioned in the Country Programme, but for UNFPA, that was basic and our bread and butter. So, I put my foot into my mouth and made an offer to the Secretary of Health to procure contraceptives. Of course, I had to give a presentation first to my own staff about the subject and how the availability of contraceptives prevents unplanned pregnancies, abortions and maternal deaths. I found strong support in a few NGOs and some members of the Senate.

Nothing can be done till the staff is motivated and convinced and get along with one another. I had two Assistant Reps; one was comparatively new and the other an old hand. There was an admin assistant and a finance assistant. An officer for Population and Development, one for Gender and one for Reproductive Health. A few assistants and secretaries were also very strong. The assistant to the senior Assistant Rep was assigned contraceptives.

Before I reached, I had taken a few days' leave, and the administrative assistant was calling and writing to me, planning a retreat as soon as I got there they love to go out and also have fun. I wanted to plan a retreat only after I settled down and had presented my credentials and after maybe a couple of months which would also give me an idea of what areas to cover. Our office was in Makati, the heart of the commercial town, we were in a building with some embassies too. A modern building with 'Fitness First' where I sometimes went during lunch, I had rented a nice apartment near the office and opposite Manilla swimming club where I crossed a small road to swim or use the gym. Location-wise, everything was perfect.

For the retreat, I called on Manford to organise a team-building retreat as I learnt that some staff were not even talking to each other: most notably the two Assistant Representatives. Manfold, who was sent to us by headquarters in Bangladesh, had their own style, and by the end of the retreat, barriers were broken, and everyone was talking to each other and promising to work well together. An instant success kept slipping back and fourth, but a good working relationship remained. I was content, and the retreat had made a major breakthrough.

During my second or third week, there was an exhibition which other staff members were going to and asked me to come. I had booked a personal car but had not got it yet and did not intend to misuse the office car. So, I went in a cab over the weekend. On the way back, my administrative assistant offered me a lift back, which I happily accepted, only to see that she had one of our office cars, and she dropped me in it. I did not say anything but thought that my action of going in a cab spoke for itself. However, after that, I kept my eyes open and saw that she was off and on using the car, and the drivers would take the car and pick up and drop her son from school. I don't know how I kept quiet even after that but, one day when she was in the office car, the car met with an accident and there was a police complaint. I learnt of it only when a copy of the complaint came in the post, I noticed that it had also gone to headquarters. There were some explanations, and the matter quietened down in a while, and she reduced or stopped using the office cars. In my first staff meeting, one of the Assistant Reps had said that there is no Representative they have not complained against, and I laughingly said that I hoped I would be the first one. The attitude of HQ always was that the Representative was troubling the local staff. In due time the Assistant Rep left of her own accord as she started her own business.

Let me tell you about my secretary, a smart girl she answered all my calls, was very good in her work and looked after my appointments quite well, but she often left as soon as office hours were over, went for a walk or eating out, I did not stop her or anyone else, but one night when I was almost asleep, I got a call from Ben de Leon who had an NGO called The Forum and was our partner, he said that he was not getting an appointment with me. I did not have my schedule next to the bed, so I told him that he could come anytime if it was urgent, and at the most, he would have to wait a bit. I went to the office and told my secretary, and she smiled. In the evening, after the day's rush was over, I remarked that Ben-de-Leon and a congressman (Edgar) who were due to be coming to see me had not come. Oh, she said, they did come, but I gave them an appointment later in the week. When I asked her why she did that when I had told her that I had given them one, her answer was "Mrs. Mukherjee, it's in my TOR to handle your appointments and not in yours". We went a long way with the Forum and other partners for the RH bill. This is the power I have, I wondered. Can I not even give appointments? So, I went slow trying to figure out how to introduce changes in the programme. In any case, routine kept us extremely busy in UNFPA, and meeting govt. officials and NGOs and understanding the concerns took some time. I also started working on safe motherhood, which was my favorite subject.

Meanwhile, there were developments on the personal front. Mitali had been seeing Rudro, and when we went to California, we found that they were inseparable, and Mitali was making attempts to include him in everything, including a family game of cards. Rudro had suggested I meet his parents when I was in Bangladesh and often came via Calcutta to Delhi. So once, when my flight was late, I called them and went over. Krishna, his mother, was sweet, but I had nothing to tell her except that I was her son's friend's mother. Sudipto did not want to go as his question always was about our not having anything to say to substantiate the relationship. Anyway, I had made a beginning, and when I met them after being posted in The Philippines, I found that they were closer and had kind of made up their minds about each other but marriage had not yet been agreed upon. However, they planned their leave in India together and were coming to Bombay, and it was nice that his parents planned to come to Bombay too. The parents wanted to do a simple ring ceremony, but the kids wanted to do that on their own, I think. So, we had dinner, and Rudro went back with his parents, and Mitali stayed with us in Bombay. There was a discussion about doing the wedding in winter. Rudro formally proposed to Mitali on Valentine's Day in San Francisco, where they were staying, and the wedding took place on 22nd November (Sai Baba's birthday) 2006.

For this, I came to India to book the venue. After a maddening and exhaustive rush to various hotels and venues, we finalised Kota House, a naval mess near Khan Market for the Sangeet on 21st November, and the Air Force Auditorium in Subrato Park for the wedding. Sudipto came towards the end before we finalised everything. He got the cards printed in Bombay while I looked after all the shopping. Much of the saree and gift shopping I did in Bangladesh. Just before the wedding, I took leave for a month and settled in HP Bhawan in Delhi, where I was most comfortable. We booked Gymkhana and Habitat for Rudro's side of the family and guest houses of a few States for our side of the family. Also, a few army messes were booked for guests. Mitali was there for about 20 days and Abu for ten days. Mitali had picked up some of her sarees and selected from the large number of sarees I had bought from Pakistan, Bangladesh, and India (I still have many leftovers with me!) Buying her lehenga for the sangeet took a long time and stitching the blouses to her liking seemed an arduous task. And she did not like any saree for her wedding. I was surprised when she asked me if she could wear my wedding saree. We quickly had it refurbished, and it was shining and bright like new. She also asked for my wedding jewellery set, and we made some additions to it to suit what she wanted. I was very happy, and she made a beautiful bride.

Sudipto had gotten used to living alone and taking unilateral decisions. Slowly he got into a united mode with all. I had suggested a family dance, and he agreed, and my cousin Gurmeet (Anu) got his son's dance teacher to teach us. I had suggested Rajasthani scarfs for the boys in the dance, and his initial reaction was no, but when we went to Lajpat Nagar, he smiled and asked, "where do you want to buy the Rajasthani veils from?" There were issues and problems but finally, everything synced beautifully for the wedding. We called Noorie, my maid from Bangladesh, and my driver Salim from Bangladesh to come and help us as they are coming from The Philippines and have been out of the country for twelve years. I could not find a reliable maid and driver in Delhi quickly, and I badly needed a maid to look after Mitali's jewellery and clothes and a driver to supervise transport provided to guests and also to take us around. All arrangements seemed perfect, as was the time of the year: the weather was perfect, and the flowers were in full bloom and seemed to be spreading their fragrance around. I had not met some relatives for almost 20 years and was looking forward to meeting them. Also, my IAS colleagues, I would see after a decade or more. However, things did go wrong as they usually do in weddings and we were no exception except that our problems were more dramatic!

The venue was perfect. The caterers had to be selected from a few on the shortlist. Also, flower decorations and lighting arrangements. We selected an outdoor venue where the stage etc., had to be constructed. Everything was going well. My parents came on the 20th but were disappointed as I did not meet them. We were practicing our dance for the Sangeet in Aju's house in Greater Kailash, New Delhi! And though I wanted to go and meet them, Mitali said it was her last night with us and wanted us to be together, so I understood and did not go, though I was sad that they wanted to meet us and we were not free. The Baratis came on the 21st, the day of the Sangeet, as did many other relatives. Sudipto went to the airport to receive the Baratis and, amidst looking after them, lost his taxi and got late. I struggled with time and attending to everyone coming to meet us. Mr. Dua was having the dance floor built outside in the naval mess, and I was in constant touch with them while visitors kept dropping by. Finally, I dashed to get into a

The family presented a dance based on song "Kajrare Kajrare..."

saree at the last minute. Mitali had gone for her makeup. I told Noorie to bring my change of clothes in which I

At the end of the performance...

was to dance and rushed to the site before guests came. As I reached, I noticed that the sky was overcast, and soon, it started drizzling. I ran indoors to find out if the hall indoors was vacant. Someone had booked it, I got details and called, and though he was not planning to use it, he, in his sleepy reluctant voice, agreed for me to use it on payment. Looking for the man who had the keys seemed so long as I saw guests, including Kiran Bedi, walk in. I abandoned my heels to run a bit and call her as well as Mrs. and Mr. N K Goyal. Goyal started chanting a few mantras for the rain to stop and it actually did! Meanwhile, with Kiran with me, I caught hold of the cleaning boy and asked him to clean the room. Kiran said that she was going to a reception being hosted by the President of India for the Chinese PM who was visiting. It was a huge affair and all top bureaucracy would be there. She promised to come after the function was over and join us. I was now checking the outside venue, when I heaved a sigh of relief as I saw Sudipto had finally come. Lo and behold, as I gave up the inside hall, it started raining again. I called Goyal, who had left, he came back and started chanting again, and I told him that his duty was now with the rain Gods!

My parents and brothers, and in-laws all started coming in slowly. I had met a lady accidentally on a flight coming from Manila, and she said that she lived in the US and was a choreographer and a singer and had come to sing for some weddings and had her team here. She started the songs with a few other girls in her team, typically Punjabi wedding songs. However, another crisis and a more serious one had brewed. As some friends from

The Philippines and US started dropping in, the military intelligence approached me to ask for the permission of foreigners at this venue. I knew nothing about this and started floundering. We had given an invite just a day before to the Naval Chief, who was Sudipto's batchmate, but he was at the President's function with the phone off. Finally, the RAW Chief, who is a friend, came, and he too was helpless with the military. So, while they were calling for the bride's mother in the songs, I was stuck here and there trying to talk to and convince the army authorities. They gave me half an hour to get foreigners off the ground. Abu had prepared a presentation on Mitali's life which he presented. And then he ran off with his cousins who were enjoying a drink. As I was often close to tears, I took hold of myself, went to the stage, announced the family dance after 10 minutes, and went to change. However, as I opened the packet of my clothes, the lehenga and the chuni were there and not the top. I got back into my saree, searched for the driver, and gave him the dupatta to bring the matching top from the bed. It seemed like forever, but he came back with the top, left the dupatta on the bed, and gave it to me as I was dancing on the stage. Abu had to change too. He was playing the role of the son Abhishek and was to look like a rogue, so he was asking loudly about the sudden hurry? Anyway, the great thing was that the dance was greatly appreciated. All the guests curved in and came close to the stage to watch, and we could see their smiles and exclamations. We were drowned in felicitations. Soon we saw the Naval Chief walk in, and he handled the situation that day. But it was clear that I would have to take permission for the wedding day as that was an air force venue.

Dancing, singing, eating, and drinking continued afterwards, but we stopped at midnight as I wanted us to rest for the wedding the next day.

We had some ceremonies the next morning, like Chura, but I was distracted and felt sad that I could not attend the ceremonies and Mitali well. Most importantly, we had to do a marriage ceremony with a tree for Mitali to ward off any problems of being manglik. I was busy contacting the foreign guests to get their passport numbers and copies of relevant pages to apply for permission for them to attend the wedding function at Subroto Park, New Delhi. I found most of the foreign guests were out sightseeing or shopping, and it was a herculean task to collect these, fill in forms, get their signatures and apply over a weekend. I was hoping that a batchmate, Ranjit Ishar, who had been posted as Additional Secretary of Defense could get this done. However, he informed me that the Joint Secretary was in Chennai. I don't know how providence helped us, and we could contact this Joint Secretary and get permission. Mitali went to get dressed and came to the venue directly. She had wanted Rudro to come on horseback, but his parents had not agreed; however, I think the local relatives persuaded them, and there were last minute delays as they got a horse and he came on horseback. The muharat or auspicious time was from about 8 to 10, so after we received the bridegroom and his team, we went straight to the marriage pandal while guests kept arriving and some came and met me in the corner the wedding was going on, and others moved toward the lovely multi-cuisine dinner laid out in the other corner. I had requested my brother and Bhabhi to receive the guests, but they did not know them, and many came after he came to the wedding site too. The wedding was fun though the mother had very little role in the ceremonies. So, even though I did not have a role, I stayed on to be with the family and be part of the ceremony. The Bengali ceremony of carrying the bride by the four brothers when she hides her face from the bridegroom till the last minute was very interesting as was hiding shoes later.

The pandal and the venue were beautifully decorated. Jasmine flowers swept your senses; beautiful and fragrant, they livened up this dreamy place. Candles and diyas were lit along the path, not only showing the path but also a feast to the eyes, looking like a reflection of stars on the ground. It was, in the words of Rashmi and Munna, "a fairy tale wedding." Mitali was tired but did not want the night to end. So, when she left for the hotel where they were spending the night, her cousins led by Gurmeet went to drop her off. Sudipto, Uncle Santokh's son, had got his car decorated for the bride and bridegroom.

They were to leave with their in-laws for Calcutta the next day. So, at night we opened and laid out the presents which they quickly came and saw in the morning and took a few things they liked and could carry with them. We made lists and packed up the rest. Sudipto quickly rushed around and settled some bills while I tried to do the same and also looked after the driver and maid who went off sightseeing to Agra. My parents and brothers left early morning. Mummy had a severe bout of diarrhoea, and I felt bad not being able to look after them. We were to go to Calcutta the next day for the reception and had this one day to tie up everything, settle accounts, thank people and say our goodbyes and express our gratitude. I bought sweets for the reception in Calcutta and to give to the groom's side, but as Abu and I reached the airport, I realised we had left them in HP Bhawan. There was no way we could go back, so I let it be, and we moved on. One day in Calcutta for the reception and then Bombay for Mitali's visit before I left back for Manila.

Back in Manila, I got acquainted with the Sallas family. Mr. Raphael Sallas was the first ED of UNFPA, and he passed away untimely from a heart attack. His wife was the Ambassador in Czechoslovakia. On his birth anniversary, Thoraiya was also to come to pay her respects, but at the last minute, Dr. Sadik came on her behalf along with Thoraiya's secretary. I again attempted a dialogue with the church. It was a good dining and good talk, but they were firm, and when they talked of abortions, we totally supported unwanted or unplanned pregnancies, which led to abortions. But they were firm, no contraceptives. But that's what prevents abortions, we would say, but they did not move from their stance. Dr. Sadik, who had a lot of experience in the ICPD, told me that I was wasting my time, but somehow, I did not give up till the end. We supported the few NGOs and legislators who were pushing for the Reproductive Health bill where apart from promoting safe motherhood, they promoted planned pregnancies. I met the then President Maria Gloria Macapagal (2001 to 2010).

She did agree with the need for contraceptives and allowed us to procure and supply contraceptives to the Ministry of Health. It was dicey as the Secretary was eyeing to become a member of the Senate, so he did this very half-heartedly. The ex-President Mr. Ramos was a strong supporter, and many of us met for dinner often at my house for discussions and planning. Janet, a member of the Senate and the Secretary for Social Services Madam Esperange Cabral, who later became Secretary of Health, also joined in sometimes. We worked slowly and surely on this, deeply committing ourselves to women's health and her right to have planned pregnancies. Our hopes increased as President Benigno Aquino 111 came into power. He was known to be a supporter of RH, and we were allowed up to 20 seconds each to speak as all the heads of agencies met him. I said: "mothers die daily in The Philippines due to maternity-related causes. Most of these deaths are preventable; one-third of these deaths occur due to unsafe abortions and can be prevented by timely contraception." The President gulped water and turned to Secretary Health (I had gone to Sec Health and shown him how I came to these figures), who confirmed it was true. The President immediately gave me time to go to his office for a discussion with him and the Secretary of Health later in the week.

The RH bill was passed but took some time and final approval came after I left, but that did not matter;

it made history, and I was invited for the final signing though I did not go.

In the third year of my stay in Manila, Sudipto joined me, and we had a ball. One can have a wonderful lifestyle in Manila. For one, massage services are regular and systematic. It is quite professional. The masseurs are all girls. Companies drop them off. They charge reasonably, bring the oil of your choice and give you a good massage for an hour, after which they are picked up. When my husband asked for a male masseur, they thought he was gay and asking for other services! In Manila, no one works during the weekends, except in emergencies, e.g., after floods. So, weekends are fun. We sometimes ran. For Sudipto, running was a passion, and while he ran 10 or 15 or 21 kms, I stuck to 3 or 5 kms only. Sudipto learnt, and we both practiced scuba diving.

Scuba diving in The Philippines

We went to Africa in 2007- Mitali and Rudro could not come because Mitali's green card was being processed which meant that Mitali could not leave the country.

We started off our trip in Kenya landing in Nairobi. This crater is a haven for wildlife, with a lake in the crater which has tens of thousands of pink flamingos turning the lake pink when seen from above.

It was an incredible experience: we saw rhinos with their babies, lions, elephants, lots of giraffe, many species of deer, hyrax, many apes including baboons who liked to show off their huge canine teeth and red bottoms. The flamingos too were a site to behold.

The next day we transferred back to Nairobi and then onto Masai Mara. We were in time to see the wildebeest migration and over 2-3 days we saw all sorts of wildlife – from a female cheetah hunting a Thomson's gazelle, bringing it down and then calling her cubs out from the bush right in front of us to eat- to lions mating, we saw so many incredible sights and sounds. We had our own vehicle and Jeep driver who was very friendly and pointed out all the wildlife. We saw hyaena, zebra, African fox, many warthogs that would scatter off at surprising pace when they saw or heard our vehicle. We also encountered large herds of water buffalo which are also deadly to humans if you get too close or they think you are threatening them. The lions were less scary lounging by the water and in the grass just yawning snoozing and grooming each other like big cats.

We spent 8 days in Egypt arriving in Cairo late at night. We explored the Pyramids of Giza and the Cairo Museum and in the evening went to the ancient perfumeries of Cairo and bought a lot of perfume having made friends with an old man whose family had been making perfume for over 200 years.

The next 3 days we went on a Nile Cruise on board a pleasant ship called MS Emperor. We soaked in the beauty of the temples along the Nile including Karnak and Luxor, we saw the Valley of the Kings, Kom Ombo Temple dedicated to the crocodile god, the Temple of Edfu dedicated to Horus, the Falcon god, and the Temple of Queen Hatshepsut the only female Pharoah ever! Sudipto and Abu had a nice long shisha session one evening by themselves in a small-town café amongst the locals! Karnak has 2 huge temples.

Once again, we had an incredible journey thanks to Sudipto's careful planning, the whole trip went without a hitch and we had memories to cherish for our whole lifetime.

We also did ballroom dancing at home in Manila with a dance instructor who would come on weekends, and 2 or 3 couples would meet and dance and have a few drinks and dinner. There were lovely markets, nice malls, and a place called Green Hills, a market for pearls and duplicate branded clothes, bags, and shoes where we enjoyed going. We had great fun. We had Ma stay with us and did not want her to go back, but she was insistent on going back home, and once she went, she never came back. She fell sick and initially thought it was a cough and cold, but it did not settle down. Sudipto went to Dhanbad and took her to Calcutta for a detailed check-up. It was quite shocking to know that she had TB of the spine. She was operated on successfully, but alas, her lungs did not recover as she found it very difficult to sit. At some point, it even seemed that she had recovered, and Sudipto, after staying a month in Calcutta next to Dada's house and re-enlivening the stagnant relationship with the family, took her to Dhanbad. Just before she left, she collapsed again, and he took her back to Calcutta, where she was often in ICU with the BiPap. She passed away from a heart attack when all her three children and daughter-in-law were in India and also in Kolkata, though none of us was actually with her when she passed away unaware that she was going. I dreamt of getting her to Gurgaon after my retirement and possibly getting older relatives to stay with her and have a good time. I regret that I did not spend more time with her. I kept thinking our time would come later. She and I were a bit of soul mates, but all this was in my heart, unexpressed in words.

Professionally during this time, we worked on MDGs. The Millennium Development Goals (MDGs) were eight international development goals for the year 2015 adoption of the United Nations Millennium Declaration adopted by all the countries in 2000. With a base year of 1994, all countries agreed to half the levels of poverty, achieve universal primary education, promote gender equality and empower women. reduce child mortality,

improve maternal health, combat HIV/AIDS, malaria, and other diseases, and develop global partnerships and development. There were 21 targets by which these goals were to be measured. We worked on them in Bangladesh and now in The Philippines but what was most important was establishing a data collection system so that we had data to measure the targets. When I was in The Philippines, the UN started a *Stand-up campaign*. This was an advocacy instrument to bring to the notice of every human being that the MDG effort was on and needed their cooperation also. A system was established to count how many people 'stood up' during a specified period for the MDGs and were aware of what they were standing up for. A kind of healthy competition started in all countries. One UN agency led and worked with Govt, Civil society, and other agencies, bilateral and multilateral. I was the Chairperson of the Interagency Advocacy Group. UNFPA led in The Philippines, and for two consecutive years, we broke the Guinness Book of Records. Agencies were hired globally for supervision of performance, and in the second year, toward the last few days, I was in the hospital with a very mild stroke, and soon, my assistant representative was there too with high blood pressure, after which I even fractured my foot and was in a wheelchair while Sudipto was in Calcutta with Ma. The head of the UN stand-up campaign was in Manila checking out how things were working, and while he thought that Bangladesh was leading this year when the final record came in, we were still at the top, and no one could match us. There were jubilations and celebrations that we were still at the top of awareness at least, and this awareness brought out and would further bring out behavioral change. We were happy that this helped in furthering the RH bill too.

The family went on a holiday to South America in 2009. It was meant to be our last family trip together for some time as Mitali and Rudro were planning for a family in the future, and we felt future family trips would be difficult to organise. Sudipto organised the whole trip, talking to various travel agencies, exploring various options and reminding us of all the formalities, vaccines and protocols that needed to be followed, as it applied to the family living in 3 countries on 3 continents entering a fourth for the first time!

We were to explore Peru, the rainforest, Cusco, Machu Pichu, and the Galapagos islands!

We landed in Lima- arriving from different continents was interesting and flew to Puerto Maldonado and went to the Reserva Amazonnica Lodge. This was in the middle of the rainforest and went on expeditions through the jungle, on canoes to see the howler monkeys, in the evenings there were tarantulas all over the resort.

After three days in the rainforest, we went to Aguas Calientes and stayed in a beautiful Inkaterra property, called Machu Pichu Pueblo which is a Small Luxury Hotels of the World member. The hotel was beautifully decorated in a rustic style, very welcoming and had fireplaces in each room with wood outside each room which was lit in the evening by bellboys who would go around replenishing the stocks. They served Pisco sours, the national drink and we had several rounds with Sudipto and Abu having 4-5 each! It was a very merry and fun evening. The hotel was built like a nature reserve and had the largest private collection of orchids in the world.

Machu Pichu was amazing, there were many llamas there which were friendly.

We then flew to Quito and onto Ecuador. Sudipto had booked a fantastic hotel called Royal Palms which was on its own secluded island, with a nature reserve and giant tortoises and other wildlife roaming around. We had a private chef in the Prince of Wales guest house who met with us the first night to get an idea of our individual tastes and how we would like our meals prepared! This was a first for all of us in a hotel abroad!

We had a 4-day itinerary- the first day we went diving to Santa Fe. The next 2 days we went to Plazas and Punta

Carrion Island and St Bartolome (on our yacht!) which were both incredible. We saw large land iguanas all over the island eating fruits that fell from the trees. They stay motionless for ages, almost looking dead then they run forward to grab some fruit very rapidly when it drops.

We saw huge colonies of sea birds. We then ventured a bit further out to the bay where we saw sea lions and jumped back into the water. They were very inquisitive, playful and swimming all around us checking us out. Soon we were surrounded by Galapagos penguins which had been relaxing out of the sun under some rocks, large flocks of these small birds started whizzing past us in the water hunting for fish which we could see right before our eyes. It was like being immersed in a Nat Geo documentary. What an unforgettable experience!

With the Secretary General Mr. Ban Ki-Moon in a meeting with heads of agencies

An important highlight before my end of tenure in The Philippines was the visit of the Secretary General Mr. Ban Ki-Moon of the United Nations. Normally the Resident Co-Ordinator (UNDP Representative) looks after the visit. Due to some circumstances, I was made the Resident Co-Ordinator during that period. Since the visits are very short (2 days), a lot of meetings and activities are condensed during that period. The meetings include the Government, the Donor community, NGOs, UN and affiliated organisations and staff. It was a very intensive and comprehensive program and we heaved a sigh of relief that it was successfully carried out.

The UN Secretary General and his wife with some of the senior UN Staff

My mom-in-law had passed away. My mom was also sick, and though her problem was related to bones, her ribs were now pressing into her lungs after they joined naturally. She was suffering, and I myself did not keep good health; apart from breaking or cracking bones often and being in a wheelchair, I had numbness in various parts of my body and was doing acupuncture through a nice Chinese doctor for that. The children came and visited us, and all learnt and enjoyed scuba diving. Sudha and her husband Manohar came too, and we went to Vietnam with them for a brief holiday. But now came the time for me to retire, and I did not want an extension as I wanted to go home and be with my mother. We had paid up for a flat in Palm Springs on Golf Course Road in Gurugram, but as usual, it was not ready for occupation, so we planned to shift to our Sushant Lok house, which we had repaired while in Manila.

I was given a grand send-off which was because of the culture in The Philippines and also as I was retiring.

My staff put up a dance on a Bollywood number; each sang and did a few ballroom steps with me.

My landlord refused to refund my security, and my maid admitted to stealing my ring but these small issues became not so important and we were soon back home. We stayed for a few days in Himachal Pradesh Bhawan till our baggage came and we could not find my passport which showed that I had been out for many years and was authorised to transfer of residence. Luckily, we found it in the bags so nicely packed by Sudipto while I was unwell!

The Philippines is the first country I visited professionally and then the last country I worked in. It has a special place in my heart and life as my husband joined me here and we had a wonderful time. A befitting place to retire from.

❐

Chapter 18
Post Retirement
(2010-2021)

What a delightful period to grow old and taste the joys of leisure

Post-retirement gave me time to do all we wanted. We looked after my parents, set up home, travelled a lot which included motorbike riding and hiking. We pursued our hobbies and tried golfing too. We loved the fitness activities we joined in Palm Springs, and our group is called the "Fit Gang". We also enjoyed being part of the Bollywood dance group with a wonderful instructor – Shashank. We enjoyed our hikes to Bhutan, valley of flowers and Hemkund Sahib as well as the most challenging one in Muktinath. And best of all was reconnecting with Sudipto's batchmates and having a new army family. However, the retirement didn't begin smoothly and required a lot of adjustments.

I screamed and got up one night as I felt and, on opening my eyes, saw a huge rat run on me. As I screamed, Sudipto put on the light, I was sobbing, and he said, "Welcome back to India. You wanted to come back!" He went on to explain that with the construction going on in the vacant plots around, these rats were being driven out of their home place. I had come home after retirement and expected to move to our new flat in Palm Springs, but it was not yet ready, and we had got our house in Sushant Lok improved with instructions from a distance, and this was not done well, so here we were struggling with lack of electricity and a hot climate and with a broken shoulder which was excruciatingly painful now that I jerked it when getting up suddenly. Thank God there was no lack of water.

But we had come back even when we could have stayed on because though we had lost my parents-in-law, my parents were around and old, and it would be good to spend some time with them. I really wanted to spend time with them, but now I feel I could have done much better. Mummy had weak bones and started taking Bonista injections daily to strengthen her bones. They had a lot of faith in PGI, and I happily took them there; with my having worked there, they got real VIP treatment. It was also an outing for them, and due to their faith, they looked forward to it.

Daddy got his regular check-ups for his heart. His eyes also needed attention, and sometimes he had gastric problems. One day his foot was swollen, and we took him to PGI only to learn it could be something serious like a clot and once an MRI was done, our fears were set to rest, but he was admitted to PGI for treatment. He recovered well, but soon Mummy broke her ribs without a fall, and it hurt her to sit, so she was often lying down while doctors kept asking her to sit and wear a belt for support. We kept going to Chandigarh from Gurugram and coming back. I had not accepted an extension in The Philippines, as I wanted to spend time with Mummy, and she was not well. A PET scan had ruled out cancer, and soon we were to repeat one, but my very brave Mother who set an example to all of us, who would first take the prick of a needle when we were to take an injection to show that it does not hurt, was now scared of the PET scan. I'm glad that we could get it done without hurting her. I remained in the scan room myself. However, though we were a lot of relief for them, I now regret that in her last days, I did not tolerate all she said more amicably.

When in Gurgaon, we were following up with possession of our Palm Springs flat and doing the interiors. And then we would go back and spend a week with them in Chandigarh trying to organise household staff and later also attendants for Daddy when we saw him falling often. On one of my visits to Gurgaon, I went to Lifestyle to buy containers for household provisions and stumbled over a tray kept in front of the cashier. I broke my shoulder in three places and was in tears with excruciating pain. I came home, had a painkiller, and went to the Medanta Hospital, and our experience there was very good with the procedures adopted by the hospital. It was a Sunday, so we came back after an Xray and first aid from the emergency and saw the doctor the next morning, who said I did not need surgery since it was only broken, not displaced. I was in a soft bandage and sling, underwent rigorous physiotherapy, and recovered in 6 weeks. I seriously started thinking about my bones, especially after seeing my Mom suffer. Our orthopaedic specialist in Delhi advised me to take Forteo injections for two years, one subdermal injection every day to be taken in the abdomen, and follow it up with a drip every six months for two years. I checked this with Dr. Sen in PGI, and he said that I really needed it as the way my shoulder had broken does not seem like a fall but like some electric shock or a car accident. I had broken my foot/leg very often, first in Bangladesh and then a few times in Manila and was often in a wheelchair. So, I started treatment in earnest and took it for one and half years each (I just felt strongly that I should not take more), and as a result, today my bones are much stronger.

Meanwhile, Mummy's situation worsened and I did not think it would end like this. Once when Abu and I were going to Chandigarh, I got a call from Sawraj that Mummy, while eating strawberry and cream after lunch which Haramrit lovingly brought, swallowed it in her windpipe and it had gone to her lungs. So, they rushed her to Fortis in Chandigarh. The liquid from her lungs was drained, and in a few days, she was ready to go home. She literally begged to come home, but by the time the family reached an agreement to take her home, she had developed a fungus infection and had to remain in the hospital for three weeks for an intravenous antibiotic treatment. We then took turns to visit her. Mitali and her family came to meet her, as did Manju. Uncle Santokh had come and met her before she left home, yet, we as children could not imagine or accept that she was going. The doctors also gave us hope, but she had stopped asking to go home., We kept being optimistic though Haramrit kept telling me that we should let her get out of this diseased body and run around as a little girl with pigtails in her new life. Once again, she was ready to come home, but in the evening before she was to come, we got a call from the hospital saying that the nurse had overfed her from the rice tube which went through her nose and from where she was being fed. The result was that the milk they had fed her had gone to her lungs. They asked if we wanted to put her on a ventilator, though we had already said no. But faced with this emergency, we all said yes. And then, she was on a ventilator for two days, and only her dead body came home. Someone who nursed and gave us all her energy and love was now lifeless in front of us, and we were helpless.

All relatives who lived close by in Punjab came and her last rites were done. Superficially Daddy went through the rituals as well as what was necessary, but he was suddenly alone. He did not open up or trust too well, and the only person he trusted completely was Sudipto, but at times he would question himself in wondering why he trusted Sudipto so much. Nothing I ever do and say can be enough to get to the essence of how Sudipto supported Daddy, especially after Mummy. We now came more often as he was very lonely, though my brothers often visited him in the morning and my Bhabhi in the evenings. Sudipto also began to write some of Daddy's memoirs and was getting down his family history, but that could not be finished.

We got one excellent opportunity to bring Daddy to Gurugram. He had been here once before and we brought him here on one New Year's Eve. But he always wanted to rush back home when he saw Mummy in his house. However, both Mummy and Daddy would hallucinate sometimes and keep insisting that the Sector 44 house was not their house and that their house was in Sector 8 and then we would remind them of the whole history. Now there was an invitation for Daddy to inaugurate the Rezangla Chowk in Gurugram, where the soldiers (Ahirs) of 13 Kumaon belonged. They made a memoir for these soldiers and translated the same poem in Hindi, which Daddy had put on the stone on the memorial of Rezangla. And it had pictures of all of them. We took him in a wheelchair, and the Chief Minister presented him with a bouquet of flowers. In his speech, Daddy gave details of his experience and he was flanked by the Commanding Officer (CO) and the Subedar Major.

Daddy making a speech with the present CO of 13th Kumaon on his right and Subedar Major on Left at the Razangla Chowk, GGN

But what was most impressive was the few soldiers who had survived flanked around him and he almost fell down. I'm glad he had this experience a few years before he left for his heavenly abode.

Daddy with the survivors of the Razangla Battle of 1962

Suddenly Daddy said he was above 90 and should be getting ready to go, but then he explained that he was in anguish. "I've not written my will. How can I go?" he said. He asked for help in writing his will, and while we were reluctant initially, there was no one else he trusted for this delicate matter. He actually dictated his and his family's life story beginning from his birth. We helped him reduce it, but it was still too long. He even visited the DC office and showed the will to the DC, who gave him the same advice on the length. So finally, he reduced it though it was still long. In the operational part, he left his portion of the house to me, and so while all of us got some portion of the property, mine was extra, and he justified it by the fact that he had already divided the proceeds of the sector-8 house with his sons. The will was registered in the Registrar's office and later shared with my brothers. I was happy that, in keeping with what he had done throughout his life, he did not give me less as I was a girl and not a boy and I am also happy that my brothers did not contest the will.

We planned to take Daddy to Srinagar on his birthday. He talked so lovingly about the hills and trees of Bhardwar, where he was born. However, closer to the date as June approached, first Sawraj cancelled his tickets and later Haramrit. Daddy, too was a bit apprehensive about how his body would take this flight and outing. So ultimately, we went to Kasauli, and though we had a good time, there was an alarm as Daddy had a chest ache.

I kept trying to keep Daddy cheerful.

We would talk of the earlier days, his childhood, his postings and his experience in the battlefields, Mummy's habits, and her overflowing love for everyone. She had looked after Daddy's extended family very well and was very loving, caring, and always making sacrifices for others. And, of course, she gave her whole life to all of us. We only saw her as a mother satisfying our needs, and she was never a woman looking after her own needs. She accepted everything about Daddy and admired and respected whatever he did. Sudipto said that the way she said "Col sahib" was if he was "General sahib". Sudipto used to tell me that I should be more like my mother. We went to Chandigarh more often, and I resigned from the Board of Members of Palm Springs, where we were staying, as I had no idea for how many years, I would now be more in Chandigarh than in Gurugram. It was difficult for Daddy with weak eyesight he could not read a newspaper and with bad hearing; the TV was also not of much use. We got him a new music system which he selected himself, though he rarely used it. I got him a new mattress and changed his sofa set in the room, so he could sit more comfortably. He could not have his evening drink often as it did not suit him, and slowly he also ate less as he started having acid reflux. I kept trying to find alternative means of keeping his nutrition up through porridge, bananas, half-boiled eggs, etc., as he could hardly chew. We had round-the-clock attendants: the night one stayed 12 hours and the daytime 10 hours and then there was an evening attendant too who also tried to keep him amused. There was also a full time girl cooking and a part-timer, cleaning. I would buy all provisions or anything he needed before I came to Gurugram, though I returned very soon.

I did not know what his death would be like and how it would come, but we were happy that he had asked us not to do lifesaving interventions as we were still struggling with Mummy's and Ma's sufferings in hospital. Even when we admitted Daddy to PGI to see his response to one of the Parkinson's medicines, the doctor agreed not even to do any blood tests aggressively.

Sudipto had been doing an astrology course on weekends in Gurugram and I encouraged him as it gave him something else to do. I used to feel sorry that after retirement, he wanted to travel and was stuck with me in this situation. He's the most tolerant person I have met, and yet I found that I was taking him too much for granted. But we just could not let Daddy be alone. So sometimes Sudipto would not come with me but follow me after the weekend course, but he also sometimes missed it. On one such occasion, when I also had a wedding to attend in Chandigarh of the daughter of a PGI employee, Daddy got up late (he often did), had breakfast at 11:00 AM, and went to the market after that. He was disoriented and impatient, kept wanting to go to his sector 8 house and I took him to Sawraj's house, where he rested and did not talk for some time. However, in the evening, he relaxed, had dinner at Sawraj's and I danced a bit and sang. Sawraj came to leave us home and had a nice conversation with Daddy before he left. Daddy asked me to sleep in his room, but I had not slept a wink the previous night in his room, as he slept only around five, so I told him I would sleep on my own, which I really regret that. He fell asleep, and I went to my room and also fell asleep. After midnight, the attendant called me, I went to the bathroom before going to his room, and when I went, she felt he was gone. He had stood up, passed urine, and then lay down and had a sharp angina pain, which he often did; she gave him Sorbitrate and yelled for me and she saw his neck jerk and felt he was gone. However, he was breathing slowly, his heart was beating, and his pulse was there, so I thumped his heart, gave him mouth-to-mouth respiration, and called the ambulance and my brothers and husband, but it was too late. While we were happy, he had not suffered, we were sad that we would never see or hear him again. Though I also knew that he would be with me always.

The ceremonies after death and other administrative matters, e.g., death certificate, will, bank accounts, etc., take up your time after a dear one passes away and, in a way, take your attention to the matter-of-fact tasks. We were in Chandigarh for about a fortnight after Daddy passed away, and we came back to Gurgaon after all three of us had handled his bank accounts and presented his will in the estate office. We emptied the house and divided or gave away his stuff almost three years later and in 2019 sold the house. He had told me that since the house belonged to the three of us, he knew it would be sold. "Please do everything happily and peacefully," he said, and that's what we did four years later.

When someone you love leaves this world, everything seems incomplete. But when we started our regular life back in Gurugram, I kept being surprised at how normal everything seemed, though I kept feeling some emptiness. I got back to my routine and joined the Board of Members again though there was some resistance. Within a year or two, we were doing very well in games, tournaments, and group classes in the gym. I was looking after the sports committee. Success, no matter how basic, often leads to jealousy, and that's what happened a few years later after completing a few tasks I had undertaken, I left. In the present BOM, Sudipto then became a member, and I am happy about that.

I was on the executive committee of IASOWA, which really is an association of spouses where the lady IAS officers are welcome. Each cadre has a member on the IASOWA Executive Committee, which looks after the activities and invites the members of the cadre in Delhi to attend. There's a function every month, and the exec com works to plan and then implement it. It is chaired by the Cabinet Secretary's wife, and two of the functions are held in the Cabinet Secretary's house; one is a Diwali dinner and another one is a tea party for the ladies. It was nice to be back and I took over HPIASOWA for two years as none of the wives of HP cadre officers was ready to take it over then. We performed a dance at least once a year and enjoyed the practices as well as the functions, which included the Diwali mela, cooking demos, dance, and other talent competitions.

Professionally I did not do much; I enjoyed preparing a draft youth charter for the SAARC countries. I facilitated and documented a global social franchising and social marketing conference for the Ministry of Health and Family Welfare. I was especially happy to do an assessment of Safe Motherhood in Sri Lanka for WHO and Amaltas joint project.

For the last few years, we have taught English in Govt. senior secondary school in Chakkarpur, near our house. A few years back, we realised that the civil hospital in Gurugram had no kitchen, and patients in a 250-bed hospital got food from outside, often made in unhealthy dhabas. So for about 2 or 3 times a week, we started cooking food at home for these patients. We would also take disposables and serve them and talk to them. We served the staff too, and since we cooked it with love and devotion, it was greatly appreciated, and no restrictions, including giving food for testing in the lab before distributing, deterred us. Sudipto, me, the maid, driver formed a team, and we were all fully committed. We were often up at 3 AM if we were taking breakfast of porridge and milk and sometimes sandwiches, eggs, and paneer. Sudipto would insist on doing all the tough parts, sometimes cutting onions for Rajmah. Once the kitchen was built and operationalised, we stopped going. We then went to earth saviours sometimes. A gentleman Rajiv Kalra set up a home for the homeless or those who don't have anyone or have lost their minds. He provides meals and medical attention to the 300 plus people he houses. Apart from contributing money, we would take someone for Bhajans or just go and talk to these souls who long for comforting hands.

Our schedules took into account our exercise classes which we enjoyed and were now being conducted in our complex by Manish Puri. And we have settled into a routine with that. Sudipto continued to do his half marathons off and on. But meanwhile, we started travelling. We travelled to London, where Abu lives

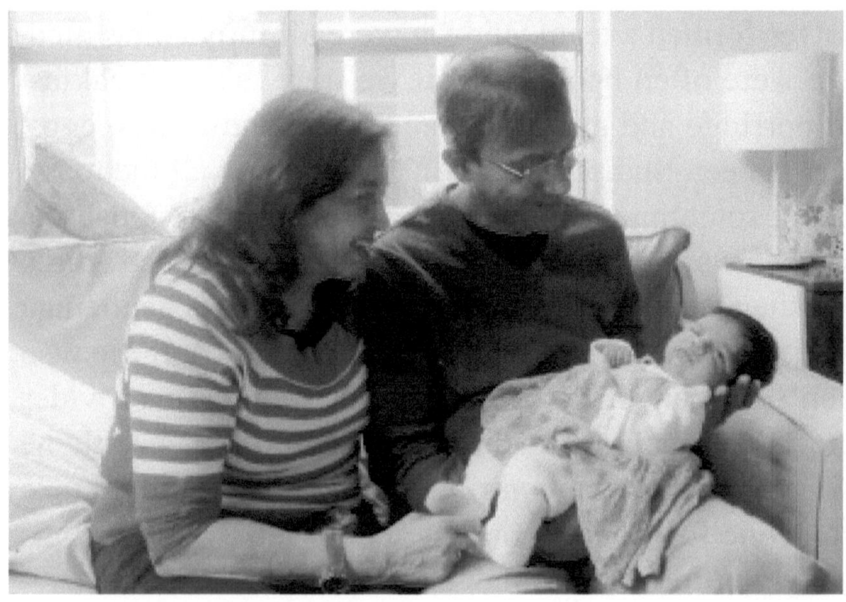

and works, and to Orinda in California, where Mitali and Rudro and Arya live. San Francisco was the only place we travelled when Daddy was here for Mitali's delivery, where we first saw our lovely vivacious granddaughter Arya I was present during her birth. It's so delightful to be grandparents that Sudipto said that, if possible, he'd opt to be a grandparent before becoming a parent!!

We visited our children every year. When we visit Abu now, we also visit some other European Countries and enjoy being a tourist. We enjoyed our visit to Czechoslovakia, where we enjoyed the local ride. We also enjoyed the coffee shops in Amsterdam and our visit to Paris and Switzerland.

Sudipto enjoyed Czechoslovakia

He also loved going to Amsterdam and the fact that Abu came with us and showed us how things are done there was very helpful, however unlike what we were expecting I took to coffee shops better than him.

We took to hiking which Sudipto is passionate about. But the most interesting has been the motorbike rides. Sudipto had sold his motorbike to buy an air ticket to come and meet my parents before we were married. Now he wanted to buy a motorbike and also go to Ladakh. Manali to Ladakh on motorbikes. I was reluctant, not too well and not ready to rough it out, but then I thought that surely, I could do this for him as he was now planning to buy a motorbike after so many years. I was also scared of falling and breaking bones, so we agreed that we would be careful not to fall and that it would not be a grilling routine. Abu also spoke to me, and we undertook a wonderful

motorbike trip from Manali to Ladakh by driving for three days. Many members of the family went with us, Our son of course but also Sudipto's sister and brother-in-law (Prachee and Shantanu came from the USA), his niece and granddaughter (Rashmi and Bitia came from Calcutta), and also one of Sudipto's colleagues.

It was a great trip, a once in a lifetime one, as Sudipto said. We also had good organisers and facilitators. Luckily, we did not have high altitude sickness due to our precautions. Ladakh is a beautiful region which is different from other mountainous regions. Snow-capped peaks, clear blue skies, and barren mountains with meandering rivers make it picturesque! What is surprising are the barren mountains with water flowing in the rivers. We went to Nubra valley one day and came back the next day and stayed in Ladakh. Next day we went to Pangong

Lake from where we also managed, with the help of a Rajput co-posted en-route, to visit Chushul, where the army organised, a small wreath laying and tree plantation ceremony. We were happy to go to a memorial Daddy had built a little less than 50 years earlier and were all tearful as the history was narrated to us, and we laid wreaths with a slow march.

Another memorable motorbike trip to Bhutan, where our son and some of Sudipto's colleagues accompanied us. Walking to Tiger Hill was the highlight, and we enjoyed the natural beauty of Bhutan. The temples, forest conservation, and the untouched prismatic beauty of Bhutan live in our memory. Their measurement of gross national happiness is unique in the world and shows what they value over material gains.

We also undertook a nice diving holiday to Andamans, which we all enjoyed though both Mitali and I could not scuba dive much because of our health issues.

All of us were by now advanced scuba divers and we wanted to renew our diving experience. Of course, the children were much better than us, especially Abu. Mitali, our daughter, is in Orinda with her husband and daughter, while Abu is in London, working as Senior Vet of a veterinary Hospital. Abu is not married but doing very well professionally he continues to be nominated as the best vet in the UK. They visit us once a year and so do we.

We like our retirement home in Palm Springs. We have a nice community here, though barely any retired or working in Govt. The residents are mostly those in the corporate sector.

We also undertook meditation at Rishikesh and slowly became a part of the Parmarth Niketan Ashram where Pujya Swami Chidanand Saraswati Jee offered us a free residence and service. We did some social services for a few weeks a few times but then our life here beckoned.

Another development was Prachee Mukherjee (Tinku) and her husband relocating from USA to Palampur. While I helped them in getting permission to buy land, the construction was messed up by the contractor and the architect and their dream of using local materials ended up in huge losses. The building that came up was not safe and had to be broken down. They had meanwhile got good jobs in Chennai and recently moved to Palampur.

Sudipto was busy with his army batchmates who got together after a long time to celebrate the 50th

honor 8Pro

anniversary of their passing out. They are fun and know how to enjoy life, so there is dancing and singing with them too. Visits to RIMC, NDA, and IMA with the celebrations have been the highlights. It was as if Sudipto had never left the army, and he got back with a quiet vengeance which was so characteristic of him.

The visit to RIMC and their golden Jublee was memorable. He took a picture in front of Ranjit Squadron and visited his classroom very fondly. I took a picture of the board where he had got a gold medal for topping all India in the NDA entrance exam. We saw a letter written by his father requesting for special leave during puja as his mother was very sad and missing him. However, he was very happy in RIMC and NDA.

Sudipto with his IMA batchmates

His meeting with his batchmate in NDA and IMA is unforgettable. They were bosum chums, quite settled. They danced in the evening together and the memories captured beautifully in pictures and stored in our hearts will remain forever.

Sudipto, on his 70th birthday, had opted to go to Amritsar to do seva in the Golden temple, and Abu accompanied us, which was priceless. We then visited Vaishno Devi too.

With Miltali, we visited Kairali, where we all took some ayurvedic health packages. Mitali said her migraine is improved, and I think it helped my involuntary head shutter. Below is the picture in Kairali with my batchmate Suvrathan and his wife. We played around with massages and treatments it was great and worth a revisit.

During Covid, a resident volunteer group was set up. Online supplies of groceries and medicines were organised. Then as the issue of migrants walking home started, we cooked for migrants at home, made packets, and handed over food and water to walking migrants. We organised this on a large scale, but it was not large enough.

Everyone hoped that Covid would settle down after the first wave, yet we also all knew that it had not yet gone. We started going cycling and when we met people, even during the walk, we wore masks.

I was once again baking a lot; I don't think I baked at all after the kids left home. I was also gardening and painting, thus making the most of the lockdown. I also finally got into some meditation and am enjoying it.

Sudipto always asked me to maintain a distance and pulled me back. He had also made the home environment more pleasant, and we indulged in singing and dancing by ourselves in the evenings. He would organise an online program with his army batchmates, and we would all dance little bits of a song, and he would put it together online. Basically, he made it fun, so we were never depressed or low but little did we know that this was not to last.

However, life is not all rosy, and nor is any place. We had a bitter experience in the 2020 elections, where the worst kind of manipulation was witnessed in this seemingly beautiful society, but I will not go into the gory details.

Rajat came after the first wave and we went to Dharamsala undertaking a memorable hike to Triund near Dharamsala. Little did we know that this would be the last hike together.

Hike to Triund

Sudipto and I marveled at our luck and togetherness and thought it would last till we grew old and faded away almost together. However, when people praised our companionship, Sudipto started saying the most unexpected thing, he felt that this continuous praise may lead to bad luck, "nazar na lag jai' he would say.

Retirement is a time to finally settle down, settle your family, relationships, finances etc., etc. Somehow for us, it continued to be a rushed time, partly because of our own desire to travel and motorbike and hike and spend time with children, friends, and batchmates and partly due to some unexpected events. How I looked forward to stress-free, relaxed evenings and walks which were to come soon after corona!

In our post retirement life, we were able to look after my parents and settle down in Palm Springs on Golf Course Road and lead the kind of life we dreamt of. But our post retirement life was unexpectedly interrupted by Corona. Was it fated?

Epilogue

On 14th May 2021, my world completely changed. Sudipto had developed a fever and cough from the third week of April; he had been going to Paras for physiotherapy as he had torn a muscle on his shoulder while exercising and started taking laser therapy in Paras Hospital, Gurugram. I tried persuading him to go to active Ortho to avoid a hospital, but the situation was not good anywhere, and active Ortho told him even after we had bought a package to take a break, they were short of therapists, and he went back to Paras Hospital. One day he came back and said that he felt he might get covid there and stopped going. However, the dye had been cast, and he got a fever and a bad cough. We all took an RTPCR test: Sudipto, the maid driver, and me. All three were positive and mine inconclusive, but soon mine became positive too!

This was the second wave of Covid-19 in India and it was terrible. It left people on the roads trying to seek hospital beds and oxygen. The medical faculty could not cope and the system just collapsed. Sudipto's fever receded, but the cough persisted, and we managed medicines and later a concentrator at home. Consultations were online and doctors could not keep the appointments they gave. Our home was sealed, and the medicine shop downstairs could not cope with demand or supplies. As Sudipto's oxygen fell short, we fixed a concentrator at home but had to move him to the hospital the next day. However, the choice of the hospital too was not right as Max Gurugram lacked equipment and perhaps sufficient doctors. A nephrologist looked after him and not the senior pulmonologist who was available, and the nephrologist asked me to call my children as he did not know what the outcome would be. When a resident from Palm Springs went and argued about this without any instruction from me, all hell broke loose and they kind of stopped treating him. His lungs had fluid, so no drip was given but no oral feeding either due to BiPap and other issues; the kitchen staff put his soup far away as he was on a breathing device; after it was taken off and he reached for the soup, it fell as it was far away and no more was given. He said he was losing weight and would fit into his old suit! I was allowed to see him for a few minutes. Sudipto asked me to consult the family astrologer, Prem Sharma and talked of children, his sister, brother-in-law, and other relatives and friends. I asked the children to decide if they could come and whatever they decided, not to feel guilty later. I emphasised this to Mitali as she had another family, but to Abu, I just asked him to come. He came on 1st May 2021. Sudipto went to Max on 23rd April, and I was coming from a quarantined home with full precautions, including a spray team walking behind me as I came and went through our building. Sudipto was in a Covid-negative ICU as he was not positive when he went to the hospital but suffering from the aftermath of Covid.

With the Max doctors not interested in treating him due to various reasons given to me no ventilators or manpower or ECMO machine which may be required, I planned to shift him to AIIMS on the recommendation of the treating doctor, nephrologist in Max. I had worked in AIIMS, and I was quite sure I would get a room. I went early morning to meet Dr. Guleria and he was positive though it took a few days to persuade Dr. Rajeshwari, head of AB8. After many days of testing and retesting, Sudipto's RTPCR was negative and he was shifted to AIIMS, where we were given royal treatment in terms of facilities.

However, probably too much damage had been done and it was too late. No one gave us the detail, and it seemed they didn't know; we also did not realise that it was too late. Sudipto was exhausted and when Abu travelled in the ambulance with him, he saw that he was too exhausted to talk. He had just been told of the condition of his lungs by the doctors and was concerned.

Sudipto had studied astrology in Delhi when my father was ailing and always told us that he would not cross 72. However, when I would protest violently at the possibility of my being left alone, he would say no, it's 74/75. Both of us will go close to each other and women have a better capacity to deal with this, so I should be with positive people and lead a good life for the short time I would be around after he goes. Just before going to the hospital with the ambulance standing down, he had opened his horoscope on his laptop and tried to explain to me how the stars were aligned and how difficult it would be for him to survive. Prem Sharma said the same but Abu had said" to hell with horoscopes, I am sure he'll recover"

In AIIMS, although he had a room in ICU, and we were allowed to go in whenever we wanted, we maintained the decorum. We could give him fresh juice only for a day or so and when he could not maintain oxygen in a prone position too, doctors put him on a ventilator early in the morning. I regret we were not with him when he asked for us while being put on a ventilation though I stayed in the guest house of AIIMs throughout. I had said that I will not go home without him. The ventilator leaked on one side one day, and he was operated, on another side the next day; and operated again and in that center, so now they proposed to put him on an ECMO machine. At this time, both Abu and my hearts were sinking as we knew ECMO had just a slight chance of reviving his lungs by giving them rest, but if they did not recover, a lung transplant was not feasible. All our friends and relatives tried to support us online, but Abu handled that; I could no longer take calls! Abu was a huge support, in fact he almost took everything. I saw how much like his father he had become.

I came to know that the ECMO machine used in the CTNS centre was outmoded and the first generation while third generation machines were now available. I messaged Dr. Guleria that Sudipto was admitted under Dr. Guleria after Dr. Rajyalakshmi spoke to me and said that we should now be prepared for an ECMO machine as that was the last option. We discussed at various levels; lung transplant was not an option. The hope was in the respite his lungs got; they may recover. But the first generation machine gave one week and the third generation machine three weeks to a person and hence a better chance of recovery. I proposed to buy them a third-generation machine and donate it to AIIMS after it was used on my husband. The supplier had it in stock, while Dr. Guleria brushed it aside, saying it was not needed at this stage, probably Dr. Rajlakshmi had not communicated with him. The supplier told me that they had earlier ordered a machine and it was ready to be delivered, but delivery was not being taken. I asked Dr. Rajalakshmi, and she confirmed that the delivery was due, but she did not have time to go to the stores and settle the matter. Here patients were dying, and the situation was ironic to say the least. Meanwhile, the machine with AIIMS was with CTNS (Cardiothoracic and Neurosciences Centre), and it was the first-generation. I, with my friends, started looking for a third-generation machine which would give the patient time for up to three weeks, so lungs have a better chance to recover. We found one in Jaipur in Fortis with the help of Sudipto's colleague, Subi and we miraculously managed to get it here when Dr. Rajyalakshmi asked for it the next day. The machine arrived after midnight and we got it into AIIMS. We were there the next morning with some hope in our hearts. We spoke to Dr. Rajyalakshmin, who made us sign a waiver but was non-committal on whether the new machine would be used. There was confusion on which doctor would come from CTNS as it seemed only they were familiar with the machine. We had been asked to procure some consumables for the old machine, in case the new machine could not be used and this included some catheters. I am told the scheduled doctor did not come, and the professor who came punctured Sudipto's vein by mistake, and Sudipto bled to death. The surgeon did not come in time to stop the bleeding and that was the end. The doctor apologised profusely and I did not express any annoyance or resentment but I had lost everything.

Though all this while, he was in AB8, a non Covid ward, I don't know why they took a biopsy of his lungs and said he was Covid positive and his body would not be handed over to us. That day was a holiday for EID and Dr. Guleria as well as head of AB8 left for the day and could not be contacted. We struggled at all levels to get hold of whatever was left of the beautiful soul and was determined to give him the best send off we could arrange. My friends in Palm springs Manisha, Manu and Rachna along with a lot of others took charge and made arrangements at home which included flowers, enlarged picture, sitting and arrangements of his sleeping on an ice bed on his last night in the house. Dhruv Bhagat and Navien Syiem came from Palm Springs to AIIMS to help us. We struggled to get the body from the mortuary and Dr. Guleria did give a final clearance for the body to be taken home. People from Palm springs community stood outside as we arrived. Sudipto and Abu got off the ambulance in a hushed atmosphere impregnated with sorrow and silence. No one could believe that this man who they considered young and who ran half marathons and shared his running skills with many, lay lifeless, ready to undertake his onward journey.

Next morning, after prayers, the cremation took place in Gurgaon and friends from Palm Springs came to a Cremation ground decorated through them with roses and rose petals. His bathmates Lt. Gen. Shamer Pal Singh Dhillon and Lt. Gen. P C Katoch from the Army and Air Marshall P K Barbora and Group Captain Lakhanwala represening and airforce came and gave the final salute as Rajat lit the pyre.

Though my friends had arranged for the ashes to be immersed in Jamuna near Delhi, I remembered Sudipto taking me to Hardwar on our way back from Rishikesh one day and showing me Har ki Pauri and saying that from near this place would start our last journey. With the help of DC Dehradun and DC Haryana, we got a passes and managed to give him a sendoff from Haridwar in a peaceful manner. What an end to a glorious life: what was and what could have been! And how will I go through life without him and the children without their father? Were my thoughts on the way back home and continue till date.

I hope you have enjoyed this rich tapestry of my life, sewn together with honesty, love and pride for all the ups and downs that have come together to make me the person that I am.

I am happy to say that I see it as not just a life well-lived, but more importantly, a life well-shared – with my colleagues who I had the great fortune to work with in my various postings to give people a better life; with my friends who have so graciously welcomed me into their lives and their homes and enjoyed smiles and tears with over so many years; with my parents, my parents-in-law and my whole extended family who have always been there to support, love and care for me in whatever I do, whichever direction I take; with my children, my greatest achievements, who have given and continue to give me so much love joy and pleasure in all that they do and achieve; and with my soul-mate, my beloved Sudipto, without whom most of this would not have been possible and would certainly not have been as enjoyable or as precious; although our physical time together has sadly come to an end, I know he is still with me every step of the way – he will always be a part of me, loving me, guiding me, cajoling me as I continue to add new chapters to my story – this is for you my darling, thank you for helping me be the best I could be and for being there in the good times and the bad and for just being you!

www.ingramcontent.com/pod-product-compliance
Ingram Content Group UK Ltd.
Pitfield, Milton Keynes, MK11 3LW, UK
UKHW041843190726
13854UKWH00002B/699